Marxist Literary Criticism Today

Marxist Literary Criticism Today

Barbara Foley

PLUTO  PRESS

First published 2019 by Pluto Press
345 Archway Road, London N6 5AA

www.plutobooks.com

Copyright © Barbara Foley 2019

British Library Cataloguing in Publication Data
A catalogue record for this book is available from the British Library

ISBN   978 0 7453 3884 2   Hardback
ISBN   978 0 7453 3883 5   Paperback
ISBN   978 1 7868 0411 2   PDF eBook
ISBN   978 1 7868 0413 6   Kindle eBook
ISBN   978 1 7868 0412 9   EPUB eBook

Typeset by Stanford DTP Services, Northampton, England

Contents

Acknowledgements

Since this book contains several decades' worth of thinking about how to teach Marxist approaches to literary criticism, I am indebted to many students, colleagues, comrades, and friends. Perhaps my greatest debt is to the many students, undergraduate and graduate, who have challenged me in my classes over the years; the questions that I ask here, and attempt to answer, derive largely from their probing and prodding. As this book took shape, Pat Keeton, Gregory Meyerson, and Bill Sacks read early versions of several chapters and offered helpful criticisms. I received useful feedback on early drafts of the section outlining basic principles of Marxism from the following young interlocutors: Kamika Bennett, Peter Foley, Mani Martínez, Jason Myers, Ike Onyema, and Grace Prial.

For my understanding of Marxist theory, such as it is, I am indebted to more people than I can begin to mention. The members of the manuscript and editorial collectives at *Science & Society* come to mind: Russell Dale, Raju Das, Sheila Delany, Martha Gimenez, Gerald Horne, Julio Huato, Gerald Meyer, Paul Mishler, Bertell Ollman, Juan Rodriguez, Rachel Rubin, Shana Russell, Jim Smethurst, Lise Vogel, Alan Wald, and above all David Laibman, the journal's learned and tireless editor. I also have benefited greatly from the wisdom of the reading group—we call ourselves the "WMDs," that is, "Wielders of Marxist Discourse"!—in which I have participated for the past decade and more: Renate Bridenthal, Hester Eisenstein, Jack Hammond, Paul Montagna, and Ellen Schrecker.

The many stimulating discussions at the summer institutes of the Marxist Literary Group have motivated me to think more deeply about historical materialism, dialectics, ideology, and political economy. I hesitate to name names in this context, largely because it is the collective conversation that makes the MLG gatherings so valuable. But I need especially to mention what I have learned from working with Anna Einarsdottir, Bret Benjamin, Beverly Best, Nicholas Brown, Kanishka Choudhury, Kevin Floyd, Neil Larsen, Carolyn Lesjak, Courtney Maloney, Tony Squiers, and Paul Stasi. I am also indebted to several leftist scholars and writers whom I know from a variety of other venues, including Roxanne Dunbar-Ortiz, Teresa Ebert, Stephen Ferguson, Katherine Fischer, Paul Gomberg, Rodney Green, Rosemary Hennessy, Michael Roberto, Rosaura Sanchez, Albert Sargis, Wang Fengzhen, and Mas'ud Zavarzadeh.

Many past and present colleagues in the English Department at Rutgers University-Newark have been companions—intellectual, emotional, and political—in a work-life at times harried, but made gracious by their presence over the years: thanks especially to Sadia Abbas, Frances Bartkowski, Sterling Bland, H. Bruce Franklin, Rachel Hadas, David Hoddeson, Tayari Jones, Mal Kiniry, Janet Larson, Laura Lomas, Jack Lynch, Gabriel Miller, Madelyn Munoz, Subramanian Shankar, Ameer Sohrawardy, and Virginia Tiger.

The crucial need to conjoin theory with practice—in the academy and beyond—has continually been impressed upon me by various colleagues in the Radical Caucus of the Modern Language Association: Michael Bennett, Finley Campbell, Norma Cantù, Anthony Dawahare, Basuli Deb, Brian Dolinar, Grover Furr, Marcial González, Paul Lauter, John Maerhofer, Richard Ohmann, Susan O'Malley, Leo Parascondola, Joseph Ramsey, and Heather Steffen. Farther removed from the groves of academe, but for that reason all the more profoundly formative, have been my experiences over the years with in-the-streets activists, some of them committed communists, who have acted upon Marx's call not just to interpret the world but to change it. Their names are legion; to list them would be to bring my entire adult life into view. I cannot thank them enough for helping me to understand the ways in which sexism, nationalism, and racism, toxic features of our past and present, connect back to the pressures of a global socioeconomic system that requires division and inequality and places profit before human need. These comrades have helped me keep in view the red line of history.

Pluto Books has been exemplary in shepherding this book quickly and efficiently through the entire publication process. Many thanks to Emily Orford, marketing manager; Melanie Patrick, designer; Sophie Richmond, copy-editor; Dave Stanford, typesetter; Sue Stanford, proofreader; Robert Webb, managing editor; and above all David Shulman, commissioning editor, who encouraged me while gently holding me to deadlines from start to finish. Thanks also to the anonymous readers of the manuscript, whose assessments of its merits have reassured me as I have worked my way through difficult moments of rewriting and reframing.

I am indebted to several people who helped me through the at times onerous task of obtaining permission to reprint the works of various poets: Joan Ashe at Henry Holt (Robert Frost); Ron Hussey at HMH Trade Publishing (Archibald MacLeish); Tamara Kawar at ICM Partners (Muriel Rukeyser); Dennis Maloney at White Pine Press (Xu Lizhi); Joan Pinkvoss at Aunt Lute Books (Anzaldúa); Robert Shatzkin at W. W. Norton (Brecht); Alex Smithline at Penguin Random House (Hughes); and Rahiem Whisgary at DALRO Theatricals (Mtshali).

My greatest personal debts are to my daughter Margaret Stevens; my son, Adam Stevens, and his spouse, Helena Ortiz; and my *compagno* and now spouse, Peter Gardner. In your various ways, you have shown me the real meaning of challenge, love, struggle, and support.

I dedicate this book to my grandchildren: Omar, Alexandra, Iliana, and Jahsiri. You are the future.

Prologue

The philosophers have only interpreted the world in various ways; the point is to change it.

— Karl Marx, *Theses on Feuerbach*

Marxism is at once a method of socioeconomic analysis and a call for revolutionary social transformation. It is also an interpretive framework indispensable to an understanding of the relationship between literature and society—and thus, more generally, of the connections between ideas, attitudes, and emotions on the one hand and their grounding in historical forces on the other. This book aims to explain key concepts in Marxism, explore their relationship to the study of literature, and examine a wide range of texts in which this relationship is displayed. As the title indicates, however, this study is premised upon the notion that such an investigation has particular importance *today*. What is the occasion, a couple of decades into the twenty-first century, for a book introducing readers to basic principles of Marxist literary criticism? What features of the current moment provide an opening—indeed, an invitation—to such an intervention?

When facing the task of describing the defining features of the present, one runs the risk of ahistoricity: either just about everything has changed, or very little has changed. In the realm of history, economics, and politics, what has happened since, say, the start of the fourth quarter of the past century, around the time when the last two introductory books on Marxist literary criticism appeared (Eagleton 1976; Williams 1977)? From one standpoint, it might seem that the fortunes of Marxism—as both a method of analysis and an inspiration to revolutionary change—have never been less promising than they are at present. The "actually existing socialism" of the Soviet Union and its affiliated nations in eastern and central Europe has imploded. In western Europe and the United States, labor movements once led by the left have been largely incorporated into ruling parties committed to the capitalist status quo. China, while proclaiming itself to be a socialist country led by a communist party, has evidently chosen to follow the capitalist path. Almost all the movements for socialism in the formerly colonized world, from Guinea-Bissau to Jamaica to Vietnam, have resulted in havens for imperialist super-exploitation administered by corrupt elites. Cuba, a last hold-out, appears to have caved in to the pressures of international capitalism; while those nations in Latin America claiming to exemplify "twenty-first-century socialism" (Venezuela, Bolivia, Ecuador) have adhered to many of the extractive and investment priorities of their former regimes and—while continually hammered by US imperialism—have also encountered their own crises in popular legitimacy. Are we witnessing, as various pundits and prophets proclaim, the final triumph of neoliberal globalization, the dropping of the curtain upon the drama of class conflict and the communist dream of a classless society? Are we in an entirely new period, one in which humanity faces new problems requiring new solutions?

This narrative of decline and fall—an occasion for celebration or despair, depending on who tells it—has routinely been accompanied by the observation that the proletariat, whom Marx and Engels described in *The Communist Manifesto* (*CM*) as the grave-diggers of capital, have failed to take up the shovel; indeed, it is argued, they have been co-opted by the social order they were supposed to overthrow. For progressives seeking to combat injustice and inequality, it is social movements based upon gender, sexuality, "race," ethnicity and environmental awareness, not class struggles against exploitation, that have been proposed as the principal sites of oppositional political practice in recent decades. This shift in emphasis has, for some observers, given rise to the conclusion that the contemporary locus of oppression is not unitary but many-faceted, situated not in capital as such but in a range of institutions and ideological formations hostile to human (and planetary) flourishing: white supremacy, patriarchy, heteronormativity, humanocentrism. Since these modes of oppression are held to spring from disparate, or at best loosely linked, causes, they need to be disarticulated, it is argued, in order to be effectively contested and then, perhaps, conjoined. Indeed, Marxism itself—with its roots in Enlightenment rationalism and its claim to offer an overarching analysis of history and economics, social relations and culture—has been charged with Eurocentricity, as well as with endorsing an authoritarian master narrative that reduces all difference to class antagonism (Mills 2003; Laclau and Mouffe 1985). Marxism is, from this angle of critique, part of the problem rather than of the solution, in need of the correctives supplied by various alternative paradigms often prefaced by "post," "inter," or "trans" (Gimenez 2005; Foley 2018).

I suggest that, for all the *frisson* accompanying such diagnoses of the staleness of old analytical frameworks and the need for new ones, it is those who have given up on the class-based critique of capital who are behind the times. In the United States, the candle of the "occupy" movement that flamed into view in 2012 may have guttered quickly; but the legacy of its principal slogan—"We are the 99%"—is everywhere evident in the discourse about inequality that has gained considerable currency in recent years. While discussions of inequality by politicians, Republicans and Democrats alike, ignore its root causes in capitalist-generated exploitation and uneven development, there is widespread acknowledgement that beneficiaries of the "recovery" from the 2008 financial crisis have been all at the top; for most people in the "working-class majority" (Zweig 2011), belt-tightening, often severe, has become the new normal. The emergence of activism in response to rising rates of police brutality and immigrant deportations directs attention to the structural racism and xenophobia undergirding a status quo reliant upon surveillance, repression, and scapegoating to ensure intra-class division and domestic tranquility.

On an international scale, the divide between the haves and the have-nots has escalated, in both "the West" and what was formerly known as the "Third World" (now routinely referred to as the "global North" and the "global South"). The rebellions against austerity led by the youth in the newly emergent "precariat," sparking in 2011 the "Arab Spring" and the massive anti-austerity demonstrations by Spain's "indignados," testify to the desperate future being faced by the rising generation of would-be workers. The increasingly intense class struggles in China point to the human cost paid by the workers who make everything from T-shirts to smartphones. International trade agreements favorable to agribusiness continually destroy much of what is left of small-scale farming in the semi-industrialized world, sending millions of former peasants, from Nigeria to Mexico, into hardscrabble informal economies or into the ranks of a barely employed proletariat (J. Smith 2016). Resource wars in large swaths of sub-Saharan Africa, along with desertification resulting from climate change—itself a product of capital's drive to accumulation—have created massive waves of emigrants, joining the tide of refugees from wars in the Middle East (Burgis 2015; Foster et al. 2010; Angus 2016). All these situations and occurrences, I propose, can be traced to the effects of capitalism in its era of "shock doctrine" (Klein 2007). While the movements resisting such trends are in many parts of the world largely unaffiliated with parties and organizations associated with the revolutionary Marxist tradition, this does not mean that class analysis has lost its relevance, or that the abolition of classes has to be stricken from the agenda of the workers of the world.

Announcements of the death of Marxism are thus premature; and while I shall primarily be arguing for the value of Marxism as methodology rather than as prophecy, it bears noting that Marx got it right about a number of historical developments. When Marx wrote *Capital*, of which volume I appeared in 1867, he focused his empirical research and economic theorizing on England—not because he felt that all parts of the world were fated to follow the English path, but because England at that time exemplified the most advanced development of capitalist forces and relations of production in the world (Anderson 2010). In its time, Marx's text was ahead of the curve, since much of the world had not yet been drawn into capital's global orbit (Chibber 2013); now, however, capital is indeed universal, penetrating to just about every corner of the world, even those zones inhabited primarily by polar bears and penguins. Against those economists who argued, in the wake of World War II, that the rising tide of capitalism was lifting all working-class boats, the income compression (that is, the shrinking of the gap between the rich and the poor) that occurred during a few mid-twentieth-century decades in a few parts of the world has turned out to be not typical but anomalous (Piketty 2013). Moreover, although the World Bank has since its founding in 1944 proclaimed its "Dream" to be "A World Free of Poverty,"[1] and incomes have risen for the small but rising middle classes in China and India, capital's ever-expanding drive to accumulation has not entailed a rising standard of living for the great majority of the globe's inhabitants. Indeed, the famed 2013 "elephant curve" graph presumably attesting to modest but significant income growth for the world's poorest people (Milanović 2018) is now being replaced by a "Loch Ness Monster" curve that illustrates stagnant or lowered incomes for most of the world's population, while the wealth enjoyed by the world's tiny richest sector—the long neck of the monster—is almost off the chart.[2] Increasing levels of under- and unemployment are in fact the order of the day for the hundreds of millions of would-be wage-workers who, separated from the land, no longer possess the means to subsist on their own (J. Smith 2016; Ness 2016). While capital has always relied upon what Marx called a "reserve army" of unemployed labor (*C* I, ch. 25) forcing workers to compete for jobs, large portions of the world's population, even in the better-off economies, are now, for all practical purposes, expendable. That widespread alienation and desperation drive millions toward religious fundamentalism, extreme nationalism, and other forms of present-day fascism makes all the more urgent the task of linking misery and inequality to the structure of the socioeconomic system prevailing on the planet. The very fragmentation of the world's producing population makes all the more urgent an understanding of the universal conditions under which it labors, as well as the need for a revived proletarian internationalism.

Finally, the instability inherent in the capitalist mode of production, which Marx anatomized so thoroughly in the three volumes of *Capital*, is giving rise to more and more frequent bubbles and crises. While there is some validity to the joke that Marxists "have predicted correctly the last twelve of the last three crises" (Harvey and Rivera 2010), Marx's reputation has made a startling comeback, at times in unexpected circles. In the wake of the 2008 financial crisis, journalists writing in a range of media outlets, from the *Wall Street Journal* to the *New Yorker* to *Rolling Stone*, have wondered whether Marx correctly understood the inherent instability of the capitalist social order (Moore 2015; Menand 2016; McElwee 2014). One *Wall Street Journal* commentator noted in 2011 that "Karl Marx got it right, at some point capitalism can destroy itself. We thought markets worked. They're not working" (Roubini in Heaven, 2011). A 2017 poll revealed that as many as 40 percent of US inhabitants "now prefer socialism to capitalism," a cause of no small consternation at the ultra-conservative *National Review* (Nammo 2017). Notably, too, the C-word—largely avoided in the discourse of neo- and post-Marxist theorists during the past several decades—has been making a reappearance, as witnessed in such titles as *The Communist Hypothesis* (Badiou 2015), *The Actuality of Communism* (Bosteels 2011), and *The Communist Horizon* (Dean 2012). Capitalism is—to alter the metaphor—no longer as seemingly natural as the air we breathe. It is a socioeconomic system that came into being in history and can therefore go out of being in history, albeit only after prolonged and intense struggle. The "today" featured in the title of this book is thus at once a call to consider the continuing need for a classless future and a reminder of the abiding presentness of the past; we are still very much in the *longue durée* (that is, long-term era) of capitalism. Reality continually changes; there is no question that Marx's world was in certain respects very different from ours. But such terms as "neoliberalism," "globalization," and "financialization," if taken as descriptors of a qualitatively new historical moment, rather than as extensions of previous phases of capitalist development, can end up obscuring more than they explain (Mavroudeas and Papadotas forthcoming).

To call attention to the threads connecting the present to a possible future of universal human emancipation is not to minimize their slenderness. Huge challenges, both theoretical and practical, face those who would like to see the world move through and past its present state—what Marx and Engels called "the realm of necessity"—and enter "the realm of freedom" (Marx *C* III, ch. 48; Engels *A-D*, ch. XI). These challenges are posed not only by the coercive and ideological power of current elites but also by certain historical limitations in the legacy inherited from Marx and Engels themselves—as well as by problems in the legacy inherited from past movements carried forward under the banner of one or another version of Marxism. But minimizing the possibilities for significant social transformation, even in our current moment, would be a greater mistake than overestimating the ease with which such transformation might occur. A fresh wind is blowing through the world. Whether or not it will drive "wither'd leaves to quicken a new birth," as Percy Bysshe Shelley hoped in his "Ode to the West Wind" (Shelley 1951, 392)—a poem written, we should note, in the aftermath of the 1819 Peterloo Massacre, when the royal cavalry trampled to death some 18 demonstrators in a crowd of 60,000 calling for parliamentary reform—remains to be seen.

* * *

Not by chance, this mention of Shelley brings us to the role that can be played in revolutionary social transformation by the study of literature and culture from a Marxist point of view. One premise of the investigation undertaken in this book is that, if we wish to recognize the promise in that fresh wind, we need to acknowledge that it has blown before—emanating from a cave as old as class society, but with particular force in the era of capital. In 1855, the English poet and critic Matthew Arnold, hardly a political radical, wrote of "wandering between two worlds, one dead / the other powerless to be born" (Arnold 1965, 123). Some eight decades later, the Italian communist Antonio Gramsci, writing from a Fascist prison, stated that "the crisis consists precisely in the fact that the old is dying and the new cannot be born; in this interregnum a great variety of morbid symptoms appear" (Gramsci 1971, 276). Arnold and Gramsci were hardly in accord about the reasons for this blockage of new birth, much less about the kind of new life that they would like to see emerge. Nonetheless, their common chosen metaphor—which, notably, recalls not only the "new birth" of Shelley's poem but also the metaphor of childbirth central to Marx's description of the process by which the new world emerges from the womb of the old—indicates their common sense of being caught in a temporal vise. The particular "morbid symptoms" of fettered human potential have changed with time, but their sources have remained fundamentally the same over a good two centuries—namely, the exploitation, alienation, and fragmentation fostered by capitalist social relations. And, although significant attempts to transcend capitalism and establish egalitarian societies occurred in the course of the twentieth century, they ultimately failed to move through and past the limits of existing class-based formations. In the early decades of the twenty-first century, we remain trapped in the same temporal vise.

This recognition of the presentness of the past guides the structure of this book in various ways. To begin with, I consider it vitally necessary that anyone interested in exploring what Marxism brings to the study of literature should have a more than passing acquaintance with fundamental principles of Marxist analysis. How can readers assess whether a given critical approach that calls itself Marxist warrants that descriptor if they do not themselves know something about the field of inquiry? Whereas other books introducing key concepts of Marxist literary criticism—even the valuable studies by Eagleton and Williams noted above—have tended to take it for granted that their readers are acquainted with the basics, this study is not premised on such an assumption. Hence the division of this book into two sections designed to address the needs of readers new to this subject matter.

Part I, titled "Marxism," sets forth concepts central to various types of Marxist social and economic analysis, not just literary criticism. Chapter 1 treats historical materialism; chapter 2, political economy; chapter 3, ideology. Within each of these chapters, certain important terms that will figure centrally in the rest of the book—for example, commodity fetishism, base and superstructure, class struggle, and interpellation—are defined. In boxes functioning as sidebars, I briefly sketch various issues— the relationship between Marxism and intersectionality, for instance, or the connection between socialism and communism, or the relationship between the internet and present-day forms of labor—that, my teaching tells me, are of general interest, even though they remain somewhat peripheral to the book's central concerns. Part II, titled "Literature," comprises three chapters that address general problems in literary study, both non-Marxist and Marxist. Chapter 4 critically analyzes various criteria that are frequently invoked, in the classroom as well as the culture at large, as grounds for defining and evaluating literature. Chapter 5

addresses a range of concerns specific to Marxist literary study—the
functioning of dominant ideologies and ideological contradictions, the
legacy of revolutionary literary traditions—as well as key issues debated
among Marxists, such as the nature of humanism and realism.

Chapter 6, aiming at a unity of theory and practice, explores various
ways in which Marxist analytical categories pertain to a broad range of
literary works drawn from different genres and periods. The organization of this section bears directly on matters of pedagogy, since texts
are grouped according to the kinds of topics often used in literature
textbooks and classroom syllabi. Some of the texts examined in this
chapter are classics, most likely familiar to the reader; others—especially
certain works of proletarian literature—are, I imagine, being encountered
for the first time. Some of these texts relate to their historical and ideological contexts in oblique and allusive ways; others wear their political
and historical situations on their sleeves, so to speak. Some are popular
and accessible, to be grasped upon a first hearing or reading; others are
couched in dense and complex language eluding ready interpretation.
Moreover, the texts display a range of political attitudes, either embedded
or explicit, from conservative to liberal to radical. The readings offered
here will demonstrate that Marxism is not a methodology that can simply
be "applied" to literary criticism—paralleled with, say, approaches drawn
from critical race studies, psychoanalytic criticism, feminist criticism, or
postcolonial theory—but instead a lens through which to view the relationship between politics and history, power and language.

In its structure and its contents, this book thus aims to set forth the
building blocks for a Marxist approach to culture, consciousness, and the
production and reception of literature. Since many of these building blocks
have been supplied by earlier practitioners in the Marxist tradition, this
study is, in many regards, and quite unabashedly, a return to orthodoxy.
Readers familiar with key figures in the Marxist intellectual tradition will
note the prominent role I assign not only to Marx and Engels themselves
but also to Georg Lukács, Louis Althusser, Bertolt Brecht, and Antonio
Gramsci. While the next generation of Marxist critics and theorists—
including Williams and Eagleton, as well as Fredric Jameson and Bertell
Ollman—have contributed significantly to this legacy, they have tended
to extend it rather than revise it in fundamental ways. In connection with
postcolonial, gender-, and race-based studies, where the classic Marxist
tradition has some significant gaps, I emphasize the new knowledges
made available by scholars in these fields who work with key Marxist
concepts. Signally absent from my treatments of both literary-cultural

and political-strategic matters, however, are references to the sizeable body of writings composed in the past few decades under the aegis of neo-Marxism and post-Marxism, which I view primarily as detours from the central concerns of Marxist theory and practice. While this book will not engage in shadow-boxing with its theoretical opponents, its emphasis upon orthodoxy is, in itself, a kind of polemical stance. To return to the basics of Marxist theory is not a rearguard position based in nostalgia, but an attempt to preserve—so that we may rethink in ways best suited to the present moment—the analytical and strategic paradigms we have inherited from the past.

Finally, a word about literary criticism. Although it may appear that this humanistic field of inquiry has relatively little to do with the formation of revolutionary consciousness and activity—Marxist critics, I readily concede, hardly occupy the frontline of the battle against the capitalist juggernaut—the project undertaken here can assist, however modestly, in developing an understanding of culture and society that has political value. The study of literary texts and traditions can reveal the inevitable rootedness of thought and writing in the tensions and pressures of history. It can heighten our sensitivity to the ways in which language functions to bind people to the status quo, as well as to imagine alternatives to the way we live now. It can demonstrate how rebellion and acquiescence frequently cohabit within the same consciousness. It can direct attention to the need for a proletarian literature attuned to the requirements of the present moment. It can connect the struggle in the mind and heart with the struggle in the streets. It can assist in the project called for by Marx in the famous "Eleventh Thesis on Feuerbach," namely, of not just interpreting but also changing the world (*Theses*, 423).

PART I

Marxism

1

Historical Materialism

It is not the consciousness of men that determines their being, but, on the contrary, their social being that determines their consciousness.

— Karl Marx, Preface to *A Contribution to the Critique of Political Economy*

Associated with the writings of Karl Marx (1818–83) and his close collaborator Friedrich Engels (1820–95), Marxism is at once a philosophy, a method of analysis, and a guide to revolutionary social change. Although, as Engels recalled, Marx himself once famously declared, "I am not a Marxist" (FE to Schmidt, 5 August 1890, *MEC*), since the publication of *The Communist Manifesto* in 1848 Marx's writings have probably had a more significant effect on revolutionary movements around the world, from Europe to Asia to Africa to the Americas, than have those of any other writer. His ideas have also had a widespread impact upon scholarship in the social sciences and the humanities.

As the most cursory library or internet search will reveal, a tremendous amount has been written about Marx and Marxism. In addition, there have been many offshoots from the original texts by Marx and Engels that have claimed the heritage of Marxism, some of these in quite emphatic opposition to one another. The brief discussion of Marxism supplied in this chapter and the two that follow will not pretend to cover these debates, let alone resolve any of them; parenthetical citations will guide interested readers to relevant primary and secondary sources. Our principal focus in Part I is on those features of Marxism that are essential to the Marxist approach to literary criticism developed in Part II. An understanding of key Marxist fields of inquiry—historical materialism, political economy, and ideology—is indispensable if we wish to devise a set of critical tools for approaching a wide range of literary texts and traditions, of varying political perspectives, as well as for appreciating the particular challenges embodied in texts committed to revolutionary social transformation.

Materialism

The term "materialism" in everyday usage is somewhat derogatory, referring to an excessive concern with shallow, consumerist values. But in philosophical usage "materialism" signifies the grounding of behavior and thought in the way a given society is organized. Its opposite, "idealism," does not refer to lofty—if somewhat unrealistic—aspirations, as we often use the term in everyday speech, but instead to the notion that the way people think and behave can be detached from the concrete conditions in which they live. For materialism, social being shapes consciousness; for idealism, consciousness shapes social being. From the standpoint of Marxism, then, these terms' usual overtones are inverted: idealism is to be avoided, materialism to be embraced. Some forms of idealism are purely retrograde. For instance, the conservative doctrine that progress in history has taken the form of movement toward the triumph of the free market is an idealist apologia for oppression and inequality. By contrast, the early Christian notion that the meek shall inherit the earth, as well as Martin Luther King Jr.'s modern liberal notion that "the arc of the moral universe is long, but … bends toward justice" (King 1965), commonly articulate a desire for a better world on the part of oppressed populations. Indeed, such idealist expressions of yearning can themselves be understood in materialist terms. Marx's famous description of religion as the "opium of the people" was premised upon the notion that, in however inadequate and flawed a way, religion recognized the needs of the "heart" in a "heartless world," of the "soul" amid "soulless conditions" (Introduction, *CHPR*). Materialism acknowledges the important role played by idealist declarations in motivating historical actors and shaping historical developments; however, it would treat neoliberal economic theory, ancient utopianism, and liberal civil rights-era political discourse alike as reflections of the pressures and limits generated by social conflicts of the day, rather than as objective explanations of why things are the way they are—much less as feasible programs for change. One of the tasks of Marxist literary criticism, we shall see, is to recognize the limits of texts that express the desire for a better world in idealist terms, while understanding that this idealism is itself grounded in historical circumstances that are comprehensible in a materialist framework.

"Historical materialism," the term Engels used to describe his and Marx's approach to analyzing society and history, is premised upon the notion that the modes of organization shaping how people live and think are constantly undergoing change. There are, for Marx, very few social phenomena that can be abstracted from history and seen as timeless; instead, just about all human habits of behavior and thought are anchored in the epochs—and sometimes the specific historical circumstances—from which they arise. Change, while slow in some periods and rapid in others, derives from the continual interaction between the level of technological development on the one hand and the division of labor on the other—an interaction in which the struggles between different social groups possessing different economic and political interests often play a determining role. The division of labor, it bears noting, pertains not just to the ways in which production and distribution are broken down into component tasks performed by different laborers. The term more generally applies to the allocation of different kinds of work to different people in various historical moments and geographical settings. These range from the original biological division of labor between women and men; to the designation of people of African descent for slavery in the United States; to the present-day division of much of the world's manufacturing labor between the so-called global North and global South. ("So-called" because there are clearly hierarchies and divisions within each of these zones, which also span both hemispheres.) While the sexual division of labor is, at least in its early phases, largely biological, based upon the child-bearing and lactation capacities distinctive of women, most divisions of labor throughout human history have been coercive, although routinely justified by ideologies of sexism, racism, and other doctrines of inherent difference and hierarchy. The identities by which people define themselves (or are defined by others) are grounded in demographic categories based in the division of labor and global uneven development; these identities can seem natural, but they came into being in history. Perhaps the most fundamental division of labor throughout the history of class-based societies has been the division of mental from manual labor, driving a wedge between those who perform a society's brain-work and those who carry out its grunt-work.

Production

Here are some key terms essential to an understanding of historical materialism. "Means of production" signifies the tools and raw materials that go into the production of something. Instances of different means of production in different phases of human development would be a stone arrowhead, an ox-drawn plow, a steam-powered engine, and a computer. "Forces of production" refers to the means of production in conjunction with labor. Important here are the type and level of technology involved. When the steam engine replaced machinery powered by mills located alongside rivers, for instance, the increased speed of production required that laborers accommodate themselves to the regime of an increasingly segmented labor process. The introduction of the cotton gin in the US South greatly enhanced the productivity of labor, thereby expanding and consolidating the institution of chattel slavery. "Relations of production" refers to the ownership and deployment of the means of production, as well as the ways in which forms of property-holding shape relationships between owners and producers. In European feudalist society, peasant families were generally bound to the land owned by the lord, for generation upon generation (except in such unusual situations as the aftermath of the mid-fourteenth-century Black Death, which produced such a dire demand for labor that formerly bound peasants were able to move from site to site and bargain for their labor). In the Latin American *hacienda* system of the nineteenth century, a combination of free and forced labor, usually performed by indigenous workers, enriched the owners of vast plantations producing commodities like sugar, wheat, wool, and hides for the world market. By contrast, in present-day capitalist society, despite the continuing presence of human trafficking and indentured servitude, most wage-earners are generally at liberty to move from employer to employer (although, as Engels ironically observed, this "fine freedom" allows "the proletarian ... no other choice than that of either accepting the conditions which the bourgeoisie offers him, or of starving, of freezing to death, of sleeping naked among the beasts of the forests!" [*CWCE*, ch. 3]). The term "proletarian" refers to a worker; "bourgeoisie" refers to those owning the means of production in a capitalist society. The paradoxical freedom/unfreedom of the wage-earning worker figures as a key theme in many literary texts from the capitalist era, from Charles Dickens's *Hard Times* (2003 [1854]) to Upton Sinclair's *The Jungle* (1906), from Thomas Cooper's "'Merrie England'—No More!" (1995 [1845]) to Ousmane Sembène's *God's Bits of Wood* (1962 [1960]).

"Mode of production," a broadly encompassing term, signifies the entire social complex constituted by the conjunction of the forces and relations of production. The different forms of social organization that people have to this point devised—ranging from primitive communalism to ancient slave society to a range of geographical variants on feudalism to capitalism—are designated as modes of production. The mode of production expected eventually to supersede capitalism is communism, which builds on the achievements developed under earlier forms of class society—often at great human and environmental cost—while reconstituting, on a higher level, the egalitarian social relations characteristic of pre-class societies. Communism is characterized by the absence of an oppressive state apparatus; the abolition of money; the disappearance of social classes; and the principle that goods and services should be produced and distributed on the basis of social need. As the poet Bertolt Brecht wrote of communism: "The exploiters call it a crime / But we know / it is the end of crime.... It is the simple thing [but] so hard to achieve" (Brecht 1965, 73).

Modes of production, while qualitatively distinguished from one another by the ways in which the few live off the labor of the many, are not static, but themselves undergo continual development. Capitalism, for instance, has evolved over hundreds of years through its merchant, industrial, monopoly, finance, and neoliberal phases, accompanied in its global dimensions by colonialism and imperialism. (The terms "neoliberalism" and "globalization," often used to describe our current moment, need continually to be anchored in an analysis of the capitalist mode of production; otherwise they can be too readily separated from their situation in the historical arc of capitalist development.) The term "social formation" describes the ways in which various traces of past modes of production, as well as features anticipating modes of production still to be fully realized, can be simultaneously present in any given society at any given time (Poulantzas 1973). The cultural historian Raymond Williams introduced the terms "dominant," "residual," and "emergent" to designate the co-presence of different historical tendencies in a given social formation at a given moment (Williams 1977, 121–27). The term "combined and uneven development" stresses both the historical and the geographical dimension of this imbalance on a global scale: the coexistence of mule-drawn plows with combustion-engine tractors, for instance, or of patriarchal forms of the family with women's independent participation in a waged workforce (Anievas and Matin 2016). Another pair of terms useful in describing different phases of economic development within a mode of production is those differentiating between what Marx calls the "formal subsumption" and the "real subsumption" of labor. The first of these denotes a phase when an emergent set of relations of production has gained a foothold but does not dominate an entire branch of industrial or agricultural production. The latter designates a phase when what was emergent is now dominant. Needless to say, what is emergent in one part of the world may already be dominant in another.

While apologists for capitalism would have us think that growth entails prosperity for all—a doctrine captured in the cliché that a rising tide lifts all boats—present-day global capitalism in fact requires that large regions of the world remain underdeveloped in comparison to others. One of the key priorities of communist societies would be—along with breaking down the division between mental and manual labor (Gomberg 2007)—the abolition of the deeply racist legacy of capitalist uneven development.

Although the distinctions between and among such terms as "means," forces," "relations," and "mode" of production may initially sound like theoretical hair-splitting, an understanding of their interrelations is, as we shall see, crucial to the methodology of historical materialism. We should also bear in mind that none of these entities is static; all are continually developing. Moreover, they constitute a totality; it is not in their isolation, but their mutual interconnectedness, that these entities—which are at once both structures and processes—describe and explain social reality. We should remember, too, that these entities are separable mainly for analytical purposes: "forces of production," for instance, includes not just technologies of various kinds but also the skills of the people who deploy them. Finally, we should emphasize that production—a much broader concept than "economics," with which it is often confused—figures centrally in Marx's materialist analysis of social formations. While the economic and psychological pressures of life in modern capitalist society often lead us to associate "production" with such negatively inflected terms as "productivity" and "productivism," which signal the primacy of profit over human or environmental needs, for Marx "production" more generally signifies any activity that contributes to the enabling, preservation, and reproduction of social existence. It is a neutral term, describing activity that is rendered alienating only by the way in which money becomes the measure of all value in our present-day socioeconomic system. Indeed, some things that people do which count as leisure-time occupations under capitalism—such as building a tower out of blocks with a child—would be considered productive in a communist society. At the heart of Marx's emphasis upon production is, simply, his understanding of the centrality of socially organized labor to the definition of what it means to be human.

Marx, preoccupied with understanding the origins and development of capitalism, focused his major writings on its emergence from feudalism in Europe, especially England. As cities gained in importance in the medieval world, the property relations and legal practices advantageous to the agrarian landed nobility were increasingly burdensome to the rising

Why do I use the term "communism" rather than "socialism" to denote the classless society superseding capitalism? Some people think of socialism as an intermediary stage between capitalism and communism, characterized by a strong state and public ownership of the means of production, in which the state will wither away and increasingly egalitarian social relations will prevail. In the more reformist versions of this model, various aspects of socialism—state-funded medical care, for instance, or a robust safety net—can be introduced under capitalism. The belief that socialism need not entail revolution, but instead an extensive redistribution of wealth within the framework of the capitalist mode of production, is better described as "social democratic" rather than "socialist." Other proponents of the view of socialism as a transitional period have not necessarily thought it could be voted in, but they have characterized it as an independent mode of production, separate from both capitalism and communism, described as the "dictatorship of the proletariat" (the term "dictatorship" here signifying not authoritarian rule, but class-based political power).

The uncertain basis for distinguishing between "socialism" and "communism" cannot be resolved by turning to the writings of Marx and Engels, who did not use the terms consistently (Chattopadhyay 2012). In their early writings, Marx and Engels declared that communism was "not a state of affairs which is to be established, an ideal to which reality [will] have to adjust itself," but "the real movement that abolishes the present state of things" (*GI*, Part 5). That is, communism was at once a political practice in the here and now and a mode of production to be realized in the future. In the wake of the Paris Commune of 1871, when the working class had briefly seized state power and organized society, Marx referred to "socialism" as "the declaration of the permanence of the revolution, the class dictatorship of the proletariat as the necessary transit point to the abolition of class distinctions generally" (*CSF*). Subsequently, however, he deployed the terms "first phase of communist society" and "higher phase of communist society" to denote different stages through which post-capitalist society would move (*CGP*, ch. 1).

While no revolutionary has ever thought that one could just wave a wand and make capitalism disappear, the use of "socialism" and "communism" to describe successive post-capitalist societies has been called into question by the history of the past century. Countries designating themselves as socialist (the Soviet Union and China figure prominently here) retained so many features of capitalist inequality—including nationalist politics, unequal wages, and continuing divisions between mental and manual labor—that they reverted to capitalism. It has thus proven highly problematic to propose that socialism is a mode of production distinctive from both capitalism and communism (Balibar, 2007, 105–6; PLP, 1982). While it is beyond the scope of this book to explore the strengths and weaknesses of twentieth-century attempts to move toward communism through an intermediary stage of socialism, we shall not muddy the theoretical waters by invoking a stage-based distinction between the two terms.

merchant class. The bourgeois revolutions in various nations—accompanied by "bourgeois-democratic" forms of government—both reflected and enabled this shift in social forces. (For Marx, the term "bourgeois" signifies a ruling elite that draws its wealth from industry or commerce—not a well-off social stratum characterized by somewhat crude tastes and mannerisms, as the term is often used today.) But the larger purpose of Marx's narrative was to understand how the contradictions within capitalism—primarily, its inevitable tendency toward self-induced crisis, as well as its creation of a class of propertyless laborers "with nothing to lose but [their] chains" (*CM*, ch. 4)—might create the conditions for the emergence of communism. This is what Marx meant when he described communism as "the complete return of man to himself as a social (i.e., human) being…. [It] is the riddle of history solved" ("Private Property and Communism," in *EPM*). Where previous aspirations toward a classless society had of necessity been idealist, confined to the realm of hope—what the revolutionary Filipino poet Carlos Bulosan called "the living dream of dead men everywhere" (Bulosan 2007, 593)—the material realization of this dream was made possible by the development of modern forces of production. What distinguishes the proletarian (that is, working-class) revolution from all previous social revolutions is that it does not substitute one ruling class for another but abolishes class as such. Indeed, paradoxical as it may sound, the goal of the proletarian revolution is the abolition of the proletariat itself, creating "an association, in which the free development of each is the condition of the free development of all" (*CM*, ch. 2). As many writers of revolutionary working-class literature (sometimes called proletarian literature) have recognized, it is by heightening class consciousness in the present that true human universality can be achieved in the future. As the potential for such transformation lurking in the present, communism—which Marx and Engels in 1848 described as a "specter haunting Europe" (*CM*, Preface)—remains the spectre that haunts the entire capitalist world order in our time.

Dialectics

How exactly does change occur, such that one mode of production emerges from, and then supersedes, another? A key analytical concept here is dialectics—a term with a long history, going back to various philosophies developed throughout the ancient world—which signifies the study of the ways in which phenomena are interconnected with one another and undergo change. The dialectical philosopher who had the

greatest impact upon Marx was G.F.W. Hegel (1770–1831), whose theorization of the dynamic nature of all processes would prove central to
Marx's analytical method. Even though Hegel was an idealist rather than
a materialist, Marx wrote:

> The mystification which the dialectic suffers in Hegel's hands, by no
> means prevents him from being the first to present its general form
> of working in a comprehensive and conscious manner. With him it is
> standing on its head. It must be turned right side up again, if you would
> discover the rational kernel within the mystical shell. (*C* I, Afterword
> to the 2nd German edn)

Key to the Hegelian method is the notion of contradiction. In our
everyday use, this word signifies an "either/or" mode of thinking:
a statement is either true or false. The dialectical use of the term, by
contrast, points to the unity and conflict of opposites that drive development within a given entity or process, causing it to come into being and,
over time, go out of being, while retaining aspects of its former mode of
existence. This process of transformation is called "negation"; the simultaneous abolition and retention of the elements of the old within the new
is designated as "sublation"; a qualitative movement from old to new is
called the "negation of negation" (Engels, *A-D*, ch. XIII). Marx deployed
the vocabulary of dialectics to explain the emergence of communism
from capitalism. "Capitalist private property," he wrote:

> is the first negation of individual private property, as founded on the
> labour of the proprietor. But capitalist production begets, with the
> inexorability of a law of Nature, its own negation. It is the negation
> of the negation. This does not re-establish private property for the
> producer, but gives him individual property based on the acquisition of
> the capitalist era: *i.e.*, on cooperation and the possession in common of
> the land and of the means of production. (*C* I, ch. 32)

The term "negation," as it figures in the vocabulary of dialectics, also
requires some teasing out. In everyday usage, "negation" signifies saying
"no" and often connotes negativity, a propensity for contrariness, as in
"having a negative attitude." From a dialectical standpoint, however,
"negation" points to the potentiality for change: while seemingly stable,
an entity or a process in fact is constantly in a state of flux, containing
within itself its negation, that is, the seed of its own undoing. This seed

is historically conditioned, setting limits as well as containing potentialities: thus communism could not emerge from ancient slave society, but became a world-historical possibility only when capitalism had developed to a certain point in some parts of the world. Marx referred to the process of negation in the realm of production as at once an "external spur" and a "bridle" of change (GR, ch. 8). Once we start thinking in terms of contradiction and negation, we see dialectics at work in many places, giving rise to all kinds of paradoxes and ironies, boomerang effects and unintended consequences. Marx's entire project in *Capital*, for instance, examines how capital's drive to accumulation—that is, its need continually to expand, just as a shark needs to keep moving in order to stay alive—results in crises that hobble the very pursuit for profit that motivates this drive to begin with. A dialectical analysis of global uneven development foregrounds the paradoxical interdependence of wealth and poverty: while capitalism expands the possibilities for personal development for some people, it deprives millions of others of the opportunity to nurture their own or their children's talents—and, in some cases, simply to stay alive. A further contradiction, however, is the moral crippling, through the coarsening effects of competitive individualism, of many of those more fortunate—a consequence ironically registered in novels representing the lives of the super-wealthy, such as Anthony Trollope's *The Way We Live Now* (2016 [1875]) or F. Scott Fitzgerald's *The Great Gatsby* (1925). But dialectics help us understand not just large-scale trends. An intimate instance of contradiction, one familiar to many of us, is the simultaneous pull toward trust and cynicism in a friendship—a struggle that can result either in heightened mutual commitment (the negation of doubt) or, conversely, in a hostile break (the negation of the relationship).

Thinking—and reading—dialectically are central to Marxist inquiry, including literary criticism; here are some key terms that will figure prominently in the analyses we undertake in future chapters. Crucially important to the vocabulary of dialectics are the terms "appearance" and "essence." The first describes a process or an entity as a kind of snapshot, frozen in its timebound "being." The latter, by contrast, stresses its "becoming," its present embodiment of its past and its possible future; essence, in other words, implies the potentiality for its negation, for its re-emergence in altered form. While appearance is not false or illusory, its truth is at best partial, for it captures only the surface of the phenomenon under investigation. Marx's critique of contemporaneous political economists, for instance, was largely based on their substitution of appearance for essence; for instance, they considered price as equivalent to value because they did not probe the process by which value takes the form of money to begin with. Another key dialectical term is "totality," which signifies not just the wholeness of an entity or a process, or the sum total of the "factors" by which it is constituted, but the dynamic interconnections, both temporal and structural, among its component parts. To "think totality" is actively to seek out such interconnections. In Marxist literary criticism, for instance, the realism of a literary work is seen as residing less in its evocation of historically accurate surface details than in its penetration to the fundamental contradictions informing the society that is being represented. A central goal of proletarian literature is to anchor its implied call for revolutionary change in a representation that establishes the causal connections between and among unequal social strata. It was this totalizing standpoint that the novelist Richard Wright had in mind when, during the Great Depression, he wrote of the need for writers:

to learn to view the life of a Negro living in New York's Harlem or Chicago's South Side with the consciousness that one-sixth of the earth's surface belongs to the working class. It means that Negro writers must create in their readers' minds a relationship between a Negro woman hoeing cotton in the South and the men who loll in swivel chairs in Wall Street and take the fruits of her toil. (Wright 1937, 62)

Wright juxtaposed these two figures not only to signify that the sharecropper's labor supplied the wealth of the financier but also to suggest that she was the specter of his symbolic negation; the fact that revolution had already occurred in the Soviet Union ("one-sixth of the world's surface") invested this view of totality with historical plausibility.

Since thinking dialectically means being critical of undialectical thought, here are some terms that will be red-flagged for critique in coming chapters. "Mid-level analytics" signifies procedures of inquiry that stop short of totality. "Arrested dialectic" alludes to the illusory perception that history has been halted. "False totality" describes idealist generalization. "Antinomy" refers to the freezing of the poles of a contradiction, substituting stasis for process. "Stand-alone concept" refers to a phenomenon that does not imply—or seem to imply—its opposite. Although some terms clearly do not have negative counterparts (apple, for instance, or table), while others are defined in terms of their negatives (up/down, for instance, or inside/outside), of concern to dialectical inquiry are terms that appear to be "stand-alone" but actually are dialectically (and politically) loaded. Some people are "rich" not just because they are lucky (much less deserving), but because others are "poor." While dialectics does not contain a magical methodology, it remains indispensable for the analysis of phenomena and processes of many kinds—including the language through which these are described.

Class

The concept of class is central to Marxist social and historical analysis. Whereas in much mainstream sociological writing "class" figures as a stand-alone term, designating different groups on the basis of criteria such as status and income, in Marxist theory social classes are constituted by their contradictory interrelation: without the bourgeoisie there is no proletariat, and vice versa. When Marx and Engels write in *The Communist Manifesto* (*CM*, ch. 1)that "the history of all hitherto existing society is the history of class struggles," they point to the fundamentally antagonistic relationship between those who labor and those who live off the social surplus—that is, the amount of goods and services above and beyond what is needed for group survival—that has been created by those who labor. (As Engels noted in a correction to the text, "the history of all hitherto existing society" referred to "*written* history," not to the primitive communalist formations preceding the differentiation of societies into "separate and finally antagonistic classes"[*CM*, ch. 1, fn. 2].) This antagonism is denoted by the term "class struggle," which describes not only those moments when social conflict bursts out in the open, as in a strike, a riot, a rebellion, or a revolution, but also the daily struggle between bosses and workers—over wages, working conditions, public expenditures, environmental impacts: the whole complex of practices and distributions within a given social formation. When captured Africans jumped into the sea rather than endure the horrors of the Atlantic mid-passage, or enslaved women in the Caribbean committed infanticide, these too can be seen as instances—even when individual and desperate—of class struggle.

Although class struggle has been especially prominent in the capitalist era, it is not a feature of modernity alone: in all modes of production following primitive communalism there have existed ruling classes (whether patriarchs, slaveholders, aristocrats, emperors, monarchs, imperialist bankers, along with their elite allies and administrators) and producing classes (whether slaves, serfs, peasants, indentured servants, or waged workers). Defining the notion of exploitation, Marx wrote:

"The specific economic form in which unpaid surplus labor is *pumped out of* direct producers determines the relations of rulers and ruled" (*C* III, ch. 47). Since the origins of class-based inequality, societies have differed in their modes of exploitation; but the extraction of wealth from the labor of the many for the benefit of the few has been common to them all. The class struggle has taken different forms in different eras. The 1850–64 Taiping Rebellion in China, the 1871 Paris Commune, the 1904–7 Herero rebellion in Namibia, and the 1937 Sit-down Strike in Flint, Michigan are relatively modern instances. They have their historical counterparts, however, in the 1170 BCE strike among Egyptian pyramid builders; the Spartacus slave revolt of 73–71 BCE (De Ste. Croix 1981); and the waves of peasant uprisings marking the transitions between dynasties over hundreds of years in China. In medieval England (Faith 1981) class antagonism is registered in such fourteenth- and fifteenth-century literary works as William Langland's *Piers Plowman* (Langland 2007 [1370–90]) and *The Second Shepherd's Play* (Wakefield 1910 [c. 1500]). Victor Hugo's *Notre-Dame de Paris* (1831 [English trans. as *The Hunchback of Notre Dame*, 2012 (1833)]), while inspired by nineteenth-century class struggles, relocates the antagonism between haves and have-nots in the Paris of some four centuries before. In all class-based social formations, there has been continual struggle between the rulers and the ruled. Reflecting in 1846 that the oppressed masses had not yet managed to wrest power from their adversaries, Marx wrote, "Irrespective of the fact that it is always the bad side that in the end triumphs over the good side ... the bad side ... produces the movement which makes history, by providing a struggle" (*PP*, ch. 2).

Three important points emerge from a Marxist analysis of class as a function of social relations of production. First, class is an objective phenomenon. While some theorists argue that classes do not exist unless people are aware of them (Hindess and Hirst 1975), the definition of social class is not contingent upon the subjective standpoints of particular individuals or groups. Second, whether they know it or not, the majority of people in capitalist society are members of the proletariat or working class. The belief commonly held in the United States today that most people belong to the middle class—a notion widely promulgated in the press, particularly at election time—is false: if you have no means of production of your own and must work for a boss for a salary or a wage to survive, you are a proletarian. But, third, the proletariat, broadly conceived in its historical development, is not confined to the group of people paid wages by their bosses. The original meaning of "proletariat," during the period of the Roman Republic over 2000 years ago, designated those who have no property other than their capacity to produce offspring. Even more than in Marx's time, wage-earners now constitute the core of the world's proletariat; indeed, while some social theorists have argued that present-day society is "post-industrial," a glance around the globe shows that a higher number of people in the world's population, in both absolute and proportional terms, are involved in wage-labor—whether in the industrial or the service sectors—than ever before. To substitute for the notion of the "proletariat" such vague notions as "the poor" or "the multitude" (Hardt and Negri 2004) deflects attention from the notion of exploitation, which, is central to an understanding of class antagonism. (The relationship of wage-labor to exploitation in capitalist society is discussed more fully in the next chapter.) But the proletariat also includes (1) those who are forced into under- and unemployment, whom Marx called the "industrial reserve army" (C I, ch. 25); (2) those who labor for a pittance in the immense informal (that is, non-waged, barter, and street trade) economies existing at the fringes of industrial economies in many places (J. Smith 2016); (3) those who provide the uncompensated labor involved in childrearing and care of the disabled or elderly (Vogel 2014); (4) the Uber-drivers, internet contributors, and other members of the steadily growing "precariat," sometimes designated as "private contractors," in what is euphemistically termed the "gig economy" (or, worse, the "sharing economy") (Standing 2011); as well as (5) the tens of millions of indentured laborers and outright slaves who are to this day hidden in plain sight in many of the world's cities, fields, and oceans (Brass 2010).

It remains a priority among leftists to organize workers who are strategically placed to bring production to a grinding halt, thereby hitting the capitalists where it hurts the most, in their pockets. But the notion that only wage-earning industrial workers are proletarians—a belief often accompanied by the notion that social revolution can be made only by blue-collar steelworkers, meat-cutters, or truck drivers—is a doctrine that distorts the racialized and gendered demographics of the global working class and inhibits the development of the revolutionary social movements needed by the great majority of the globe's inhabitants. (This doctrine is sometimes called "economism" or "workerism.") When Marx and Engels published *The Communist Manifesto* in 1848, they asserted that the communist revolution would speak to the needs of the "immense majority"—even though in nineteenth-century Europe wage-earning factory workers were a distinct minority (*CM*, ch. 1). The Russian revolutionary leader Vladimir Ilyich Lenin, similarly, wrote that the Bolsheviks should defend the rights of all oppressed sectors of the population, even though they needed to concentrate their efforts on urban workers best positioned to lead the revolutionary charge (*WITBD*). The sociologist and historian W.E.B. Du Bois, writing about post-Civil War Reconstruction from the vantage point of the 1930s, designated the freedmen and freedwomen newly emancipated from the plantations as "proletarians," possessing a common interest (if not always a shared consciousness) with their white peers (Du Bois 1998 [1935], chs 1 and 2). For these and other theorists of revolutionary change, the proletariat is to be defined not just by its empirical make-up at any moment in time—that is, as a "stand-alone" term—but what it is, actually or potentially, in the process of becoming. At present, the generation of a unifying class consciousness in the immense, disparate global proletariat—enabling its objective existence as a class in need of self-abolition to develop it into a historical force capable of carrying out this task—is perhaps the greatest challenge facing those who envision social revolution as necessary for human survival and flourishing, not to mention the continuation of all life on the planet. This revolutionary project is called "proletarian internationalism," designating the need for the world's workers to repudiate nationalist allegiances and recognize their common interests as a class.

What does it mean to say that class is the "primary" analytical category for explaining social inequality and leveraging revolutionary social change? What about sexism and racism as modes of domination, and gender and race as modes of identity? While it is important, both theoretically and practically, to embrace as broad a definition of the proletariat as possible, it is equally important that class not be simply equated with other types of social positions, much less viewed primarily as a matter of identity. It is incontestable that members of the proletariat who occupy lower positions in hierarchies established on the basis of gender and race—and, often, geography—generally experience the greatest degree of economic hardship, encounter the greatest amount of coercion, and possess the fewest illusions about the legitimacy of the status quo. The standpoint generated by this positionality has often given rise to distinct forms of consciousness that have figured as primary motivators in struggles for radical social change (Hartsock 2004; Mohanty 1997). But this does not mean that gender, race, and class function along comparable axes.

Class, as a social relation of production, directs attention primarily to exploitation (see chapter 2). Gender and race, by contrast, are connected with modes of oppression (brutal treatment) and domination (control) that have historically emerged from the division of labor in different modes of production. Gendered oppression, Engels argued, came into being with the emergence of class societies out of primitive communalism (*OFPPS*). Racialized oppression—including the concept of "race" itself—took shape more recently, in the context of modern chattel slavery (L. Bennett 1975; Fields 1990; Allen 2012) and colonialism (Cabral 1970; Fanon 1963). These modes of oppression are closely linked to exploitation, past and present; much of the literature registering the effects of sexist, racist, and colonial oppression thus possesses a "materialist heartbeat" (Lazarus 2011, 79). In combination, moreover—as illustrated amply in writings by women of color, from Alice Walker's *The Color Purple* (1982) to Helen Maria Viramontes' "The Cariboo Café" (1985)—oppression based upon gender and race, an especially toxic brew, is often experienced more directly and coercively than class-based exploitation; it can be the proximate cause of the violent fist in the face. As we shall see, the conjunction of class, race and gender can be usefully addressed through the concept of "structure in dominance."

Nonetheless, sexism and racism (conceived of as causal matrices), remain analytically distinct within the capitalist world order. After all, gender does not cause sexism; race does not cause racism (Aguilar 2015; Meyerson 2000). By contrast, class analysis not only directs attention to the totality in which various sectors of the proletariat are all situated but also supplies the grounds for a broad-based strategy for opposition to sexism, racism, and a host of other oppressive "isms." For class analysis demonstrates that—contrary to popular conceptions of male dominance—the majority of men, as members of the proletariat, are not in fact benefited but instead disabled by sexism, even if the prevailing culture often leads them to feel more powerful than women (Leacock 1981). Comparably, most members of the proletariat designated as "white" end up being hurt by racism, which can lead them to align themselves with their class enemies of the same color and scapegoat workers of darker hue or foreign origin as the source of their hardships (Painter 2011; Taylor 2016). Such terms as "white skin privilege" (McIntosh 1989) and "white advantage" (Roediger 2017, 20–22) translate the differential treatment generally accorded to whites into an objective benefit; white antiracism thus signifies not material self-interest but missionary self-sacrifice. The core problem with these formulations is not that they focus on racialized differentials—which are very real—but that they adopt the wrong standard for measuring their significance, based upon the actual capitalist present rather than the potential classless future. To say that most whites—who are after all workers—are "less oppressed" rather than "more privileged," "less deprived" rather than "more advantaged" compared to their darker-skinned equivalents is neither a verbal quibble nor an evasion of reality that buries race in class (Isenberg 2016). Instead, this formulation takes as its basis of measurement actual human need—and points to the necessity for communism as the necessary negation of all systemic inequalities.

Base and Superstructure

Before we examine the economic basis of designations of social class in chapter 2, we need to tackle a concept central to historical materialist methodology—namely, the relationship between what has been called the "base" and the "superstructure." (Sometimes "base" is translated from German as "infrastructure.") Marx's clearest description of this relationship is presented in his 1859 Preface to the *Contribution to the Critique of Political Economy*:

> In the social production of their life, men enter into definite relations that are indispensable and independent of their will; these relations of production correspond to a definite stage of development of their material forces of production. The sum total of these relations of production constitutes the economic structure of society—the real foundation, on which rises a legal and political superstructure and to which correspond definite forms of social consciousness. The mode of production of material life determines the social, political and intellectual life process in general. It is not the consciousness of men that determines their being, but, on the contrary, their social being that determines their consciousness. (*PCCPE*)

In setting forth the contrast between materialism and idealism, Marx uses two key terms—"determine" and "correspond"—to account for material causality in its temporal and structural aspects. (The German term, *bestimmen*, signifies "determine" not as fixing, but instead as shaping or conditioning, a given outcome.) The contradiction between forces and relations of production constitutes the base (the "real foundation") in the historical development of modes of production. The superstructure denotes the historically varying social institutions that accord with the different ways in which surpluses are extracted from living labor at "definite stages of development" of productive forces. These social institutions supply the basis of the cultural practices and belief systems—"different forms of social consciousness"—prevailing in different social formations. (The "intellectual life process" is where literature and literary criticism come in for consideration.)

Examples from different eras illustrate the historically determined nature of the base–superstructure correspondence. In the transition from feudalism to capitalism, for instance, the movement from bound to free labor is accompanied by changes in modes of government, from aristocracy to democracy, and, accordingly, in dominant ideas of what it means to be a member of society. Hence the supersession of feudal-era notions of obligation and dependency, such as those celebrated in the stories of King Arthur and the Knights of the Round Table, by capitalist-era notions of individual freedom and autonomy, such as those featured in the "rags to riches" stories embodied in the best-selling dime novels by Horatio Alger. In the nineteenth-century United States, where principles of formal democratic equality, extended to larger numbers of white men, coexisted with the institution of chattel slavery, it became increasingly necessary to justify slavery by means of pseudoscientific theories of racial hierarchy rather than older notions of paternalistic responsibility (Fredrickson 1987; Kendi 2016). Developments in employment patterns in present-day capitalist society—where unstable, short-term employment and Uber-driving "independence" are increasingly the order of the day—and the emergence of a fluid, free-floating conception of selfhood, often manifested as "intensifying processes of self-individuation" and rationalized as "entrepreneurship," offer another instance of the ways in which social being determines consciousness (Dean 2016, 31).

Central to the superstructure—and to the continuation of ruling-class hegemony—is the state. Many people think of the state as a neutral institution that acts to reconcile the different interests of different social groups. The state has the appearance of a stand-alone entity—an impression visually enhanced by the monumental buildings testifying to its self-sufficient solidity. Actually, however, there has not always been a state: the long stage of primitive communalism—constituting, anthropological studies conclude, at least 90 percent of human history (Gowdy 2004)—is marked by the absence of any type of state apparatus. In societies based upon collective production and distribution and the absence of private property—among the Sān of the Kalahari Desert (Barnard 2007) or the Inuit of Greenland, at least until recently—control is exerted over individuals who stray from the rules of the group by mechanisms like shaming and ostracism. In these societies, however, there are no courts, no police, no prisons—features of future classless worlds hypothesized by writers like William Morris in *News from Nowhere* (1994 [1890]) and Marge Piercy in *Woman on the Edge of Time* (1976). Rather than constituting a necessary means of social organization that has existed throughout time, the state in fact emerged historically as the negation of such egalitarian arrangements. Although the historical form of the state has varied with the mode of production, wherever the private property of the wealthy has needed to be protected from appropriation by the producers and the poor—whether slaves, serfs, peasants, wage-earners, or the unemployed—there has existed an apparatus of legally sanctioned institutions designed to enact this preservation, by any means necessary. Marx and Engels thus defined "the executive of the modern state" as "but a committee for managing the common affairs of the whole bourgeoisie" (*CM*, ch. 1). Lenin applied this formulation equally to all forms of bourgeois rule. "To decide once every few years which member of the ruling class is to repress and crush the people through parliament," he wrote, "this is the real essence of bourgeois parliamentarism, not only in parliamentary-constitutional monarchies, but also in the most democratic republics" (*S&R*, ch. 3). The modern bourgeois-democratic state controls the masses as fully as did the kingdoms presided over by Egyptian pharaohs or the monarchy ruled over by Louis XIV, the "Sun King," from seventeenth-century Versailles. Indeed, since capitalism relies much more on economic coercion than on state intervention in controlling the behavior of the producing population, it can be argued that the modern state has perfected the mechanisms of class rule in a way unimaginable to past elites.

While the state regulates everyday life to keep things moving—traffic is directed, wages are (sometimes) paid—the essence of the state remains its capacity to use force to maintain order so that capitalist money-making can proceed with minimal interruption. This is especially true in connection with racialized populations subjected to colonial oppression or, in the core capitalist nations, to heightened levels of surveillance and police violence (Fanon 1963; Alexander 2010). One of the markers of capitalism's movement into a fascist phase is the extension of such repression to broader and broader segments of the population, even as certain sectors are bribed with differential rewards—a process that Jack London illustrated with chilling prescience in his 1908 dystopian novel, *The Iron Heel*. But ruling classes have always preferred to exercise social control through systems of ideas and beliefs that, possessing the aura of common sense, discipline the producers to remain on the treadmill of daily life of their own accord. Hence the importance of viewing such institutions as organized religion, the mass media, or the educational system as structures embedded in the "state" broadly conceived. The French Marxist philosopher Louis Althusser terms these institutions "Ideological State Apparatuses" ("ISAs," for short—Althusser 2014, 232–72). The Italian communist leader and theorist Antonio Gramsci used the term "hegemony" to signify the "combination of force and consent" by which a "social group" aiming at "domination" and "intellectual and moral leadership" asserts its control throughout society (Gramsci 1971, 57). As we shall see, the ways in which "ideology" and "hegemony" at once reflect and reinforce the base–superstructure relationship have proven foundational to Marxist analyses of a broad range of literary texts and traditions—those affirming the status quo as well as those contesting its legitimacy and calling for revolutionary change.

Can the base–superstructure paradigm supply a universally applicable account of social change? Or is Marxist class analysis bound to its European origins, and therefore blind to the particularity of colonialism and imperialism, as well as of racist oppression in the nations of the global North? Some postcolonial and critical race theorists have argued that the "modes of production narrative" they find embedded in Marxist theory has limited applicability to world history, and that, when taken as a universal description, embodies a presumption of superiority on the part of "the West" (Said 1994; Chakrabarty 2007; Mills 2003). A further conclusion sometimes inferred from Marx's writings— that all societies need to undergo full-fledged capitalist development before making the transition to a post-capitalist social order—has been criticized as mechanical and "stageist." Once capitalism has achieved full realization in some parts of the world, it has been argued, other regions, especially those where development has been fettered by colonialism and imperialism, should be able to bypass the slow and painful stages by which capitalism emerged from feudalism in Europe and move directly to egalitarian social relations (Anievas and Matin 2016).

There is some basis for this critique of Eurocentrism in early writings of Marx and Engels; in *The Communist Manifesto*, for instance, they praise capitalism's historically progressive function in drawing all parts of the globe— including "barbarian nations"—into a single world market. It bears noting, however, that even here Marx and Engels referred ironically to capitalism's imposition of "what it calls civilisation" (*CM*, ch. 1). In subsequent writings, Marx increasingly denied that the development of capitalism in England supplied a model for historical development elsewhere; his methodology was retrospective, tracing origins and presuppositions, rather than prophetic, prescribing law-governed development with universal applicability (Anderson 2010). In his *Ethnographical Notebooks* and other late writings studying Asia, Africa, and Latin America, moreover, Marx investigated the distinctive forces and relations of production—and possible alternative paths to communism—in non-Western societies. In correspondence with the Russian revolutionary Vera Zasulich, he pondered whether the residual presence of the *mir* or *obshchina*—that is, the peasant commune—supplied the basis for an immediate transition to a classless society, thereby bypassing capitalist development (Marx to Zasulich, 1881, *MEC*; Kalmring and Nowak 2017).

During the second half of the past century, it further bears noting, the practical utility of Marxist theory as a guide to revolutionary practice was tested out more fully in largely agrarian nations—from China to Cuba—than in more industrially developed parts of the globe. In Africa, anti-colonial theorists such as Amilcar Cabral in Guinea-Bissau, Frantz Fanon in Algeria, and Kwame Nkrumah in Ghana queried whether it would be possible to graft socialist revolution onto the abiding features of pre-class society in nations struggling for freedom from European economic, political, and cultural domination. For Fanon, "whether the bourgeois phase can be effectively skipped [in the history of underdeveloped countries] must be resolved through revolutionary action and not through reasoning" (Fanon 1963, 119). Some African movements for national liberation ended up caving in to the internal contradictions produced by the consolidation of national bourgeoisies replacing the colonial rulers—a development to which the Kenyan writer Ngũgĩ Wa Thiong'o testified with biting satire in *Matigari* (1986; English trans. 1989). Movements in other nations were violently suppressed: Cabral, who had called upon the intelligentsia to commit "class suicide" if they wished to serve the masses, was murdered by Portuguese agents in 1973 (Cabral 1966). The austerity regimes imposed in subsequent decades by the International Monetary Fund (IMF) and the World Bank would complete the task of drawing these and other nations into the stranglehold of capital. Nonetheless, a number of these postwar national liberation movements were initially guided by the theory that instituting a distinctly African "scientific socialism" (Nkrumah 1965) was compatible with a relatively low level of development of productive forces. Rather than seen as irremediably tainted by its European origin or relevant only to countries with majority-white populations, Marxism significantly influenced many of the past century's social revolutions.

Relative Autonomy

As we make use of historical materialism in literary analysis, we need to be methodologically self-conscious and ask: what are the advantages, but also the possible shortcomings, of the base–superstructure paradigm as a way of understanding the linkages between and among literature, culture, consciousness, and material reality? This explanatory scheme enables us to anchor both social institutions and modes of thinking and feeling in the structural imperatives of class rule. It invites us to remove the legitimating veil from seemingly neutral institutions and conventional practices and examine critically their functions in sustaining social hierarchies. It helps us see how all literature is in some sense political. It reminds us, moreover, of the historical embeddedness of just about every social phenomenon and practice, from markets to forms of marriage to assumptions about what it means to be a human being. "Always historicize!" we shall see, is a cardinal principle of Marxist literary analysis (Jameson 1981, 9).

A potential shortcoming of the base–superstructure model, however— at least of its undialectical application—is that it can encourage a reductive (that is, one-sided and oversimplified) notion of causality, too readily linking cultural phenomena to class-based practices and giving too short shrift to what has been termed the "relative autonomy" of superstructures. ("Autonomy" signifies the independence of one entity or practice from another, while "relative" qualifies the degree of this independence.) Put to use in a mechanical way, the base–superstructure model can underestimate the contradictory nature of many superstructural institutions and processes (Althusser's "ISAs"). Clearly the educational ISA functions to impose a pro-capitalist regime, as is illustrated, for instance, by a 2012 ruling by the Texas Board of Education that the phrase "Free enterprise system" had to be substituted for the word "capitalism" in all economics textbooks used in the public schools.[1] But to acknowledge that the ruling class directly or indirectly controls the educational apparatus from K-12 (i.e. kindergarten to grade/year 12) through graduate school does not mean that schools and universities cannot be important sites of ideological struggle against the very class by which they are financed, licensed, and legitimated. The terrain of the educational apparatus is not neutral, but neither is it uncontested—a matter of no small importance to teachers and students striving to change campus practices they find unjust or oppressive. Often related to this underestimation of contradiction is an overestimation of the inflexibility of the ruling class. Although Gramsci, imprisoned by the Fascists for most of the last decade of his short life, was well acquainted with the coercive power of the state, in his prison writings he argued that bourgeois hegemony is unstable and insecure, constantly in need of reinforcement and renewal. Indeed, he argued, for the exploiting class to continue enjoying the fruits of political power and economic enrichment it has to keep adjusting the terms of its domination over those inhabiting the lower rungs of society (Gramsci 1971, 257–64). Perhaps the most famous literary expression of this ruling-class imperative is the statement by the wealthy landowning Prince of Salina in Giuseppe Tomasi di Lampedusa's historical novel *Il Gattopardo* (1958; English translation 1960 as *The Leopard*) to the effect that "If we want things to stay as they are, things will have to change" (Tomasi di Lampedusa 1960, 40).

Reductionism can also result from too literal an interpretation of the spatial dimension implied in the base–superstructure model. The architectural metaphor can be taken to posit that the basement and first floor—often construed as simply "the economic"—are fundamental, while the higher stories rising into the sky possess less causal importance. One need only consider the Nazi regime's increasing obsession with the mass murder of Jews during World War II—even when this obsession interfered with military necessity—to see the shortcomings of an argument insisting upon the secondary importance of ideological motivations in all situations (Mayer 2012). Late in his life, Engels criticized self-proclaimed inheritors of Marx's method for ignoring the reciprocity—that is, back-and-forth influence—between base and superstructure. He wrote:

> According to the materialist conception of history, the *ultimately* determining element in history is the production and reproduction of real life. Other than this neither Marx nor I have ever asserted.... The economic situation is the basis, but the various elements of the superstructure ... also exercise their influence upon the course of the historical struggles and in many cases preponderate in determining their *form*. (FE to Bloch, 21 September 1890, *MEC*)

Althusser, wary of versions of Marxism positing all phenomena as produced by a single unitary cause, proposed a revision of the base–superstructure model stressing the causal role of various "structures in dominance" that are determined only in "the last instance" by economic forces (Althusser 1969, 161–217; Resch 1992, 52–57). In his view, the Church, while ultimately tied to the class structure of feudalist society, performed this dominant function in premodern European times; the school system, comparably enacting the needs of the bourgeoisie, performs this function in modern capitalist society.

In addition, the base–superstructure metaphor can be interpreted too literally in connection with time: first comes the impetus for change from the dialectic of the forces and relations of production; then come such institutional transformations as the supersession of monarchy by democracy; then come alterations in consciousness. Again, this is a mechanical reduction of a complex process. Although the historical development of modes of production allows for various ways of thinking and believing to be operative in a given social formation at a given time, such indicators of uneven development are primarily linked not to a chronological "lag" between base and superstructure. Instead, the residual presence of regimes of power in a given social formation coexists with emergent tendencies that will possess hegemonic status at a future time. A somewhat macabre instance of the emergence of capitalist financial practices amid residually feudalistic social relations is contained in Nikolai Gogol's novel *Dead Souls* (1842; English translation 1886), which describes a trickster who buys up the names of deceased serfs to use this phony "property" to leverage a huge bank loan. An ironic testament to the conjoined interests of aristocratic landlords with capitalist factory owners is featured in the parliamentary election portrayed in Robert Tressell's *The Ragged-Trousered Philanthropists* (2012 [1914]), where the aptly named Tory landowner D'Encloseland loses by a narrow margin to the equally well-named Liberal industrialist Sweater, but the two remain good friends (Tressell 2012 [1914], ch. 48). (Enclosure refers to the process by which wealthy landowners dispossessed peasants of commonly held lands as agrarian capitalism took hold in the English countryside.)

The notions of relative autonomy, structures in dominance, uneven development, and reciprocity all play central roles in Marxist literary study, since historical actors—including writers—are often motivated by cultural affinities, political loyalties, and ideological doctrines that are only indirectly linked to what Marx called the "production and reproduction of real life." Of particular importance is an appreciation of the extent to which various writers—some of them explicitly revolutionary, others simply insightful and prescient—have been able to discern in the present the lineaments of a qualitatively transformed future. At times this prophetic strain—dubbed as "utopianism"—has taken idealist form. Henry David Thoreau, for instance, wrote that "If you have built castles in the air, your work need not be lost; that is where they should be. Now put the foundations under them"; but his experiences at Walden Pond hardly embodied a plan for social transformation (Thoreau 2000 [1854], 257). Marx and Engels, while appreciating the egalitarian experiments of certain figures—Robert Owen, Henri de St. Simon, and Charles Fourier—devoted an entire section of *The Communist Manifesto* to a critique of the idealist shortcomings, and at times reactionary underpinnings, of contemporaneous Utopian Socialists (*CM*, Part 3; see also Engels, *SUAS*). Especially in times of crisis, however, when relations of power and domination are laid bare, social revolutions are possible largely because historical actors can glimpse the outlines of a future that does not yet exist. In *What Is To Be Done?* (1902), Lenin quoted the observation of the Russian revolutionary writer Dmitry Ivanovich Pisarev that "if [the person who is dreaming] attentively observes life, compares his observations with his castles in the air, and … works conscientiously for the achievement of his fantasies … the rift between dreams and reality causes no harm"; to which Lenin added, "Of this kind of dreaming there is unfortunately too little in our movement" (*WITBD*, ch. 5). Gramsci, contemplating the role played by literature in preparing the way for new social formations, wrote that "every new civilization … (even when held back, attacked and fettered in every possible way), has always expressed itself in literary form before expressing itself in the life of the state" (Gramsci 1985, 117). The German philosopher Ernst Bloch made an important distinction between texts that supplied what he called "compensatory utopia"—a consoling vision of an unattainable better world—and "anticipatory utopia," signaling a "Not-Yet-Conscious [and] a Not-Yet-Become" that might still come into being (Bloch 1986, Introduction; Levitas 1990, 83–105). The US proletarian writer Tillie Olsen—inspired by Bloch—wrote of the need to be "strong with the not-yet in the now" (Olsen 1960, 109; Dawahare 2018). The base–superstructure paradigm proves indispensable to an analysis and assessment of the utopian dimension of various literary texts and traditions.

Mediation

Also indispensable to Marxist explorations of causality is the notion of mediation. In its most general sense, mediation signifies the process by which two phenomena that may appear to be unrelated to one another can be shown to be vitally linked by means of a third term that expresses an important inner connection between them. For example, labor mediates between humanity and nature. Money—which Marx referred to as "the pimp between need and object" ("Human Requirements and Division of Labor," *EPM*)—mediates between the market and human subsistence. The state mediates between the rulers and the ruled. A revolutionary party mediates—or at least aspires to mediate—between the proletariat and communism. Revolutionary literature mediates between "class consciousness and the historical situation" (San Juan 1976, 156). Mediation can play a broad range of roles. The way in which labor mediates between humanity and nature constitutes a primary mediation, existing in all modes of production, whether classless or class-based. Secondary or "second-order" mediations, by contrast, are specific to particular modes of production. When these serve to reinforce ruling-class hegemony, they can be termed, in the words of the philosopher C.J. Arthur, to be "alien mediations" (Arthur 1986, ch. 11). The specifically racist form taken by the division of labor in colonial situations, for example, is a second-order mediation distinctive of capitalist modernity. Similarly, under capitalism, the key function of money is to guarantee the whole matrix of social conditions—from paying wages to bundling mortgages to funding imperialist armies—that facilitate the accumulation of capital in the hands of ruling elites. The key function of the nuclear family is to supply the owners of the means of production with a steady source of ideologically disciplined labor. The key function of the state is to tamp down the irreconcilable antagonism between classes. When the second-order mediations characteristic of historically specific social formations serve to buttress class rule, they constitute, in their mutual reinforcement, what the Marxist philosopher István Mészáros has termed a "vicious cycle" (Mészáros 1995, 108–9). Even under communism, it bears noting, there would still be second-order mediations; but these would constitute a cycle serving rather than fettering the primary needs generated by productive human activity. A well-organized system for the distribution of social goods not based upon the market—indeed, free from the mediation of money—would constitute one such set of second-order mediations. A form of the family altered in ways we cannot yet anticipate—continuing to reproduce people capable of contributing to the welfare of society, but without the alienated relationships too often accompanying the reproduction of the family under capitalism—would be another.

Mediations, both primary and second-order, exist in reality. But they are also concepts competing for explanatory adequacy; we should recall that "thinking about totality" is also a matter of "thinking totality." It is obvious that we need agreed-upon vocabularies if we are to communicate at all. While a term like "the family," for instance, runs the risk of being taken to signify only the heterosexually based nuclear family as it has evolved in capitalist modernity, the term's usage remains indispensable nonetheless. How otherwise might we even begin to explore the dynamics among characters in a novel like *Jude the Obscure* (Hardy 2009 [1895]) or in plays from *Medea* (1964 [431 BCE]) to *King Lear* (1972 [1605–6]) to *Long Day's Journey into Night* (O'Neill 2014 [1956]), much less examine how these texts embody historically and geographically specific conceptions of family that diverge in crucial ways? But we need to be sensitive to the meanings and implications of certain terms, especially when these function as at once explanations and remedies in important debates of the day. For both Thomas Carlyle and Karl Marx, for instance, the term "cash nexus" signaled the brutal impersonality of the wage relation and the market. Whereas the term motivated Carlyle to long for a return to medieval times, however, for Marx "naked self-interest ... callous 'cash payment'" could be superseded only by communist revolution (Carlyle 1970 [1843]; *CM*, ch. 1). The word "abolitionist" makes comparably divergent appearances in nineteenth-century US literature. For Frederick Douglass, understanding the word's theoretical and practical meanings enabled him to realize the historicity of his situation: that he need not be a "slave for life" (Douglass 1996, 51). For Huckleberry Finn, by contrast, his decision to try to help Jim escape from slavery brands him in his own eyes as a "dirty low-down abolitionist"—a verbal mediation setting firm limits on his moral development (Twain 1995 [1886], 65).

Because it is often easier to see the politics of language at work in the past than in the present, however, we need to be especially cautious regarding the meanings clustered around terms mediating present-day realities. The term "the West," as noted previously, serves as convenient shorthand to signify the historical role of Europe and the United States in colonialism and imperialism; but it can also negatively tar with the brush of domination anything emerging from that part of the planet over the past few hundred years, as is implied by the frequently negative associations of the phrase "Western rationalism." "Race" is routinely acknowledged as a biological fiction—and hence as a word without, strictly speaking, any referent at all. Nonetheless, the term—whether or not it is enclosed in quotation marks—continues to be invoked in discussions of social inequality, even though "racism" is arguably a more productive analytical term for examining the mediations between oppressive behaviors and the beliefs by which they are motivated. The same problems accompany such terms as "black," "white," "latino/a/x," and "Asian"—including when or whether these terms are to be capitalized. Although words are obviously indispensable if we are going to explore causal connections, we need continually to be alert to their simultaneous function as descriptors and as embodiments of the second-order mediations central to our common-sense understandings—which are not infrequently misunderstandings—of how the world works. As Althusser has noted, the struggle over language, over what something should be called, is a "political, ideological and philosophical struggle. [T]he words are also weapons, explosives or tranquillizers and poisons. Occasionally, the whole class struggle can be summed up in the struggle for one word against another word" (Althusser 1971, 21).

As we attempt to formulate models for understanding causality that are attuned to the complexity of actual phenomena and processes—not least of these being the production, reception, and analysis of literary works—consideration of relative autonomy and mediation will help us steer away from devising what can be called "vulgar" formulations of the role played by economics and social class in shaping history, society, and culture. Marxism is not economic determinism. Nonetheless, without a fundamental commitment to historical materialist determin*ation*— which is not at all the same thing as determin*ism*—Marxism simply is not Marxism. The base–superstructure relationship is indispensable to a totalizing understanding of what Marx called the "real foundation" of consciousness and activity in social being. Although anti-Marxists continually try to reduce Marxism to a rigid model of purely economic causality, and therefore in need of explanatory supplementation from other modes of social analysis, the best correctives to vulgar Marxism come from within the Marxist tradition itself. The cost of abandoning the base–superstructure paradigm, however, is that we are stranded in the zone of mid-level analytics, where different levels of causality are viewed as "factors"; "interaction" substitutes for "determination"; and cultural developments end up being explained in terms of—what else?— culture (Ebert and Zavarzadeh 2008, 28–29). As we navigate the waters of Marxist literary criticism, where the shoals and whirlpools are many, we will bear in mind that literary works are always bound to the societies from which they emerge—even though this knowledge never tells us exactly how that connection functions with respect to any given text, let alone how to read it.

Levels of Generality

Finally, as we consider the methodological issues associated with historical materialist analysis, we should be aware that what we will discover depends on what we are looking for. The Marxist philosopher Bertell Ollman has usefully suggested that the social relations relevant to a dialectical under-standing of a given phenomenon or process can be mapped out on seven planes of generality (Ollman 1993, 53–67). Several of these correspond with different phases of history, ranging from (1) the immediate cir-cumstances surrounding unique individuals; (2) the particular epoch in capitalism informing the moment under examination, a period of some 20–50 years; (3) the era in which capitalism has been the dominant mode of production, some 300–500 years; (4) the still longer timespan consti-tuted by class society, some 5000–8000 years, depending on location; and (5) the timespan common to all humans since their evolution into *Homo sapiens*. The two remaining levels of generality can take us beyond history to ontology (that is, the nature of being): (6) denotes the features that all forms of human and animal life have in common; while (7) comprises the material qualities that humans share with all other existing matter, organic and inorganic. While these levels of generality are connected with different degrees of temporal specificity, Ollman cautions against viewing them, especially the first five, simply as "'slices of time,' since the whole of history is implicated in each level" (Ollman 1993, 56). In *Adventures of Huckleberry Finn*, for instance, the relevant time-frames range from the immediate history of the 1830s–40s, during which the novel is set; to the longer timespan, including post-Reconstruction, when the novel was written; to the centuries-old history of racialized US capitalism; to the geological movements creating the Mississippi River basin in the remote past of the planet.

Ollman's discussion of the different levels of generality involved in base–superstructure analysis not only helps us investigate the different types of causality relevant to different types of inquiry but also cautions us to look out for the mistaken conclusions we can reach when we confuse different levels of generality. Many non-Marxist philosophers and cultural commentators, Ollman remarks, characteristically locate their causal analyses in either the first level—where each "unique individual ... has a proper name"—or the fifth, where a person is considered as "a member of the human species" (1993, 58). This maneuver enables them to deny, or at least minimize, the types of causality operative on levels two through four—that is, the levels where class analysis, especially of capitalism, figures prominently. Not the least of the consequences of this proclivity for levels one and five, along with relative inattention to levels two through four, is that causality comes to be construed either as, on the one hand, the exercise of distinct individuality or, on the other, the fatalistic pressure of an unchanging human condition. Level five is especially prone to the promulgation of false universals about the nature of social being. This tendency is, we will see, especially important in connection with literary criticism, where some of the most influential schools have proven prone to bypassing historically based causal analysis and positing abstract notions of human nature and language, often premised upon the belief that the most general statements about what it means to be human are for that reason the most valuable and profound (Ollman 1993, 63–64).

While the Marxist approach to base–superstructure analysis does not preclude attention to the full range of determining forces potentially operative in a given phenomenon, it encourages us to focus on the kinds of causal explanations most relevant to what we wish to understand more fully. It also cautions us to take care in the use of such words as "always" and "never." It is not true that sexism has been with us "always"; a historical materialist approach to gender relations traces the origins of male–female inequality to the early formation of class societies, level four (Engels, *OFPPS*; Lerner 1987). Racism, often treated as an intrinsic human propensity for abhorring difference, is comprehensible primarily within the framework supplied by a focus upon level three, the capitalist era (E. Williams 1994 [1944]; Baptist 2016)—as is also true of nationalism, being "the most pernicious form of 'identity politics'" in our time (Nguyen 2014; Hobsbawm 2012). The notion that people have never functioned in a collective manner, conversely, is largely refuted if we turn our attention to level five, comprising the entire span of human societies, including the tens of thousands of years lived in situations of primitive communalism.

In order more fully to understand the specifically economic forces operative in the capitalist mode of production, however—and therefore operative in the levels of cultural analysis most relevant to the concerns of this book—we need to examine some key tenets of the Marxist approach to political economy. It is to this task that we now turn.

2

Political Economy

Capital is dead labour that, vampire-like, only lives by sucking living labour.

— Karl Marx, *C* I

In Marx's time, the term "political economy" signified the study of what we now know as "economics"—practices of buying and selling, working, and investing—at the level of both households and states. "Politics," in other words, was not seen as separate from everyday economic activity, at once "macro" and "micro" (terms often used in mainstream economics to denote different levels, large-scale and small-scale, of economic activity). We should keep this dual focus in mind as we consider the various ways in which political economy supplies a framework not only for understanding systems of ideas but also for subjecting to critical scrutiny the social system giving rise to these ideas. It bears noting that, when Marx subtitled *Capital* "a critique of political economy," he was indicating that his study aimed both to correct the errors of other theorists of political economy—some of whom he viewed as pioneering intellectuals, others as crude apologists for existing social hierarchies—and to supply his own analysis of the object of inquiry.

Commodities

Certain keywords are of vital importance in our inquiry, quite different from the terminology used in mainstream economics, where supply, demand, and markets are viewed as the principal determinants of economic activity. First and foremost is the commodity, which is defined as an entity consisting of two components, use value and exchange value. A commodity must be useful to humans (a single fallen leaf does not figure as a commodity, since it has no imaginable use, at least to most people) and must have the capacity to be bought and sold, that is, it must be produced for the purpose of exchange. (While we might think that a breath of fresh air cannot be a commodity because it cannot be packaged and placed on the market, this is not quite true. In 2015 I learned of a restaurant in Beijing that charges its customers an additional fee if they wish to sit in the "clean air room."[1] I suspect that by now there is more than one.) The use value of a commodity is qualitative, for it cannot be measured; its exchange value is quantitative, for it can be described in terms of numbers. In capitalist society, the market—so pervasive that its existence is invisible—is the principal mediator between use value and exchange value. Those Mastercard commercials that proclaim as "priceless" the loving family relationships presumably facilitated by expensive vacations—financed of course by Mastercard—cynically play upon people's longing, however suppressed, for the non-market-based experiences associated with use values. While in some pre-capitalist societies the medium serving as a measure of exchange value could vary—from seashells to cattle hides—throughout the world today the universal medium of exchange value is money. Money, for many people, is the most "real" thing in their world, since, if they have enough of it, it can get them whatever their hearts desire. But money is actually a somewhat mystical entity, embodied in the things that people use but at the same time curiously abstracted from them. Marx wrote, "Since gold does not disclose what has been transformed into it, everything, commodity or not, is convertible into gold. Everything becomes saleable and buyable.... [Nothing is] able to withstand this alchemy" (*C* I, ch. 3). Yet money is also utterly dependent upon the social relations that give it reality and authority. This point is often made in cartoons featuring castaway people on desert islands where one coconut is worth more than a wallet full of dollars, euros, or yuan. It is also central to works of utopian fiction like William Morris's *News From Nowhere* (1994 [1890]), where inhabitants of a future classless society view coins as relics belonging only in museums.

But we are jumping ahead: how is value, as when measured by money, actually determined? That is, what is the property of the commodity that gives it the value that takes the "form of appearance" of exchange value, and that makes it interchangeable, through money, with commodities of so many different kinds (*C*, ch. 1)? For Marx—at once drawing upon and refining the work of two earlier political economists, David Ricardo and Adam Smith—exchange value is a quantification of the socially necessary labor time embodied in a given commodity. This doctrine, which is called the labor theory of value, is premised on the notion that the amount of work that went into the production of a given commodity is what determines its value. The proposition that labor enters into the determination of the basis upon which one thing would be exchanged for another makes intuitive sense: five pounds of bleached raw wool can be made into a heavy Shetland sweater, for instance, but, under most circumstances, no one would think of simply trading the wool for the sweater, since clearly much more labor has been expended on the sweater beyond the original shearing of the sheep. But why "socially necessary" labor time? Because one knitter who works at half the speed of another, but produces a similar article, is not going to be able to sell her sweater for twice as much: the faster knitter has established a generally applicable norm for determining price. In industrial capitalism, of course, most commodities are not produced by individual craftspeople, but in factories where machines establish the speed of production. As Marx pointed out in *Capital*, one of the major incentives prompting capitalists continually to invest in new technology is the need to undercut the competition in the race to reduce the amount of time involved in the production of a given commodity. After all, if the time-saving machinery purchased by capitalist #1 enables his factory to produce more widgets in an hour than capitalist #2, capitalist #1 can make more money—until, that is, capitalist #2 gets hold of the same machinery, in which case things even out and the race starts all over again. While competition for profits thus continually reduces the amount of socially necessary labor time required to produce a given commodity, this phenomenon has a boomerang effect, since capitalists are forced to invest in more (and often more expensive) technology in order to retain their share of the market. In Marx's analysis, the paradoxical pressures resulting from capital's unending drive to accumulation are at the heart of the inherent tendency of the rate of profit to fall, leading to periodic crises resulting from the unplanned character of competition among capitalists (*C* III, chs 13–15).

But before we touch upon some details of these self-destructive contradictions—which bear a more than passing resemblance to the uncontrollable monster in Mary Shelley's *Frankenstein; or the Modern Prometheus* (2018 [1818])—we need to consider some other important features of commodities. In social formations not yet subdued to the universal rule of capital, markets and money function primarily to facilitate the circulation of commodities between and among people for whom use value predominates over exchange value. Person A, an eighteenth-century dairy farmer, goes to the weekly market and sells three cases of eggs; with the money gained from this transaction, she goes to the stall of a wheelwright in another part of the market where she buys a new spindle for her spinning wheel, which she needs to make clothes for her growing family. (She may have been able to raise her chickens on communal land not yet enclosed by the wealthy local landlord, a process condemned by the poet Oliver Goldsmith in *The Deserted Village* [2002 (1770)]). Our dairy farmer has not created any wealth or gained any profit through this transaction; money has served simply to enable the selling of one article to one person in order to facilitate the acquisition from another person of a different article that will then be used by the buyer. Marx designated such a circuit as C-M-C (commodity-money-commodity), in which money serves to connect the sale and the purchase (*C* I, ch. 3). At present, it bears noting, the relationship of most workers to commodities and money can also be described by the C-M-C circuit (that is, commodity-money-commodity). In other words, workers sell their labor power (a term that will be defined more precisely in a moment) for money, their wage; this money enables them to purchase different commodities that they will use. For example, a worker who packages DVDs takes $20 from his weekly paycheck to purchase a T-shirt bearing the logo of his favorite baseball team. After it has been removed from the cellophane package and worn, however, the T-shirt will no longer be a commodity; it will have reverted to a simple use value, since most people—other than those frequenting vintage clothing stores—will not want to buy a well-worn T-shirt.

While both the eighteenth-century dairy farmer and the twenty-first-century DVD packager relate to both commodities and money through the C-M-C circuit described above, there is a crucial difference between their experiences of exchange. For in a capitalist society premised upon industrial mass production, exchange value predominates over use value; indeed, many things that were not commodities in earlier forms of society undergo a process of commodification. Think of ways in which spectator sports have supplanted street stickball and the village soccer match, and even double-dutch jump-roping has become a money-making operation complete with corporate sponsors and competition for cash prizes. Moreover, the basis for the exchangeability of commodities varies considerably in historically different kinds of markets. In the example of the dairy farmer and the wheelwright, money serves as only an approximate measure of the amount of work involved in the raising of chickens on the one hand and, on the other, the making of the spindle. Although the wheelwright would no doubt be unwilling to exchange the spindle for the money the farmer gains from selling a mere half-dozen eggs, neither participant in this exchange has kept a precise log of costs, expenditures, and hours spent at work. We may whimsically speculate, indeed, that the inability of pre-capitalist participants in the marketplace to engage in precisely quantified acts of exchange is obliquely reflected in the story of "Jack and the Beanstalk." Jack's trading of the family's sole cow for a handful of magic beans is a blatantly foolish act of exchange, given the desperate poverty in which he lives with his mother. But the ability of the seeds to generate wealth far beyond the market value of the cow—through Jack's ascending the giant bean stalk and robbing the drunken giant in his castle in the sky—testifies not just to the longing of the poor for magical rescue (or revenge against their oppressors) but also to the historical existence of markets where value and exchange value were not automatically seen as equivalent. Our present-day habit of quantifying exchange based upon the socially necessary labor time embodied in commodities is neither natural nor transhistorical.

Commodity Fetishism

When commodification becomes universal, however, the origin of commodities in specific acts of human labor is lost, as well as their destinations in specific acts of consumption. The so-called "law of value," which makes commodities exchangeable with one another on the basis of their embodiment of socially necessary labor time, results in their becoming invested with a kind of magical aura. Invoking the definition of a fetish as an inanimate object that appears to take on mystical meaning, Marx designated this phenomenon as commodity fetishism: "A commodity is therefore a mysterious thing, simply because in it the social character of men's labour appears to them as an objective character stamped upon the product of that labour; because the relation of the producers to the sum total of their own labour is presented to them as a social relation, existing not between themselves, but between the products of their labour." As a result, "a definite social relation between men ... assumes ... the fantastic form of a relation between things" (C I, ch. 1); the realm of exchange is a mystified (and mystifying) site where appearance substitutes for essence, surface for depth. While taking the form of a "thing" that people will use, the commodity is also a ghostly entity, an embodiment of invisible social relations. Although it was created and transported by any number of workers, it appears on the shelf as if it gave birth to itself. When the DVD packager purchases his cotton T-shirt at the Sports Authority for $20, he may see the label "Made in China," but he probably does not think about the worker who bent over the assembly line in Guangdong Province to stamp the logo on the shirt that he plans to wear to the ballgame. Nor does he give any thought to the container ship sailors, longshoremen, truck drivers, advertising copy-writers, and stock clerks whose labor has collectively delivered the shirt to its shelf in the local Sports Authority outlet. If he goes through the automatic check-out line at the chain store, moreover, he does not even have any contact with the saleswoman at the cash register (unless, given the cannibalization of retail jobs by e-commerce, she has lost her job). And while he knows that he worked hard for that $20 in his warehouse job, where his own boss, in search of greater profits, may have sped up the assembly line or cut back on the length of the workers' coffee breaks, he probably does not think much about how the thousands of music videos that he loads into boxes every day are used by the various people who buy them. (When he loses his job because streaming has completely replaced DVD use, though, he may give some thought, belatedly, to this question.)

Two other terms from Marx's lexicon—"concrete labor" and "abstract labor"—are central to an understanding of the nature of commodities, as well as to the way in which value gets expressed as exchange value. Another way of describing the experiences of the Chinese and US workers mentioned above is to say that the concrete labor connected with the use value of a given commodity—that is, the actual labor put forth by the actual worker who ran the actual machine used to stamp the logo on the actual T-shirt—is subordinated to the abstract labor that renders the Chinese T-shirt-maker's labor exchangeable with the labor that the DVD warehouse worker performed to earn the $20 that he spent on the shirt. The process by which abstract labor predominates over concrete labor, to the point where only the posited equivalence of quantities of labor, measured by money, is what matters, further clarifies the nature of the law of value. Indeed, the abstraction of labor is in some ways the linchpin of Marx's critique of capital. For while he was more than willing to concede that fluctuations in markets could create conditions in which commodities might be exchanged at prices corresponding only loosely with the amounts of socially necessary labor embodied in them, his critique of a social system in which value is measured by quantified labor, and labor has to be quantified in order to have value, is unremitting.

As we shall see, the psychosocial effects of commodity fetishism are far-reaching, penetrating not only into the consciousness of individuals involved in acts of labor, purchase, and exchange, but also into the literary works that emerge from a society in which the law of value prevails. As Marx noted, the commodity is thus a kind of "social hieroglyphic" that contains the key to understanding the workings of capital (C I, ch. 1). Just as nineteenth-century archeologists needed the multilingual Rosetta Stone to crack the code of ancient Egyptian writing, enabling them to read inscriptions and papyri previously impervious to interpretation, modern political economy needs to grasp the dual nature of the commodity if it is to comprehend how capital shapes social life. It is no wonder that Marx chooses to begin his exposition of political economy with the chapter titled "Commodities"; he focuses upon the thing that we all take for granted—the object for sale on the shelf—in order to peel away layer after layer of the historical processes and economic practices that have brought it into existence. To investigate political economy is not only to lay bare the workings of capital; it is also to examine the disparity between appearance and essence that at once obscures and naturalizes the inequalities to which capital gives rise. The philosopher Étienne Balibar has dubbed the notion of commodity fetishism "one of the great philosophical constructions of modern philosophy" (Balibar 2017, 56).

Labor Power and Exploitation

If we wish to penetrate through the first few of these layers, Marx shows, we need to take into account the standpoint of the capitalist. After all, capitalists are not in business to facilitate the circulation of use values among ordinary people; they are in business to make money. Their motivating circuit is not C-M-C (commodity-money-commodity), but M-C-M (money-commodity-money): as the comptroller of Bethlehem Steel once proclaimed, "We're not in business to make steel, we're not in business to build ships, we're not in business to erect buildings. We're in business to make money."[2] But why should capitalists bother with the circuit of M-C-M if the M ending the circuit is of the same magnitude as the M that began the circuit? How can the second M be made greater than the first?

Many commodities are "things" that can be seen and felt, whether items purchasable by average people like ourselves, such as T-shirts or DVDs, or huge means of production like the logo-stamping machine that the Chinese textile factory owner purchases from the maker of large-scale industrial machinery. The use value of commodities, remember, is determined by their utility to their buyers, their exchange value—approximately—by their prices. What enabled Marx to crack the code of the hieroglyphic of the commodity was his discovery that, in the regime of capital, labor power—that is, a quantity of labor capable of being expended in a given period of time—is itself a commodity. Its exchange value is measured by the wage; its use value is determined by its ability to expand value, thus creating additional wealth for the employer who has purchased the worker's labor power. Since the capitalist is motivated by the desire to turn his initial investment into a greater amount of money, he needs to find a way to make that second M bigger than the first one. The purchase of labor power, which has the capacity to increase the value of the original M, accomplishes this goal. The capitalist has managed to move from M-C-M to M-C-M + ΔM, in which M represents the amount of money initially invested; ΔM represents the increment in value added by the labor of the worker; and M + ΔM represents the augmented total value of the initial investment. This new circuit can be designated by the notation M-C-M', in which M' signifies M + ΔM; to the delight of the capitalist, value has been expanded (*C* I, ch. 6), which means that profits can be gained.

It bears noting that the distinction between labor and labor power—which it took Marx a good twenty years to come up with—is vitally important. Labor is the activity, taking place in real time, that engages in the production and reproduction of human life; decontextualized from a historically specific social formation, however, it has little economic meaning, leading Marx at one point to joke that the phrase "'price of labour' is just as irrational as a yellow logarithm" (*C* III, ch. 48). Labor power, by contrast, is the potential capacity of the worker to produce value for the capitalist; it can be quantified in terms of wages, outputs, and profits. As a commodity—indeed, as the commodity of greatest value to the capitalist—labor power itself may be intangible and invisible; unlike labor in general, however, it bears all the marks of its origin in time and space. Indeed, it is the quintessential product—and, arguably, producer—of modernity.

The commodification of labor power and the extraction of surplus value are what distinguish the exploitation of wage labor under industrial capitalism from the exploitation of labor in earlier modes of production. A medieval serf worked four days a week on the lord's lands and two days on his own—in addition to performing occasional stints of compulsory labor required by the lord (in France called the *corvée*) and yielding up additional surpluses when tax time came around. A slave on a plantation in the United States or the Caribbean was owned outright: she did not sell her labor power as a commodity but was herself a commodity, to be bought or sold. By contrast with an enslaved worker, the individual wage-laborer under capitalism is at liberty to quit her job and change employers; she is not bound to any given boss. As a class, however, wage-laborers are bound to the class that employs them (or not) as surely as chattel slaves were bound to their individual owners, a reality signaled by the term "wage-slavery." As Marx observed, "[The worker] belongs not to this or that capitalist, but to the capitalist class" (*WL&C*, ch. 2). The essence of this bondage lies in the ability of the capitalist class—through both coercion and ideology—to close off workers' access to the means of survival unless they submit to exploitation.

What is the difference between chattel and free labor? Are they features of qualitatively different modes of production, or can they exist within a single social formation? To posit a qualitative difference between free and enslaved labor is not to claim that they cannot profitably—from the point of capital—exist side by side, at least for a significant period of time. Marx, while well aware of the difference between the political economy of ancient slave society and that of industrial modernity, argued that "[t]he veiled slavery of the wage workers in Europe needed, for its pedestal, slavery pure and simple in the new world" (*C* I, ch. 31). The fortunes generated in Manchester, England, depended upon the fortunes generated in Barbados, Georgia, and Alabama. If anything, however, Marx underestimated the extent to which US chattel slavery was part and parcel of capitalist modernity. Marx wrote, "The fact that we now not only call the plantation-owners in America capitalists, but that they *are* capitalists, is based on their existence as anomalies within a world market based on free labour" (GR, ch. 9). Recent studies of the political economy of slavery have called into question this "anomalous" relationship, revealing the extent to which enslaved labor drove the development of capitalism not just in England but throughout the United States, North and South, from the nation's founding onward. Indeed, the labor of enslaved workers generated enormous profits, their bodies even functioning at times as the basis of collateralized loans not all that different from the bundled securities involved in the financial crisis of the early twenty-first century (Baptist 2016). While the regime of free labor would ultimately prevail, this was not because chattel slavery was—or is—inefficient; to this day slavery persists in labor markets in many parts of the world (Brass 2010).

Surplus Value

The relationship between labor power and surplus value can be more fully understood if we add two new terms to our lexicon and if we do some very simple arithmetic. Think of the capitalist who owns the T-shirt factory in China. In a given day, an individual worker works for eight hours and earns a wage of $15, (actually a very generous exaggeration, since the capitalist is more likely to be paying as little as $10 a day, or even less). From the standpoint of the capitalist, this wage is an expenditure of what Marx called "variable capital." The worker uses up in the course of a day's labor, say, $500 worth of raw materials, including the cost of one day's energy, one day's wear and tear on machinery, one day's rent on the factory, one day's worth of insurance, etc.; the expenditure on these costs of doing business is—from the standpoint of the capitalist—called "constant capital," namely, the value invested in means of production. The T-shirts are sold for $1000 to the merchant who will then transport them overseas. As mentioned before, there are several further steps in what has been called the commodity chain, involving oceanic transportation to the United States, unloading by longshoremen, trucking, advertising, placement of the T-shirts in stores or online, and handling by stock clerks and salespeople, resulting in their eventual purchase by consumers shopping at the Sports Authority, where they sell for a total of $10,000. At each link in the commodity chain, there occurs an exploitation of labor—provided by different laborers—that hikes up the exchange value of the T-shirts. (If they are associated with a desirable brand, like Tommy Hilfiger, they may go for as much as $50 apiece, unlike the $20 that our DVD packer paid for the generic Sports Authority brand.)

But what has expanded the value of the original $500 of constant capital invested by the owner of the T-shirt factory, enabling all these subsequent operations to occur? The labor power purchased from the original textile worker, which has yielded up $485 in surplus value. Even if the local Chinese capitalist is under pressure from the "just-in-time" requirements of the Sports Authority—which is demanding that he update and speed up his assembly line in order to have the latest T-shirt designs ready for the new season—he has gained a tidy profit from the labor performed by the worker on the factory floor. If we divide up her day's labor into the time in which she earned her $15 wage and the time she devoted to producing $485 in surplus value, we see that she has spent the great preponderance of her eight-hour work shift essentially working for free: that is why wage-slavery is called wage-*slavery*. Sports Authority, it bears noting, has made far more than the Chinese factory owner (who has of course not done badly), since the final selling price of the shirts, even after the other costs incurred in the commodity chain have been covered, amounts to an even tidier profit (a profit that is tidier still if the shirts are marketed under the Tommy Hilfiger monopoly label).

Some additional terminology helps us grasp the process by which surplus value can be extracted from the labor of our T-shirt maker. The term "surplus labor" denotes the labor expended after she has earned the amount of her wage; "surplus labor time"—illustrated just above—denotes the time she has worked for free. The term "rate of surplus value" signifies the ratio between the surplus value she created and her wage, in this case a whopping 485:15. The terms "absolute surplus value" and "relative surplus value" help us differentiate between the ways in which profit can be extracted from her labor. The former term describes her situation if she works in factory where the machinery is unsophisticated, but throngs of people like her work long hours for very low wages, enabling the owner to pile up his profits. The latter applies to a labor process in which advanced technology is deployed, so that profits are accumulated by reducing the socially necessary time required for production (Marx *C* I, Part V). While the general tendency of capitalist development, shaped by competition, is toward a greater and greater reliance upon the extraction of relative surplus value, both methods prevail in the world today, indicating why capitalists often choose to invest in parts of the world—from El Salvador to Bangladesh, China to South Africa—where labor is cheapest. The most exploited workers in the world are the brown-, yellow-, and black-skinned workers, many of them women, laboring in the global South's "dark satanic mills," to quote the poet William Blake's description of early industrialization in England (Blake 1953, 244–45). Although it is a term that can be misused when applied broadly to demographic groups which contain significant gradations in income and wealth, "super-exploitation" usefully describes the extraction of surplus value—in either its absolute or its relative form—from the workers who earn a mere pittance for the enormously profitable labor that they perform. Indeed, these workers are often paid less than the very minimum they need to keep themselves and their families alive, requiring that their children and elderly parents scrounge for small change—or, worse, pick through mountains of garbage—in the vast informal economies of the global South (J. Smith 2016; Ness 2016).

The preceding description of surplus labor extraction helps us correct some common misunderstandings about the connections between and among commodity fetishism, exploitation, and productive labor. One is the notion that commodity fetishism manifests itself principally in the sphere of consumption, where the articles produced by abstract human labor confront one another in the marketplace as quasi-mystical embodiments of value. To be sure, commodities need to be made into desirable objects of consumption if the capitalist is to realize profit from their production: as Theodore Dreiser wrote in *Sister Carrie*, the objects produced by concrete human labor call out seductively to would-be consumers in department stores (Dreiser 1967 [1900], ch. 3). (These days, the advertisements crowding onto computer screens are increasingly important feeders of desire.) But the essence of commodity fetishism is the commodification of labor power, whose invisibility obfuscates the process by which wages—the exchange value of labor power—are falsely equated with the actual value of the labor that the worker

What is the particular relationship of work characteristically performed by women to the political economy of capitalism? While women workers are paid less than men in most of the highly gendered job situations around the world—that is, their labor yields up an additional increment of surplus value—there is another way in which the labor of women augments capital accumulation. This is in connection with the unwaged labor that women perform in producing the commodity that is labor power. In all modes of production, women perform the bulk of the labor involved—whether child-bearing, child-rearing, or caring for the elderly or those unable to work—in creating and reproducing the workforce needed to sustain production and produce a surplus for the owning class. (To make this claim is not to deny that men too at times perform such labor—except, obviously, for child-bearing—but to designate the particularity of the role played by women.) Under capitalism, however, the fact that women reproduce the commodity that is labor power means that they perform unwaged labor in the home. In 2017 the *New York Times* reported that "the economic value [of the care supplied by family care-givers] is estimated at $470 billion a year—roughly the annual American spending on Medicaid" (*NYT* January 19 2017). But since this labor is not compensated, it is (while vitally necessary for the survival of capitalism, let alone the human species) devalued.

In earlier modes of production—whether primitive communalism or situations in which the principal circuit of exchange is C-M-C rather than M-C-M'—household production is clearly central to the domestic economy of a family (Leacock 1981). When only waged labor is seen as productive of value, however (as is the case with capitalism), the work that goes into making sure that children are raised and that adults eat and have clean clothes to wear is—while it uses up many hours of a woman's time—invisible as work. It is seen, instead, as simply what women do, because they are women. The associated ideology of gender dualism—the notion that there is a fundamental and hierarchical difference between women and men—functions powerfully to legitimate and perpetuate the regime of women's unpaid labor in the home, sometimes called "the patriarchy of the wage" (Federici 2004, 98). That this ideology can motivate men's violence toward women, in the process entrapping the perpetrators in the web of their own actions, is a theme illustrated in many literary works—albeit from widely varying political perspectives—ranging from Frank Norris's *McTeague: A Story of San Francisco* (1994 [1899]) to Gayl Jones's *Corregidora* (1975).

performs. Critical examinations of modern consumer culture that bypass the grounding of commodification in exploitation may usefully describe the deleterious psychosocial effects of marketing and branding, but such commentaries rarely get beyond mid-level analytics in their discussions of capital. In order to understand the essence of exploitation, wrote Marx, it is necessary to enter "the hidden abode of production on whose threshold there stares us in the face 'No admittance except on business.' Here we shall see ... the secret of profit making" (*C* I, ch. 6).

A second misunderstanding consists in the definition of exploitation. For Marx, the extraction of surplus value at the point of production constitutes exploitation; it is a scientific concept, one that can be quantified. Its meaning is quite different, then, from the way we often use the term in everyday speech, when we might refer, for instance, to one person's "exploiting" another person's goodwill, or to a politician's "exploiting" popular prejudices for personal gain. Exploitation is often confused with oppression and domination—terms that usefully describe the unequal power relations in class-based societies, but that are not explicitly economic. Even when confined to economic matters, however, the term "exploitation" is often used only to describe wages in sweatshop conditions, to be counterposed with the notion of a "fair wage." From a Marxist standpoint, this distinction is inaccurate, indeed misleading. Any appropriation of surplus value through the purchase of labor power con-stitutes exploitation; in the regime of capital, there is in fact no such thing as a "fair wage," even if workers in different job sites may receive vastly different incomes. Textile workers in the sweatshops of the global South produce high levels of surplus value, not only at the point of production but also when we correlate their meager wages to the profits generated at every step in the commodity chain. But hydro-fracking workers in the global North making use of advanced technology also produce high levels of surplus value in proportion to their wages. (The distinction between relative and absolute surplus value extraction is often relevant to the difference between the concrete labor performed, respectively, by the two groups.) The fact that the individual Canadian hydro-fracking worker receives a much higher wage than the Indonesian textile worker— and that he probably lives somewhat more comfortably than she, at least until his job is wiped out by automation or a bursting bubble in energy markets—does not mean that he is receiving a "fair wage": both are exploited in that both produce surplus value. And while—as long as he has his job—it might be argued that he benefits from being able to buy the product of her labor at the local Wal-Mart, the relative cheapness of her product enables his boss to hold down his wage (J. Smith 2016).

While differentially positioned and compensated, both workers—the T-shirt maker and the hydro-fracker—have an interest in abolishing the conditions of wage labor. Ideologies of racism and nationalism play no small role in preventing some workers in the global North from recognizing the commonality of their interests with those of their counterparts in the global South. Given the increasing brutality and instability of the regime of wage labor for the great majority of the world's workers, North as well as South, however, as well as the continuing threat of armed conflict among imperial powers seeking planetary hegemony, the need for proletarian internationalism is now as urgent as it has ever been. Moreover, while throughout this discussion we have been using the terms "global North" and "global South" as a crude shorthand to distinguish different geographical zones of imperialist exploitation—second-order mediations of some kind, we will recall, are required for purposes of description—these terms' analytical limitations need to be kept in mind. Not only are there significant numbers of super-exploited workers in the global North, but also even those who are *merely* exploited have a far greater objective interest in abolishing the conditions of wage-slavery altogether than they have in maintaining their precarious—and often temporary—position of what appears to be a relative advantage.

A third misunderstanding connected to the notion of surplus labor extraction has to do with the distinction between so-called "productive" and "unproductive" labor in Marxist theory (*TSV*, Part I). Marx insisted on a clear differentiation between labor that can be commodified as labor power, serving as the basis of surplus value extraction, and labor that does not yield up profits but performs useful services: our worker in the T-shirt factory exemplifies the first, while a domestic servant in the house of the factory owner exemplifies the second. The servant might put in as many hours per day as the assembly-line worker—perhaps even more—be as badly paid, and experience at least as much unpleasantness on the job; she certainly feels "productive" as she bends over her mop, as well as oppressed by the sexual attentions of her boss's teenage son. But the servant is not technically exploited, for she is paid out of revenue—that is, income—whereas the assembly-line worker produces the surplus value that makes it possible for the factory owner to be in possession of that revenue in the first place. When Marx designates the servant's labor as "unproductive," he does not mean that her work does not fulfill social needs (although the boss's definition of his "needs" very likely includes various luxuries outstripping most people's conception of the meaning of human requirements). Marx further notes, however, that workers who perform services—from cooks to schoolteachers, clowns to tailors—produce surplus value if they perform waged work for a business owner or a master who—at times calling them "apprentices"—has hired out their services. If they sell their services directly to the person who benefits from them, though, they are deemed unproductive. We can include William Blake's young chimney-sweepers, described in a series of poignant poems, in this ambiguous category of workers—although from their standpoint, "lock'd up in coffins of black," a distinction between employers would no doubt have been a distinction without a difference (Blake 1953, 26). While Marx makes an important point about political economy in differentiating between these two types of labor, he is also pointing up, with considerable irony, the distortion that the category of productive human activity undergoes when production is yoked to the generation of surplus value. One of the many benefits of advanced communism, along with the abolition of wages and money, would be the abolition of the distinction, required by the regime of capital, between productive and unproductive labor. All socially necessary labor—from floor-mopping to child care to the making of steel—would be treated as equally productive.

What is the relationship of surplus value to profit? Why is it important to distinguish between the wealth that capitalists and their families squander on yachts and fur coats and that which pertains to their conduct of business? Surplus value is not after all sheer profit, all of which the individual capitalist can take home for personal use. The industrial capitalist finds himself forced to reinvest a good deal of the surplus value gained from the exploitation of labor into buying more efficient machinery, so that the increased output per worker-hour can enable him to beat out the competition from the owner of the factory next door (or thousands of miles around the world). If he does not succeed in wringing more surplus value out of his workers, he risks being put out of business by his competitors, who are bound to attempt the same. As was noted previously, getting hold of the most advanced machinery and technology becomes a matter of life and death for a capitalist as capitalist, whether he wants to or not; competition—a relationship among capitalists—becomes the external and unintended force that drives each capitalist to reduce socially necessary labor time, even to automate. Our factory owner may then engage in a price-war with his competitors, even for a while selling his product at below the cost of production to gain, if not a monopoly, at least a larger market-share. He must pay off the creditors from whom he borrowed money to purchase the up-to-date logo-stamping machinery enabling his firm to be competitive. He also has to pay taxes—even though he has various tax havens in the Bahamas, and his buddies in government will keep his tax bill as low as possible.

Moreover, unless he owns the entire vertical operation connecting his product to the store where it is sold—which these days is highly unlikely, given the complex nature of global supply chains—the industrial capitalist has to sell the product to the commercial capitalist who eventually delivers it to the market, an obligation creating additional pressures on the level of profit. The result is that, from the standpoint of the capitalist, "labor" appears as simply one of several expenses, or "inputs"; its crucial role in enabling the amassing of profit through the extraction of surplus value is obscured from his view (as well as from the view of the capitalist's supporters, including economists and historians). Most importantly, we need to realize that profit does not derive from the capitalist's simply adding on a charge to the value at the point of sale, as is often claimed, but rather is already embodied in the value of the commodity, in the form of unpaid labor, as the commodity rolls off the assembly line and begins its journey to the store.

Alienation

Thus far we have considered the appropriation of surplus value and the reproduction of the proletariat from the standpoint of the capitalist. As far as the capitalist is concerned, the need of the worker consists in earning a wage—as low as possible—sufficient to reproduce her labor power, and perhaps that of her family. Indeed, from the standpoint of the capitalist, she *is* her wage, simply another cost of production. But what about the standpoint of the worker? Even before he had come up with the concept of labor power as commodity, Marx was concerned with what he termed the alienation (or estrangement) of labor. In an early (1844) essay whose title is usually translated into English as "Estranged Labor," Marx set forth a range of ways in which the worker experiences alienation in a regime defined by private ownership of the means of production ("Estranged Labor," *EPM*). To begin with, the object of her labor—the embodiment of her engagement with the natural world through productive activity—is whisked away from her into the realm of an impersonal marketplace. The eighteenth-century dairy farmer who took the three crates of eggs to the county market not only owned her means of production, however modest; she also interacted directly—maybe even shook hands—with the wheelwright from whom she bought the spindle. By contrast, the worker in Guangdong Province has no connection with the purchaser of any of the hundreds (or maybe thousands) of T-shirts that she stamps over the course of a day. Moreover, she has had no role in designing the machine that controls the actions—or speed—involved in her labor process; she is thus alienated from the capacity for thinking and planning how production should take place that she shares with other workers in the factory. Borrowing a hard-to-translate term from Hegel, Marx referred to this human need for productive creativity as "species being"—a critically important concept, for it alludes to what is, for Marx, perhaps the core feature of human nature. "The whole character of a species—its species character—is contained in the character of its life activity; and free, conscious activity is man's species character" ("Estranged Labor," *EPM*). The division of mental from manual labor—a feature of the exploitation of labor in all class-based modes of production—is exacerbated under capitalism, where many jobs are broken down into increasingly mind-numbing segments to maximize the extraction of surplus value at all points along the commodity chain.

As a consequence of alienated labor, however, "life appears only as a *means to life*" ("Estranged Labor," *EPM*; italics in original). The worker feels herself to be most human only when she is away from work, satisfying her personal needs in the private sphere of the home; insofar as these needs are largely the needs that she shares with non-human animals—to eat, to sleep, and perhaps, if she has the time or the will, to reproduce—she is thus also alienated from herself. Indeed, the whole conception of a private sphere—that is, a personal life separate from the exigencies of the market—is itself testimony to the power of the market to determine all aspects of her existence. Individualism—whether experienced as ambition or loneliness—is, however paradoxically, a profoundly social product. Finally, but not least, the competition in which she is thrust vis-à-vis other workers—whether in her own factory or in the one opening up in another county, or for that matter another country—alienates her from her fellow human beings. Her individual wage packet supplies the modest sum upon which she and her family try to live, but she is continually aware that the factory in Guangdong Province may close down and reopen in Ho Chi Minh City or Addis Ababa, where labor is cheaper still. Her sense that she is up against the rest of the world and has to fend for herself has its foundation in the capitalist-engendered alienation of labor.

The alienation of labor is not absolute; like all dialectical processes, it contains its potential negation. The worker's home life can isolate and privatize her sense of herself as a human being; her provision of unpaid labor can lead to an undervaluation of her human worth, by others and even herself. At the same time, while not supplying "a haven in a heartless world" (Lasch 1995), the family can, to a degree, sustain its members in their daily encounters with the harshness of the regime of capital; both tendencies are displayed in Tillie Olsen's proletarian feminist novel *Yonnondio: From the Thirties* (1974). Although workers are often pitted against one another on the job, moreover, an awareness of their common exploitation can also create solidarity; indeed, understanding the totality of class-based social relations from the standpoint of exploitation is essential to the formation of the theory and practice—as well as the internationalist working-class identity—necessary for communist revolutionary activity. Nonetheless, in the absence of a social movement enabling history to move forward, albeit through its bad side, the main aspect of alienated labor is the toll it takes upon the worker, which extends beyond the low wages, harsh working conditions, long hours, and insecure employment to which the majority of the world's waged workers are subjected. As Marx wrote, capitalist production:

> squanders human lives, or living-labour, and not only blood and flesh, but also nerve and brain. Indeed, it is only by dint of the most extravagant waste of individual development that the development of the human race is at all safeguarded and maintained in the epoch of history immediately preceding the conscious reorganization of society. (*C* III, ch. 5)

Where communism envisions the creation of fully realized human beings as the goal of social development, capitalism, for many, reduces human need to bare subsistence, occasionally brightened by the purchase of a seductively marketed commodity whose use value is—somewhat paradoxically—of questionable social use.

It bears noting that Marx's approach to the problem of alienation is quite different from the way in which the term appears in most sociological writing and everyday language (Musto 2012). We speak of people as being "alienated" when they display a feeling of disconnection from other people, a sense that life is meaningless; the sociologist Émile Durkheim theorized this despairing condition as "*anomie*" (Durkheim 2002). Even when it is attributed to the way that society is organized—and not just individual psychology or an unchanging human condition—alienation is often ascribed to the impersonality and anonymity of life in a mass industrial society, as in David Riesman's description of the "lonely crowd" (Riesman, with Glazer and Denney 2001 [1950]). In theorizing how individuals are alienated from themselves and their fellow humans,

Marx clearly associates this sense of fragmentation and purposelessness with modernity. But he anchors this phenomenon in the market-based relations of production associated with the abstraction of labor in *capitalist* modernity, not with industrialization or technological development in themselves. Indeed, he views the material achievements of capitalism as a precious legacy to communism, all the more precious for the price paid in "squander[ed] human lives." The abstraction of labor, which estranges workers from their human essence, their "nerve and brain," and denies access to the reality of interconnectedness underlying the appearance of fragmentation, is, for Marx, the material basis of alienation. The effects of alienation are frequently registered in works of literature produced in the era of capital. One of the tasks of Marxist criticism is to distinguish between and among works that treat alienation as an inevitable feature of the human condition; those that ground it in historically specific social relations; and those that gesture toward the possibility for dialectical inversion to supersede those social relations through the revolutionary abolition of classes.

While grounded in exploitation—and hence the product of ruling-class hegemony—alienation pervades society as a whole, not just the working class; even those members of the bourgeoisie who live off the fat of the land, so to speak, are affected by the fragmenting and dehumanizing impact of inhabiting a society based upon universalized commodification. Often formulated as "reification"—based upon the Latin word "*res*," meaning "thing"—this "thingification" of human existence under capitalism is, we shall see, a key concern of Marxist critics, whether they approach texts by writers from working-class backgrounds like Thomas Cooper or writers from ruling-class backgrounds like Edith Wharton. What bears noting, however, are the different material interests that different classes have in either perpetuating or abolishing the conditions giving rise to alienation. Marx wrote:

> The propertied class and the class of the proletariat present the same human self-estrangement. But the former class feels at ease and strengthened in this self-estrangement, it recognizes estrangement as *its own power* and has in it the *semblance* of a human existence. The class of the proletariat feels annihilated in estrangement; it sees in it its own powerlessness and the reality of an inhuman existence. (*HF*, ch. 4)

The universality of alienation cannot be abolished by a trans-class recognition of its harmful psychological and moral effects; it will be superseded, in a process sometimes called disalienation, only when productive human activity is freed from its commodification as wage labor—that is, only when society has made the transition from capitalism to communism. Disalienation clearly entails far more than the redistribution of some of the wealth of the greedy "1%" to the needy "99%," which is the pipe dream of liberals; it requires dismantling the entire system of capitalist social relations, starting with the sale and purchase of labor power.

Alienation is not, however, a stand-alone term; it implies its own negation. For Marx, the very concept of alienation is premised upon the possibility of its nonexistence; its criticism of the present prefigures an alternative future, one in which there are no classes, only people, and in which there are no commodities, only things and services produced and distributed on the basis of social need. Like other key concepts in Marx's lexicon—proletariat and bourgeoisie, use value and exchange value—the notion of alienation is intrinsically dialectical; it carries the implication that only the practical achievement of its opposite, via the negation of negation, will divest the word of its power of reference, enabling it to disappear, through gradual disuse, from the vocabulary of humanity. In Jack London's dystopian/utopian novel *The Iron Heel* (2006 [1908])— narrated 400 years into a communist future after 300 years of violent plutocratic domination—the text's "editor," Anthony Meredith, has to footnote for the text's twenty-eighth-century readers such words as "proletariat" or "insurance" (London 2006 [1908], 30, 46), with which they are completely unfamiliar. The very fact that alienation is seen as a problem means that its negation is imaginable. As Marx wrote, "Mankind always sets itself only such tasks as it can solve" (*PCCPE*).

Capital

If capitalism is a mode of production characterized by the antagonistic contradiction—that is, the directly clashing class interests—between the capitalist ruling class and the proletariat, what, then, precisely, is capital itself? Marx wrote thousands of pages on this subject; depending on the angle from which he was viewing capital, he defined it in a range of ways. Sometimes he stressed its material aspect, as the raw materials and machinery needed to initiate a given production process. Sometimes he stressed its monetary aspect, as wages to be paid to workers, interest to be paid to bankers, profits to be cleared and then reinvested to renew and expand the cycle of accumulation. Sometimes he stressed its social aspect, as a coercive relationship between classes differentially located in production. Sometimes he stressed its monolithic character, sometimes its multiplicity, the "many capitals" emerging from competition. The three volumes of *Capital* (the last two of which were edited by Engels after Marx's death) show Marx examining capital from a variety of angles. Embedded in all these approaches, however, is the notion that capital requires an entire mode of production as a presupposition: "Capital is not a thing," Marx wrote, "but rather a definite social production relation, belonging to a definite historical formation of society, which is manifested in a thing and lends this thing a specific social character" (*C* III, ch. 48).

But even this formulation, Marx knew, begs the question of capital's origin: where did these caches of raw material and machinery, as well as of investable money, come from, and how did all this stuff end up in the hands of the capitalist? In part this origin consists in violent historical processes. These processes were global: "The discovery of gold and silver in America, the extirpation, enslavement and entombment in mines of the aboriginal population, the beginning of the conquest and looting of the East Indies, the turning of Africa into a warren for the commercial hunting of black-skins, signalized the rosy dawn of the era of capitalist production" (*C* I, ch. 31). These processes were also internal to the countries where industrial capitalism took root: the proletarianization of peasants who were, through the landlords' enclosure of commonly used lands, forcibly dispossessed of their means of survival and compelled to labor for wages. These processes of extraction and compulsion, designated by Marx as "primitive accumulation" (or, in an alternative translation, "original accumulation"), are not, it bears noting, confined to capitalism's past (*C* I, ch. 26). They have taken violent—indeed, genocidal—form as capitalism has spread around the globe: in the "settling" of the US West in the nineteenth century; in the imposition of the plantation economy upon the Kenya of the 1950s; indeed, in most places where the regime of capital, in the form of colonialism and imperialism, has opportunistically seized hold of, and then displaced, earlier modes of production. Marxist geographers and political theorists increasingly stress the ongoing nature of this process, designating it as "so-called primitive accumulation" or "accumulation by dispossession" to indicate that it is by no means part of a buried past (Singh 2017; Harvey 2003).

But the origins of capital are not only world-historical; they are also embedded in the very machines at which wage-earners labor. For these machines—like the logo-stamping machine in the Chinese textile factory—were themselves once commodities before they entered the labor process as means of production; they were produced by other workers whose past expenditures of surplus labor are contained in the machinery itself. These workers may now be literally dead—although they also may be alive hundreds or even thousands of miles away from the textile worker, busily producing more logo-stamping machines. These machine-making workers, in turn, have been preceded further back along the commodity chain, temporally or structurally, by the workers who refined the steel, and before them by the workers who mined the iron, etc. The machines thus represent the congealed labor of legions of workers in the industrial army who, after producing the machines' components and then the machines themselves, have passed from the scene; in that sense, capital, constituted by "dead" labor, possesses a ghostly aura. Focusing on the power exerted by dead labor over living labor through the regime of the machine, Marx wrote, "Capital is dead labour, that, vampire-like, only lives by sucking living labour, and lives the more, the more labour it 'sucks'." If money "'comes into the world with a congenital bloodstain on one cheek,'" Marx writes, "capital comes dripping from head to foot, from every pore, with blood and dirt" (*C* I, chs 10, 31). The trope of Gothic haunting that appears frequently in the writings of Marx derives in no small part from this paradoxical understanding that capital, for all its energetic creation of modernity, does so by harnessing the labor of the dead (Nucleous 2003).

Is Marxist value theory obsolete in the era of the internet? Theorists of so-called "cognitive capital" ask, is surplus value being created electronically without the exploitation of labor? Anyone contemplating the impact of information technology (IT) on the political economy of twenty-first-century society has to acknowledge a qualitative shift in what Guido Starosta has called the "knowledge dimension of the productive subjectivity of the collective laborer as a whole" (Starosta 2012, 388) or what Michael Hardt has called the "technical composition of labor" (Hardt 2010, 132). It is evident, too, that well-situated companies are getting rich through the private appropriation of the social wealth—often dubbed "the commons"—that is embodied in the creative knowledge displayed and shared by sophisticated internet users. But to propose that the internet has thereby become a site where new value is created, and where the participation of its users constitutes exploited labor, is a mistaken departure from the labor theory of value (Reveley 2013). Users of the internet leave digital footprints, and the data these generate are a happy hunting ground for advertisers, who track their consumer prey relentlessly, as shown in scandals associated with Facebook's sale of mountains of personal data to customer-seeking businesses. But the profits generated from such sales signify the realization of surplus value in the realm of circulation, not the production of new value (Buzgalin and Kolganov 2013).

Some "cognitive capital" theorists' fixation upon IT workers as the possible leading force of revolutionary social transformation leads them to conclude that the new forms of knowledge-based labor have opened up possibilities for an immediate communist transformation of society, insofar as the capitalists benefiting from their brazen theft of social wealth do not involve themselves in micro-managing the creation of value by squeezing every possible drop of productivity out of the IT worker. Google's headquarters, where IT workers can apparently leave their desks and pick up ping-pong paddles at will, becomes the prototype of collective, unalienated labor. It may be true that the relatively small and elite group of computer-savvy creative workers in technologically advanced economies experience a relative freedom from the pressures most workers experience. Early twenty-first-century incidents in which rogue computer spe-cialists managed seriously to disable governments and businesses indicate, too, the increasing centrality of these workers' labor to the everyday workings of capital. But to view this sector as a political vanguard not only attributes undue radicalism to a relatively privileged stratum of the global workforce but also solidifies the so-called "digital divide" in ways that reinforce rather than contest the effects of racism and imperialism. This romance with the figure of the key-clacking tech worker also glosses over the ways in which the now-invisible labors of the workers who expend "not only blood and flesh, but also nerve and brain" in sweatshops like Foxconn's produce the computers enabling netsurfers of the global North to use their Apple computers for creative purposes. Every time these information workers' fingers hit the keys, they are touching dead labor—a reality cruelly exhibited, we shall see, in the fate of the "Foxconn poet" Xu Lizhi, author of "I Swallowed an Iron Moon."

It is only through the procedures of mystification embedded within capital itself that its historical—and ongoing—genesis in human suffering can be replaced by the seemingly common-sense notion that capital is, well, just capital, "an inevitable feature of 'overwhelming natural laws' … to be confront[ed] … as blind necessity." This obfus-cation of the structural nature and historical roots of capital, Marx concludes, "simultaneously corresponds to the interests of the ruling classes by proclaiming the physical necessity and eternal justification of their sources of revenue and elevating them to a dogma" (C III, ch. 48). Marx's relentless insistence upon uncovering origins—of a single commodity, of capitalism as an entire mode of production—was not the hobbyhorse of a history buff; it was only by thinking historically that he could attempt to penetrate from appearance to essence and peel away the layers of apologia supplied by contemporaneous political economists. It was only by thinking historically that he could discern the specter of negation hovering behind the specter of the vampire. In order to perceive the totality of capitalist social relations, we must not only strip away the "eternal justification" supplied by the perpetrators of ruling-class "dogmas," but also penetrate through the false appearance of equal exchange generated by the market itself.

We need to enter the realm of ideology.

3

Ideology

The ideas of the ruling class are in every epoch the ruling ideas.
— Karl Marx and Friedrich Engels, *The German Ideology*

What is ideology, and how has it been defined and discussed in the Marxist tradition? What is its connection to the relationship between base and superstructure? To legitimation? To obfuscation? To revolution? We all have some unformulated notions about what the term entails. It has something to do with ideas, beliefs, and attitudes. It has something to do with social power. Most of the time, though, it is vaguely disreputable, smacking of dogma and closed-mindedness: other people's thinking may be ideological, but mine is not. We need to tease out this contradiction.

It bears noting, for starters, that not all explanatory or judgmental propositions are ideological. For instance, the statement that the earth revolves around the sun is an assertion of scientifically agreed-upon fact (although articulating this proposition several hundred years ago would have been regarded, at least by the Church, as an ideological move, one that in Europe would likely have gotten you burned at the stake). Nor does a preference for spinach over broccoli, while perhaps passionately held by a particular individual, count as ideological, since there is nothing much at stake in a preference that is purely individual and does not enter the arena of public discourse (unless, of course, for that person spinach is associated with the hyper-masculinity identified with the cartoon character Popeye, in which case the preference has ideological overtones). When it comes to notions about what it means to be both an individual human being and a member of society, however, ideology inevitably figures in framing the terms in which these ideas and assumptions are set forth. A metaphor comparing a monarch to the sun and the rest of society to planets, moons, and asteroids, for instance, is ideological, since it not only proclaims the superiority of the monarch and the dependence of others on him for their survival, but also, through the astronomical metaphor itself, naturalizes (that is, treats as natural) relationships that have in fact come into being in history—and that can go out of being in history as well. Insofar as the premises embedded in ideology are often unspoken, indeed unconscious, their presence in language—and literature—calls for interpretation and critique; this is one of the principal tasks to be taken up by the Marxist literary critic.

Three Definitions of Ideology in Marx

What did Marx have to say about ideology? In his early writings—for example, *The German Ideology* (*GI*), co-authored with Engels—Marx framed his commentary on the Young Hegelians as a critique of ideology. (The Young Hegelians were a grouping of philosophers who purported to have come up with a radical critique of Hegel's idealism; while Marx was originally close to some of them, he concluded that they had retained Hegel's idealism while losing the explanatory power of his dialectical method.) Whereas the Young Hegelians:

> descen[d] from heaven to earth ... we ascend from earth to heaven....
> The phantoms formed in the human brain are ... sublimates of their
> material life-process.... If in all ideology men and their circumstances
> appear upside down as in a *camera obscura*, this phenomenon arises just
> as much from their historical life-process as the inversion of objects on
> the retina does from their physical life-process. (*GI*, Part 1)

(In a *camera obscura*, a predecessor of the modern camera, images were produced upside down; a mirror was needed to produce an image that was right-side up.) Ideology here is equivalent to distortion, indeed falsehood. Marx argued, moreover, that ideology is produced by philosophers detached from the real work that makes society possible, thereby both reflecting and legitimating the class-based division of labor. Ideology is thus complicit in disseminating and reinforcing the standpoint of those possessing property and power, who in effect hire the ideologists to shore up existing class hierarchies. "The ideas of the ruling class are in every epoch the ruling ideas," Marx wrote. "The class which has the means of material production at its disposal has control at the same time over the means of mental production." While different classes rule in different modes of production, each ruling class "is compelled ... to represent its interests as the common interest of all the members of society ... it has to give its ideas the form of universality" (*GI*, Part 1).

The medieval doctrine of the Great Chain of Being—which situated God at the top, peasants at the bottom, with angels, kings, and nobles ranged in between, and commoners, wild beasts, and plants and minerals at the bottom—would be a premodern example of an ideology, elaborated by the priesthood, that clearly rationalized the rule of royalty, aristocracy and priesthood (Lovejoy 1976 [1936]). Perhaps the most prevalent modern ideology legitimating unequal social relations has been the mystification of the capitalist market as a reflection of historical and social necessity. The self-appointed task of many works of proletarian literature—from Robert Tressell's *The Ragged-Trousered Philanthropists* (2012 [1914]) to the Depression-era poetry of Langston Hughes (1994) and Muriel Rukeyser (1978)—has been to undermine the notion that competition and individualism are intrinsic human traits, with the corollary that those who have been excluded from a life of wealth and ease deserve their fates. Whether deliberately promulgated by ruling classes or absorbed through the pores of everyday life, such ideologies reinforce exploitation and oppression by treating as eternal truths the false universals serving those with power and wealth.

Marx articulated a somewhat different definition and explanation of ideology some fourteen years after *The German Ideology*, in the Preface to *A Contribution to the Critique of Political Economy*. (This passage was quoted in part previously in connection with materialism and idealism, as well as the base–superstructure relationship.) After describing the ways in which the "real foundation" of society gives rise to different "forms of social consciousness," and the fettering of productive forces by relations of production produces an insurmountable crisis, Marx wrote:

> Then begins an era of social revolution. The changes in the economic foundation lead sooner or later to the transformation of the whole immense superstructure.
>
> In studying such transformations it is always necessary to distinguish between the material transformation of the economic conditions of production, which can be determined with the precision of natural science, and the legal, political, religious, artistic or philosophic—in short, ideological forms in which men become conscious of this conflict and fight it out. (*PCCPE*)

This formulation shares with the one presented in *The German Ideology* the notion that ideology is grounded in material circumstances and does not float freely above particular social formations. The 1859 text differs, however, in its stipulation that "ideological forms" constitute a terrain where ideas "fight themselves out"—that is, they reflect a kind of class struggle in the realm of concepts and beliefs. The logic of this position is that any class—the proletariat as well as the bourgeoisie—can have its "ideologists." Ideology here signifies not distortion, as in the earlier text, but the outlook of a given class, its partisan stance in the class struggle. In this context, "ideology" is not in and of itself a pejorative term.

This conception of ideology as class-based political standpoint would be taken up by Lenin, who asserted in *What Is to Be Done?* that there were only two ideologies available to the proletariat in the class struggle: "bourgeois ideology" and "socialist ideology." He added, "There is no middle course (for mankind has not created a 'third' ideology, and, moreover, in a society torn by class antagonisms there can never be a non-class or an above-class ideology)" (*WITBD*, ch. 2). For Lenin, the opposition of these two forms of ideology did not constitute an absolute dualism. "Bourgeois ideology" consisted not so much of outright falsehood as of "partial" or "relative" truth; while the lived experience of the proletariat did not spontaneously produce "socialist ideology." Indeed, it was the role of a revolutionary party to help the proletariat transcend the limits of its experience—which he termed "economism," or "trade union consciousness"—by introducing "from outside the economic struggle" the totalizing understanding supplied by Marxism (*WITBD*, ch. 3). ("From outside" did not signify elitist political control, but an epistemological standpoint—that is, a basis for seeing and knowing—that challenges the familiar categories of common sense [Lih 2006; Shandro, ch. 4].) For Lenin, the ideologies of the bourgeoisie and the proletariat were reflections of class standpoint: the former required that social reality be, to one degree or another, obfuscated; while the latter, if it wished to liberate itself, needed as fully as possible to understand things as they really are. The ideology of the proletariat could thus aim at being at once partisan and objective; what was at stake was not epistemological relativism—that is, the notion that truth does not exist, but is only a matter of competing views—but fundamental class interest.

Lenin's conception of "ideology" as a weapon that can be deployed by contesting sides in social struggles would be widely used by revolutionaries in the past century. Mao Zedong, contrasting communism with the dead and dying "ideological and social systems ... of feudalism [and] capitalism," viewed the revolutionary reality emerging in 1940 as "at once a complete system of proletarian ideology and a new social system" (Mao 1940, 360). Amilcar Cabral critically remarked that "Africa's post-colonial history is one of unfulfilled missions because the national leadership has been lacking in revolutionary theory and ideology" (Cabral 1966). The Black Panther Party unabashedly declared that its "ideology was the historical experience of Black people and the wisdom gained by Black people in their 400 year long struggle against the system of racist oppression and economic exploitation in Babylon" (Cleaver 1967, 1). For these and other radical theorists of the past century, the construction of a new social order necessitated the development and deployment of an "ideology" that could contest and supersede existing ruling-class paradigms. This usage of the term "ideology" has nearly disappeared from leftist discourse of the past several decades. In its founding statement, for instance, the Combahee River Collective—a black feminist organization that coined the term "identity politics"—speaks of the "narrowness" of the "ideology" on the left it has had to confront and supersede (Combahee River Collective 1983 [1979]). The negative overtones of "ideology" prevail in the rhetoric of many present-day social movements.

In *Capital*, notably, the term "ideology" does not appear. But Marx's theorization of commodity fetishism, which is premised upon the prevalence of abstract labor and exchange value in human interactions, guides his entire analysis of the ways in which capital generates all kinds of contradictions between appearance and essence. The consciousness of both the proletariat and the bourgeoisie mirrors a clouded and distorted reality. "The advance of capitalist production," he writes, "develops a working class, which by education, tradition, habit, looks upon the conditions of that mode of production as self-evident laws of Nature.... The dull compulsion of economic relations completes the subjection of the labourer to the capitalist" (*C* I, ch. 28). Indeed, the rulers themselves also remain largely unaware of the causes and consequences of their actions: hence their acceptance—indeed, elevation—of the explanatory power of such ideologically saturated notions as "supply and demand" and "the fair price of labor." One difference between the arguments set forth in *The German Ideology* and in *Capital* is that, in the former, Marx and Engels viewed ideology as illusory consciousness, warping one's perception and understanding of a reality that is, by implication, otherwise transparent and knowable. In the latter text, it is the workings of capital itself that produce the proliferation of false appearances: that is, the very truth of capital consists in its masking of the truth.

There are thus three overlapping but distinct definitions of ideology in the works of Marx: as illusory consciousness; as the standpoint of a class; and as socially necessary misunderstanding (Eagleton 1991, ch. 2). In one of his late letters, Engels, alluding to his and Marx's joint project, referred to ideology as "a process accomplished by the so-called thinker consciously, indeed, but with a false consciousness. The real motives impelling him remain unknown to him, otherwise it would not be an ideological process at all" (FE to Mehring, 14 July 1893, *MEC*). Marx himself never used the phrase "false consciousness" to denote the blinkered modes of perception and cognition produced by capitalist social relations (Pines 1993, 1–16). Moreover, he continually distinguished between the "vulgar economists" like Say and Malthus—whom he viewed as "perpetuat[ing] a senseless confusion ... in the interest of the ruling classes" (KM to Kugelman, 11 July 1868, *MEC*)—and the classical political economists like Ricardo and Smith, whose theories were limited by the horizon of what they took for granted in the workings of capital. "Classical Political Economy," he wrote, "nearly touches the true relation of things, without, however, consciously formulating it. This it cannot, so long as it sticks in its bourgeois skin" (*C* I, ch. 19). While he did not group all his intellectual antagonists in the same category, the Marx of *Capital* clearly believed that his "critique of political economy" was needed precisely because of the proliferation of inadequate, indeed false, explanatory paradigms produced by the analytical vocabulary of the economic theories enjoying mainstream status in his time. The alternative vocabulary he developed to analyze the workings of capitalist society—"abstract labor," "surplus value," "constant" and "variable" capital, for starters—was necessary to interrogate everyday economic concepts, historicize the conditions of their emergence, and jar his readers into a realization of the need to move beyond the immediacy that passes for common sense to a deeper truth. (The term "immediacy" here signifies categories of perception and analysis that rest at the level of appearance, failing to draw the necessary connections between and among phenomena.) While Marx's chosen terms for describing economic processes are scientific in the sense that they denote—far more accurately than the vocabulary of bourgeois economics—actual realities and processes, they are at the same time partisan, in that their function is to produce the understanding needed to dismantle the existing social order. His battle is, after all, not so much with bad ideas as with the social order that has brought them into being. Without naming itself as such, then, *Capital* can also be seen as an "ideological" text in the second sense of the word noted above; it is a weapon in the struggle for proletarian liberation from the yoke of capital.

Dominant Ideology

We can begin our investigation into the conceptions of ideology relevant to literary criticism by focusing upon dominant ideology, that is, what

Marx and Engels called the "ruling ideas" serving the needs of the class with property and power. Codified in belief and emotion and materialized in action, dominant ideology can take a variety of forms, from doctrines disseminated by ruling elites for crudely manipulative purposes to largely unconscious systems of belief that spring spontaneously from the way we live. Dominant ideologies have also changed over time: the doctrine of original sin prevailing in the premodern West, for instance, has largely been displaced by the no less idealist notion of an inherent human nature. But it is not always easy to distinguish between dominant ideology as overt ruling-class doctrine, disseminated through various ideological state apparatuses, and dominant ideology as the common sense guiding everyday behavior. People can readily view as ideological the ideas and beliefs that have either functioned historically as a means of social control or that currently fulfill such a function elsewhere in the world. Many inhabitants of the modern world look upon emperor-worship, for example, as a relic of premodernity, and they are likely to view as backward any society that perpetuates such idolatry of its ruler; the comically racialized—and demonized—portrayal of North Korea's President Kim Jong-Un in the Western press supplies a case in point. It is less easy to view taken-for-granted practices in one's own society as reflections of a dominant ideology. Arguably, however, the ritual of covering one's heart and pledging allegiance to the US flag in school assemblies performs the function of binding (and subordinating) the individual to the state in ways not all that different from the methods of securing the state's legitimacy that are practiced in North Korea. It is this kind of ideological control that Langston Hughes contests when he places workers and leaders on an equal—and internationalist—plane, calling for the recognition of "[a] real guy named/ Marx Communist Lenin Peasant Stalin Worker ME—/ I said, ME!" ("Goodbye, Christ" in Hughes 1994, 166).

Religiously coded ideological practices are comparably susceptible to differential judgment. A person raised in a heavily Catholic country might not bat an eye when a habit-wearing nun—who has taken the paradoxical vow to be the virginal bride of Christ—walks past. But he might consider a Muslim woman wearing a burqa as she does her weekly shopping—or a burkini when she goes to the beach—to be the oppressed object of primitive patriarchal institutions (if not, given the Islamophobia currently functioning as dominant ideology, as the bearer of a bomb under her clothing). The point is not that burqas are a good thing whereas nun's habits are a bad thing, but that the exemption of the nun from a comparable judgment about patriarchal control is a sure marker of ideological thinking. Indeed, the stigmatization of the burqa and acceptance of the habit deflect critical thinking about how both outfits rationalize women's inferior status—as well as the unpaid labor women perform as a group—by associating female virtue and value with a spurious sexual purity that must be protected by men and institutions run by men. The tendency to view the group behaviors of "others" as ideological, and one's own cultural practices as normative, to no small degree reinforces the hold of dominant ideology by rendering it largely unheard and invisible.

The concept of "fettering"—meaning binding, constraining—usefully describes large-scale diachronic (that is, historical) movements, such as the ways in which the relations of production governing feudalism came to function as a restraint upon the development of the forces of production associated with incipient capitalism, resulting in bourgeois revolutions of various kinds. This concept also helps us understand reality from a

Why not follow Lenin's practice and use the term "bourgeois ideology" to denote ideas and beliefs supportive of the status quo? This term has the advantage, after all, of keeping in view the class whose interests are served by many of the concepts and attitudes that we act upon unknowingly. Certain Marxist theorists continue to deploy the term to denote dominant ideology (Ollman 1993). One disadvantage, however, is that "bourgeois ideology" pertains only to the period of capitalism, and not to earlier forms of class society characterized by different—but no less powerful—forms of dominant ideology. Another disadvantage is that the somewhat accusatory tone of the phrase can leave little room for consideration of ideological contradiction, which is, we shall see, vitally important to Marxist literary analyses that view dominant ideologies often locked in combat with their dialectical counterparts in given texts and traditions.

Finally, the term "bourgeois ideology" can give rise to a somewhat conspiratorial conception of the origins of dominant ideologies, as if ruling classes routinely form huddles and decide to broadcast ideas reinforcing their standpoints. While we would be naïve not to realize that this at times occurs—especially in periods of crisis, when the rulers' ideological hold over the masses becomes precarious—we would be equally naïve not to see that some ideologies emerge more or less spontaneously from historical developments and are then reinforced ex post facto. The weighting of the male–female binary in favor of male superiority, for instance, gradually emerged with the institution of private property and monogamy; that this opposition has proven immensely profitable to capitalism and continues to be affirmed ideologically among many sectors of the population does not mean that the capitalist ruling class cooked up sexism in advance in order to justify the exploitation of women's waged and unwaged work. Things are a tad more complicated. Throughout this book, then, the terms "dominant," "prevailing," and occasionally "mainstream" will usually be deployed to indicate ideological formations supportive of ruling-class interests.

synchronic (that is, snapshot) standpoint: the profit-making imperatives of capitalist medical care, for instance, operate as a fetter upon public health. But the notion of fettering also helps us theorize the role played by dominant ideologies in constraining the imaginations and aspirations of people who might otherwise be able to view the world more objectively and act more decisively in their own interests. As described above, patriotism and patriarchy (which share the same etymological root in the Latin word "*pater*," meaning father) are ideologies that tie people to inherited ways of thinking and doing, and thus to the ruling classes that have, as Marx and Engels wrote, supplied "the dominant ideas of any age." This kind of ideological constraint is what the poet William Blake referred to as the "mind-forg'd manacles" binding people to the regime of "Palace" and "Church" (Blake 1953, 46); it is what the "Internationale"—the song of the worldwide communist movement—alludes to in proclaiming, "No more tradition's chains shall bind us" (Poitier 1871). The fettering that occurs in the realm of ideology is a major impediment to human liberation.

When considering the ways in which ideology pervades everyday life and fetters our political imaginations, we should be especially alert to how things that we encounter in everyday life, and that we take entirely for granted, often reflect and reinforce dominant relations of power and property. Museums, for instance, are not just repositories of science, art, and history, but embodiments of highly selective narratives about what is valued in societies of various kinds, and why; a Sunday afternoon trip to the local museum involves much more than pure entertainment or enlightenment. Public parks and college campuses are full of statues of famous people (almost always men, often astride horses) and buildings named after benefactors. Who decided which figures should be memorialized, and why? Where did the money come from that made these people rich and famous to begin with? Why are there virtually no statues of women? Of people of color? Recent controversies in the United States over whether or not statues of Confederate generals should be removed from town squares, or whether campus buildings named after racist politicians should be re-designated, have brought to the fore the ways in which dominant ideologies are at once asserted and confirmed in public places.

But what about "factual" representations, like maps? Aren't these objective representations of the world, unshaped by ideology? If we think about it, though, maps function as mute testimonies to past and present divisions of power and property. Who, after all, decided upon the borders between counties, states, provinces, and nations—much less called these entities into being in the first place? A pre-1848 map of North America would have shown Texas, Arizona, Nevada, New Mexico (note its name), and large portions of California as part of Mexico—a history largely pushed to the margins in mainstream texts, though often figuring centrally in works of Chicano literature. On what basis are some land masses treated as separate continents, but not others? Europe, after all, could more logically be designated as a peninsula of the Eurasian landmass than as a continent in itself. What assumptions about the presumed center of the civilized world are built into the terms "Near East" and "Middle East"? Through what ideological process were the names chosen for various streets and cities? Once we start peeling away the layers of congealed history, we see that many of the names we view as self-evident descriptors often contain buried narratives of colonialism, imperialism, and, not infrequently, genocide. To draw attention to the politics of map-making and map-reading is not to claim that, in a communist society—where there would be no more nations or borders as we know them—there would be no ways of differentiating between various parts of the globe, or that streets and cities would be nameless. But it is to acknowledge that there are very few ways of representing space and place that are free from ideology.

Relative Autonomy and Mediation Revisited

The above examples of the ways in which dominant ideologies like nationalism, sexism, racism, and religious doctrine function largely on an unconscious level to legitimate current power relations invite us to reconsider certain features of the base–superstructure relationship. Relative autonomy, we will recall, denotes the ways in which ideas and beliefs so fully permeate a social formation that they do not require explicit and continual reinforcement, but "go on automatic," as it were. In societies based upon slavery, colonialism, or fascism, the relationship between dominant ideology and ruling-class coercion is out in the open, forcibly renewed every day through the functioning of private property and the state. As Frantz Fanon observed in *The Wretched of the Earth*, unabashed doctrines of racial superiority and inferiority are indispensable to the colonial project, where "what parcels out the world is to begin with the fact of belonging to or not belonging to a given race or species" (Fanon 1963, 40). European claims that the "essential qualities of the West [are] eternal" (Fanon 1963, 46) have routinely been directly—and dialectically—premised upon the denial of the humanity of racially sub-ordinated peoples. In times of war, moreover, regimes of power in just about all countries operate in a fairly concerted and unsubtle way: hence those blatantly propagandistic World War I recruitment posters depicting Germans as ape-like monsters assaulting lily-white women passively draped in one or another flag of the Allied powers. In the everyday life of so-called liberal democracies, however, the processes of status quo ideo-logical reinforcement, like the habit of standing and singing the national anthem, are for the most part quasi-automatic and self-perpetuating. For this very reason, relatively autonomous institutions can be adjudged more effective in reinforcing ruling-class ideological hegemony than openly coercive ones. For instance, even though both major political parties in the present-day United States have firm ties to Wall Street, the fact that Democrats and Republicans vie for control of Congress gives the democratic system of government greater legitimacy—at least in the eyes of many—than would be the case if there were just one ruling-class political party; similar illusions are promoted in parliamentary electoral systems elsewhere in the world. Even though voters in capitalist society have essentially no control over any of the social forces that shape their lives, the relative autonomy of the state reinforces its hold—both ideo-logical and coercive—over the average citizen.

Another important term associated with base–superstructure analysis that we can usefully revisit is mediation, which is, like relative autonomy, essential to an understanding of the ways in which ideology flows through the bloodstream of society. While it is not always clear, at the level of appearances, why and how various phenomena and social practices can be correlated with class-based social relations, mediation enables us to think through the possible causal connections between seemingly disparate zones of causality and the ideologies to which they give rise. Take, for instance, the ways in which attention to mediation can help us ground dominant notions of gender and sexuality in capitalist social relations. Heteronormativity—the ideology presuming that maleness and femaleness are defined in binary contradistinction to one another, and that only heterosexuality is natural and should be sanctioned in insti-tutionalized social practices like marriage—can without much difficulty be seen as a second-order mediation of the gender dualism deeply rooted in capitalism. (Indeed, in all forms of class society: by contrast, it bears noting that, in some pre-class societies—e.g. various Native American/ First Nation groups—the figure of the "Two Spirit," a person possessing multiple gender identities, is frequently honored rather than frowned

upon [Estrada 2011].) As a form of dominant ideology, heteronormativity not only justifies highly profitable wage differentials based upon
gender but also supplies the rationale sustaining the heterosexual nuclear
family as a favored economic site for the reproduction of labor power
and a favored ideological site for the transmission and reinforcement of
normative values.

Although it is fairly easy to see how heteronormativity functions to
the advantage of capital, however, it is not equally clear how homophobia
may serve the same end, except in the general sense that it is one more
toxic ideology that—like religious fundamentalism, racism, or nationalism—instills fear of "the other" and discourages working-class unity.
Mediation helps us establish the necessary connections by enabling us
to view homophobia as a mediation of a mediation: that is, antipathy to
those engaged in nonconforming sexual behaviors is shaped by the heteronormative assumptions accompanying gender dualism without being
directly caused by class-related pressures and limitations. Especially if
we bear in mind Engels's caution that "various elements of the superstructure ... exercise their influence upon the course of the historical
struggles and in many cases preponderate in determining their form," as
well as Althusser's theorization of "structures in dominance" determined
by economic forces "in the last instance," we can discern the causal
connections between the imperatives of capital on the one hand and,
on the other, the motivations that prompt homophobic discrimination and violence. Capital's drive to accumulation need not function as
the rock tossed into the pool of historical causality, so to speak, with
every ripple resulting from that primal event. While heteronormativity
mediates between the requirements of capital and homophobic attitudes
and practices, it serves as a much more powerful locus of proximate
causality than do such fundamental features of capitalist social relations
as, say, alienation or exploitation. Without resorting to a model of plural
causality—the notion that social phenomena result from a mass of disarticulated "factors," in which none exercises final determining power—the
view of homophobia as a mediation of a mediation can help us theorize
the role of homophobia in reproducing capitalist social relations without
asserting a direct line of historical or sociological genesis.

To link homophobia as an ideology to capitalism is not to assert
that homosexuality—and other non-conforming sexual practices—are
themselves *caused* by capitalism; as various historians of sexuality have
pointed out, the category of "homosexual" as an identity may have
emerged as a consequence of the altered work and family relations enabled

by capitalism, but same-sex practices have been part of human (and for that matter some animal) experiences for a very long time (Floyd 2009; D'Emilio 1998). Nor does designating the ideology of homophobia as "relatively autonomous" and as a "mediation of a mediation" mean for a moment that it cannot have immensely destructive consequences for people whose lives enact patterns of sexual difference—as displayed, for instance, in the June 2016 massacre of patrons at a queer lounge in Tampa, Florida; the criminalization of same-sex marriage in Uganda; and the enduring patterns of police violence against people of nonconforming sexual orientation (Ritchie 2017). Nor, again, does this mean that LGBTQ people are not discriminated against in job hiring and promotion in many industries, or that their medical needs are as fully covered by health insurance as are those of straight or cis-gendered people. The terms "relatively autonomous," "mediation," and "structure in dominance" function to designate a mode of causality, not an assessment of its intensity or its effects.

It is important to bear in mind, however, that at any given moment dominant ideologies can function in quite contradictory ways in connection with different demographics and shifting ruling-class imperatives. The gender dualism upon which homophobia is premised, and by which it is continually reinforced, remains firmly in place in the economic and familial situations of many inhabitants of the globe—reinforcing, on the one hand, the approximately 20 cents an hour wage gap between women and men in the United States (AAUW 2018); on the other, the so-called "honor killings" of Pakistani or Afghan women who have stepped outside their arranged marriages and run away with their lovers (Chesler and Bloom 2012). In many parts of the world, the conjunction of sexism, homophobia, and religious fundamentalism constitutes an especially poisonous combination, all the more potent because of its unquestioned acceptance by large sectors of the population. Yet at the same time heteronormativity, as dominant ideology, is gradually being eroded in various social sectors of some capitalist countries, where many people, especially young people, increasingly resist traditional ideological constructions of gender. Even as this shift in beliefs reflects widespread rejection of gendered inequalities, however, capital can take advantage of the change, as the fashion industry is supplied with highly profitable images of gender nonconforming coolness and an expanded market for commodities. This shift in mainstream attitudes indicates the extent to which liberal multiculturalism has—at least among certain sectors of the population in the global North—proven a more reliable ideological accompaniment to capital than old-fashioned heteronormativity. Even as what Marx called "the dull compulsion of economic relations" becomes increasingly onerous for many members of the world proletariat, and the state shows itself to be increasingly coercive and violent toward both straight and queer people who transgress traditional gendered boundaries in many parts of the world, same-sex social practices are celebrated in some countries and regions as signaling an expansion of personal freedom. Attention to relative autonomy and mediation enables us to think dialectically about the complexity of capitalist social relations without resorting to pluralist models of causality, much less culturally relativist explanations characterizing some societies as more "advanced" or "backward" than others.

Ideology as Smorgasbord

Ideology is fluid; ruling-class hegemony, as well as enhanced possibilities for capital accumulation, can be secured by any number of routes of ideological transmission, combined with varying degrees of economic and institutional coercion. Racism, for instance, has taken a variety of forms since it emerged as central to the apologia for slavery and colonialism in the modern era (L. Bennett 1975; Fredrickson 1987). The kind of blatant racism described by Fanon may now be officially frowned upon in some presumably enlightened parts of the world, where the biologically based theories of race that prevailed in the nineteenth and early-to-mid twentieth century have been—at least scientifically—rejected: hence the currently popular enclosure of the word "race" in quotation marks. But, for all this attunement to fashionable linguistic convention, it is all too evident that racism remains alive and well in the lives of billions, both as a material practice and as an ideology rendering acceptable differential levels of suffering, from Yemen to Myanmar to South Sudan to Italy. Whether it be the lethal forced migrations caused by imperialist wars and increasing desertification; the mass drownings of the inhabitants of low-lying areas; the magnified violence experienced at the hands of the state; the disproportionate levels of sexual slavery; the payment of sub-subsistence wages, or of no wages at all to those of undocumented status: all these brutal situations and practices arouse far less indignation when involving the globe's darker-skinned inhabitants than when affecting those of lighter hue.

Language functions as a crucial ideological mediator enabling—indeed at times augmenting—all kinds of racial disparities that serve the interests of capital. In the presumably "post-racial" society of the United States, for instance, patterns of differential treatment that are the product of deliberately instituted state and corporate policies are justified—sometimes obliquely, sometimes quite directly—by ideologically charged rationales disguised as neutral descriptors. During the financial crisis of 2008–12, for instance, the housing bubble—a product of Wall Street's compulsive addiction to what Marx called "fictitious capital," itself a response to falling rates of profit in the industrial economy—was routinely blamed upon racialized working-class homeowners. The polite substitution of "urban" for the "n-word"; of "blight" for the differential delivery of public services to racially coded zipcodes; "non-payment of loans" for the constraints imposed by selective patterns of predatory lending: these kinds of rhetorical moves shifted the burden of explaining the spiraling numbers of foreclosures onto the shoulders of their victims. The effect of such misleading, indeed dishonest verbal ploys has been not only to blame minority mortgage holders for their own distressed circumstances but also to invite the sector of the working-class population designated as white—itself also prey of the big banks, and also experiencing, if to a somewhat lesser degree, foreclosure and homelessness—to deny its commonality of interests with those sectors designated as black or brown (Taylor 2016). That a government facilitating the policies noted above could have been presided over by a president of partial African descent in the early decades of the twenty-first century indicates the extent to which racism, as both dominant ideology and material practice, is not a matter of individual behavior and belief, but is instead structurally embedded in the imperatives of class rule. That this president's successor managed to be elected largely by white voters misled into seeing the nation's nonwhite inhabitants as the source of their felt insecurity speaks volumes not only about the abiding heritage of chattel slavery but also about the continuing reinforcement of racist attitudes in mainstream political discourse.

Capitalism's enduring capacity to rule hinges, to no small degree, upon its making available a range of ideological options to the populations inhabiting its domain. For, situated among the various ideological alternatives supplied by capitalism, any given individual would seem to have access to a veritable smorgasbord of possibilities; false universals abound to satisfy a range of individual and group tastes. (A smorgasbord is a buffet-style meal in which the diner has many options from which to choose.) One can reject segregation and embrace diversity; one can reject misogyny or homophobia and adhere to a doctrine of gender

and sexual equality. Yet none of these more progressive stances is necessarily anti-capitalist. Indeed, if it is identified with the "true" mission
of enlightened modernity—and celebrated by such uplifting chants as
"This is what democracy looks like!"—a pluralistically inflected liberal
nationalism can end up reinforcing capitalist class rule as effectively as an
overtly nativist racism. Whether liberal or conservative, all standpoints
that take as given the exchange of labor power for wages fail to call into
question the material basis of existing power relations. Indeed, as long
as widely circulated beliefs and assumptions about the social order obey
the dictum of ABC—"Anything But Class"—all is well in the ideological realm. After all, in any smorgasbord the provider of the feast, or the
owner of the restaurant, establishes the choices made available to those
who dine. That this host need not be a purposive agent writing out the
menu of the week, but instead an impersonal system functioning through
ideological state apparatuses on the one hand and plain old common
sense on the other, makes the task of contesting the available options all
the more challenging—and necessary.

Reification

Thus far we have been examining modes of dominant ideology that
are embedded in particular sets of codified ideas and beliefs. "Ideology"
in this sense is plural, in that religious fundamentalism, racism,
nationalism, sexism, homophobia and so on can be seen as specific
doctrines—"ideologies"—that are connected with social practices and
serve ruling-class needs in specific historical situations. But dominant
ideology—conceived not as a set of specific beliefs, doctrines, and
attitudes, but as a more comprehensive relationship between thoughts
and emotions on the one hand and the world of lived experience on the
other—can also be seen to function on a deeper level, one more difficult to
pinpoint and associate with material causality, but for that reason all the
more important to identify and understand. The abstraction of labor, we
will recall, has the effect not only of masking exploitation but also, more
generally, of instilling modes of perception that remain focused on the
surface of phenomena, conceiving of them in their isolation rather than in
their interconnectedness—that is, of precluding access to totality. While
in the time of Marx and Engels this habit of fetishized perception was
on the increase, it was, in its novelty, still visible as a social phenomenon.
Their admiration for the novels of the early nineteenth-century realist
novelist Honoré de Balzac is traceable in large part to Balzac's ability

to anatomize the configuration of post-French Revolution society that was changing before his eyes, with members of different social groups scrambling either to retain their old class status or secure a new one.

When capital has come to suffuse every crack and corner of social existence, however, its tendency to fragment, obfuscate, and mask is universalized as reification. Describing the ways in which the "vulgar economists" took words like "labor," "land," and "capital" as a "trinity formula" that treated these historically determined aspects of production as self-evident entities existing throughout time, Marx wrote that there results:

> the complete mystification of the capitalist mode of production, the conversion of social relations into things, the direct coalescence of the material production relations with their historical and social determination. It is an enchanted, perverted, topsy-turvy world, in which Monsieur le Capital and Madame la Terre do their ghost-walking as social characters and at the same time directly as mere things. (*C* III, ch. 48)

For Marx, this "conversion of social relations into things"—alternatively translated as "reification"—that arises from capitalist social relations is necessarily reflected in the language used to describe those relations; ideological mystification is a result both of reality and of the reified vocabulary corresponding to that reality.

The definitive analysis of reification as a prevailing social phenomenon produced by the universal abstraction of labor was undertaken in the early twentieth century by the Hungarian Marxist Georg Lukács, who argued that "the problem of commodities" is "the central structural problem of capitalist society in all its aspects" (Lukács 1971, 83). The effects of reification are registered, Lukács argued, not only in the "fragmentation of the object" through the dominance of exchange value over use value, but also in the "fragmentation of the subject." The "fate of the worker"—whose alienated "self-objectification" forces him into the "contemplative consciousness" that leads him to view his own activity from the outside—thus becomes "the fate of society as a whole" (Lukács 1971, 89–91). Phenomena resulting from historical causes appear self-evident and natural; "the unexplained and inexplicable facticity of bourgeois existence ... acquires the patina [that is, surface appearance] of an eternal law of nature or a cultural value enduring for all time" (Lukács 1971, 157). In the lived experience of advanced capitalist society, the tendency toward commodity fetishism that Marx discerned in his early writings on alienation is writ large. Not only is exploitation veiled; the habit of not-seeing the totality, of living and perceiving at the level of appearance, becomes simply the exercise of common sense. An immense fetter on the development of human potential, reification is, for Lukács, the principal process, both material and ideological, that mediates between labor and capital, the individual and the social totality. It at once creates the conditions of existence in capitalist society and produces the beliefs and conceptual frameworks through which this existence is rationalized and legitimated.

There is, however, an antidote to reification, Lukács argued—namely, the "standpoint of the proletariat" (Lukács 1971, 149–209). While the proletariat "shares with the bourgeoisie the reification of every aspect of its life" (Lukács 1971, 149)—that is, both are experientially restricted to a semi-blinded immediacy—the material interests of the two classes remain diametrically opposed. As the only class in need of its own self-abolition as a class, the proletariat has an objective interest in seeing through and past the veil that reification imposes upon reality by developing categories of perception and understanding that accord—or at least more closely accord—with the truth of its life as an exploited class. For Lukács, mediation as a conscious act on the part of the proletariat—that is, an attempt to understand the layered levels of causality that explain the origins of thought and behavior in capitalist social relations—is not simply an exercise in trying to understand why things are the way they are; it is a means of class-based self-emancipation that, especially at a time of crisis, emerges as historical necessity. Totality is thus not just the "big picture"; it is the necessary framework for overcoming fragmentation and seeing reality in its interconnectedness, as well as for affirming the proletariat's claim to human universality—that is, to representing the interests of humanity as a whole. In grasping the causes of its own objectification, the proletariat retrieves its subjectivity; realizing its potential as a revolutionary force, it becomes—in an admittedly ponderous Hegelian phrase—the "identical subject-object of history" (Lukács 1971, 199–200). In other words, the proletariat, as collective subject, attains awareness of its selfhood by understanding—and, through class struggle, negating and sublating—the sources of its objectification. Marxism, for Lukács, is "the ideological expression of the proletariat," the theoretical ground enabling the proletariat to transform its reified state of "being" into a state of revolutionary "becoming" (Lukács 1971, 258–59). Immensely influential in Marxist theorizing about ideology, political economy, and class struggle in the past century, Lukács's discussion of reification and the standpoint of the proletariat has also played a central role, we shall see, in historical materialist literary criticism.

Interpellation

Althusser—whom we have mentioned previously in connection with the notions of ideological state apparatuses and structures in dominance—approaches the nature and function of ideology from a significantly different angle. Where Lukács stresses the fragmenting function of reification but argues that the class-conscious proletariat can make the journey from immediacy to totality, Althusser focuses upon the ways in which Ideology—which he counterposes to the Science of Marxism—is lived and cannot be escaped. He grants that, as a plural term, "ideologies" signifies different doctrines that people may consciously embrace—but also, upon seeing them as illusory, reject. As a single (and capitalized) term, however, Ideology functions largely on the unconscious level. Representing "the imaginary relationship of individuals to their real conditions of existence," it has a "material existence" that is manifested in people's living and acting in certain ways (Althusser 2014, 256, 258). (By "imaginary" Althusser means "image-like," not "false" or "made-up.") As an "imaginary relationship," Ideology mediates between reality—"the Real"—and the ways in which people represent reality to themselves and others (Irr 2017). For Althusser, ideology may derive from the socially necessary misunderstanding generated by the workings of capital; but it is also consummately practical. For instance, when a young woman in the twenty-first-century UK thinks that it is "natural" to graduate (or try to graduate) from college, get (or try to get) a nine-to-five job, open a bank account (if she has not yet established a poor credit rating), etc., she is living the dominant ideology of her time and place; her ideas are insepa-rable from her actions. Critically analyzing literary works that naturalize historically grounded beliefs and practices is, we shall see, one of the important tasks facing the Marxist literary critic.

To describe the mechanism by which Ideology positions people in such a way that they are unaware of their positioning, Althusser has introduced the notion of interpellation, which signifies a kind of "hailing," or recog-nition, as in, "I know who you are! You are an American!" (or, a housewife, or, perhaps less weightily, a Subaru owner). In Althusser's seminal for-mulation, the key person doing the interpellating is characterized as a policeman, thereby emphasizing the role of the State—a key source of both coercion and ideology—in determining identity (Althusser 2014, 261–64). Yet, Althusser points out, we are also continually being inter-pellated by friends, who "recognize" us and make us feel "recognized" by them. Thus it is not any specific interlocutor, but the Ideology embedded in language and everyday social practice, that is doing the hailing which produces the desired response, "Yes! That's me! That's who I am!" Any of the tags mentioned above—American, housewife, Subaru owner—may, of course, have some descriptive accuracy. Yet each tag supplies not just partial recognition but often, more fundamentally, *mis*recognition, in that it affirms an identity that is loaded in advance with all kinds of ideolog-ical assumptions—whether about nationalism, the nuclear family, status consumption, or whatever. The key effect of interpellation is that indi-viduals, in acknowledging the hailing, internalize the category of identity in question; they police themselves, thereby taking the burden for social control off the coercive policies of the state.

People can, of course, refuse to be interpellated, especially if the appeal is somewhat out of date. Many present-day readers of the poetry of Rudyard Kipling, for instance, do not readily rise to salute the empire when reading his 1899 call to Theodore Roosevelt, "Take up the White Man's burden / Ye dare not stoop to less" (Kipling 1922, 322). People can also choose to un-learn patterns of interpellation that they have grown up taking for granted. For instance, a person living in the United States can choose to reject being designated as an "American" by doing some research and finding out that inhabitants of the Caribbean or Central or South America are equally entitled to claim this label. Becoming uneasy when hearing a politician intone, "My fellow Americans" or referring to Puerto Rico as "America's backyard," she may move on to a broadly critical awareness of American Exceptionalism, that is, the doctrine that the United States is uniquely positioned to give moral guidance to the rest of the world. In moving through and past identification with the nation, she has repudiated interpellation by ideology with a small I, which is no mean achievement. An important task of Marxist pedagogy is to assist in such procedures of de-interpellation. Hence the usefulness to teachers in US classrooms of myth-blasting books like James Loewen's *Lies My Teacher Told Me* (2007); Howard Zinn's *A People's History of the United States* (2015 [1980]); Roxanne Dunbar-Ortiz's *An Indigenous People's History of the United States* (2014); Edward Baptist's *The Half Has Never Been Told: Slavery and the Making of US Capitalism* (2016); and Gerald Horne's *The Counter-revolution of 1776: Slave Resistance and the Origins of the United States of America* (2014).

Althusser's main point about Ideology with a capital I, however, is that the act of interpellation, as well as the affirmative response that it evokes, foster the addressee's notion that she is an autonomous individual, a subject who has freely chosen to be recognized by means of the category in question. The catch is that this very illusion of subjectivity, that is, of being a self-governing "subject," marks her "subjection to the Subject." (In older social formations this Subject was God or the Church; in modern formulations it is Capital or the State [Althusser 2014, 268–69].) The belief of the "subject"—small "s"—that, as an individual, she has opted for one identity or another reflects the pervasiveness, under capitalism, of the mystified assumption that the presumably free (that is, uncoerced) exchange of labor power for wages is premised upon her actual freedom as an individual. Ideology is thus unconscious because it presupposes fundamental assumptions about what it means to be a social being that do not necessarily involve any given set of codified doctrines: it is inseparable from what we think of as "identity." Indeed, Althusser proposes that even in a communist society ideology would function to furnish people with a practical framework guiding their everyday lives: that this framework would entail beneficial rather than destructive perceptions and activity, giving rise to identities based upon social rather than individualistic notions of selfhood, does not mean that it would not be ideological (Althusser 1969, 231–41). The principal tasks confronting revolutionaries aspiring to replace the ideological state apparatuses of the capitalist state with those promoting the "proletarian ideology of the proletarian state" (Althusser 2014, 90), however, is a formidable one; so long as capitalist relations of production are retained in what purports to be a post-capitalist society, inherited modes of ideology—and Ideology—will, he warns, maintain their sway.

Both Lukács and Althusser view Marxism as at once a methodology for penetrating from appearance to essence and a weapon of the proletariat in the class struggle; their theorizations encompass the view of ideology as necessary distortion as well as the view of ideology as partisan knowledge (Read 2017). But Lukács and Althusser differ in some important ways: the former is a humanist who views reification as the principal impediment to human freedom, while the latter is a militantly anti-humanist structuralist who finds the very notion of human freedom to be a capitalist-generated mirage. Moreover, both are potentially vulnerable to critique. In the case of Lukács, it is not clear how the empirically existing proletariat can break free from reification and attain the standpoint of true class consciousness; even if what is at stake is not

the consciousness of an individual proletarian but the objective positioning of the proletariat as a class (Stasi 2015), the inadequately specified
transit between "being" and "becoming" invites the charge of idealism.
In addition, the designation of reification as the key force foreclosing
revolutionary change may underplay the repressive role of the state, as
well as pertain more fully to social formations permeated by the real subsumption of labor than to those in which the regime of the wage relation
is less fully universalized, but racialized coercion is the order of the day
(Fanon 1963, 35–106; Bewes 2002, 81–85).

In the case of Althusser, it can be objected that the assignation of
such overwhelming epistemological power to "the Subject" makes it
near-impossible to see how individuals—or, for that matter, a class constituted by individuals—might free themselves from the straitjacket of
Ideology and attain the superior vantage point of Science. Nor does his
formulation of interpellation pertain equally to all instances. As Fanon
pointed out in *Black Skin, White Masks* (2008 [1952]), a white child's
spontaneous outburst on seeing a black man, "Look! A Negro!", surely
derogates the humanity of the colonized person. In its lack of direct address
to the black man, however—the child in fact speaks to his mother—his
exclamation ends up telling us more about the child's self-recognition
as white than about the man's as black (Fanon 2008 [1952], 89–119;
Macherey 2012). Moreover, Althusser's insistence on the permanence
of Ideology, regardless of mode of production, invites the criticism that
the transparency of economic relations in communist society need not
entail the mystification of social relations so essential to the functioning of Ideology under capitalism (Eagleton 1991, 149–50). Finally, for
all its value in pinpointing false identities that bind people to the state,
Althusser's formulation of identity as intrinsically linked to misrecognition cannot provide a lens through which to read the significant body
of literature that seeks to develop the revolutionary class consciousness
needed to abolish the exploitation that produces misrecognition in the
first place—as he himself puts it, the "proletarian ideology of the proletarian state." When the communist poet Carlos Bulosan concludes his
poem "If You Want to Know What We Are" with the words, "WE ARE
REVOLUTION!", he is interpellating a "you" whom he invites to be part
of the speaking "we" (Bulosan 2007, 294). Here interpellation does not
affirm misrecognition, but instead supplies recognition of an alternative
identity, one that will try to change the world.

Neither Lukács's theorization of reification nor Althusser's theorization of interpellation is without its shortcomings; moreover, these key

concepts draw upon quite different philosophical sources. Nonetheless, both will prove useful in our examination of the workings of dominant ideologies—and Ideology—in literary texts and traditions. Both concepts help us theorize the second-order mediations that supply the false notions of totality that guide uninterrogated, but widely accepted, understandings of the world. Both concepts help us examine the ways in which literary works, read symptomatically—that is, as indirect ideological reflections of their origins—at once gesture toward and mask their foundations in history.

Hegemony and Alternative Hegemony

If we wish to get a firmer grip on the ways in which works of literature are routinely riddled with ideological contradictions, containing both oppositional and dominant ideological tendencies, we need to revisit Antonio Gramsci's notion of hegemony, mentioned briefly in chapter 1. Gramsci defined hegemony as a combination of force and consent, in which the ruling class continually adjusts its means of achieving consent in its attempts to stabilize its dominance over the exploited masses. Accordingly, wrote Gramsci, "The active man-in-the-mass has two *theoretical* consciousnesses (or *one contradictory consciousness*): one which is implicit in his activity and which in reality unites him with all his fellow-workers in the practical transformation of the real world; and one, superficially explicit or verbal, which he has inherited from the past and uncritically absorbed" (Gramsci 1971, 333; italics in original). Despite all the pressures for consent exerted by what passes as "common sense"—the Italian *senso commune* signifies not just conventional wisdom but also all that is taken for granted in everyday life (Crehan 2016, 43–58)—the proletariat continually contends with a gap between what it knows—if only in raw and experiential terms—and what it has been taught to think. In times of heightened class struggle or capitalist crisis, this contradiction, at once material and ideological, can be intensified, producing "a new social group"—a "historical bloc"—that "enters history with a new hegemonic attitude" characterized by a "new way of feeling and seeing reality" (Gramsci 1985, 98). In this new mode of perception, what was once obvious, to be taken for granted, is obvious no more; new frameworks for thinking about human need have emerged.

The emergence of such a "historical bloc" is hardly spontaneous, however. Gramsci designates as "organic intellectuals" those members of the proletariat who have grasped a totalizing framework—that is,

Marxism—both for criticizing the dominant ideology that the prole-tariat has "inherited from the past and uncritically absorbed" and for supporting the proletariat in its "practical transformation of the real world." Alert to the multiple obfuscations embedded in ruling-class hegemony, these organic intellectuals are tasked with the responsibility of uncovering within the popular culture enjoyed by the masses—even when it is suffused in ruling-class ideologies—those kernels of hope for a better world that have the potential to develop in the direction of a radical transformative politics. Organic intellectuals shape and encourage the growth of "new popular beliefs, that is to say a new common sense and with it a new culture and a new philosophy which will be rooted in the popular consciousness with the same solidity and imperative quality as traditional beliefs" (Gramsci 1971, 424). Contradistinguished from the "traditional intellectuals" who supply ideological legitimation of the status quo, the organic intellectuals in the ranks of the proletariat are class-conscious communists. Mediators between what is and what can be, they are vital to the process whereby the new social group—that is, an awakened proletariat and its allies among the other "subaltern" classes—can emerge as a potentially revolutionary force in a time of crisis and upsurge. But such an emergence is possible because, even when the class struggle is at low ebb, capitalism cannot exist without producing intense social contradictions: these may be papered over, but they can never be abolished. While organic intellectuals are usually thought of as political organizers who, in a Leninist sense, come "from outside" the immediacy of working-class experience, the term encompasses a wide range of functions. Proletarian writers, for instance—from the Clifford Odets of *Waiting for Lefty* (1979 [1935]) to the Robert Tressell of *The Ragged-Trousered Philanthropists* (2012 [1914])—count as organic intel-lectuals, as do the radical anti-capitalist mentor characters appearing in their works (Foley 1993, 249–83).

The term "alternative hegemony"—sometimes translated as "counter-hegemony" and linked with the notion of "counter-discourse"—designates the process of class-wide rethinking of possibilities for social transformation that takes place when organic intellectuals insert themselves among the subaltern masses. "Alternative hegemony" reminds us that ideology is a terrain where battles are continually fought out—that ideology is not stand-alone but relational, and that even dominant ideologies of the crudest kind bear internal traces of the opposed understandings of the world that they function to suppress. Religious fundamentalism, for instance, is always implicitly engaged in a kind of ideological shadow-boxing with secular understandings of the world that locate causality in the here and now. Jingoistic nationalism takes proletarian internationalism as its unspoken opponent. Alternative hegemony is thus the ruling hegemony's dialectical counterpart, generated by the same set of contradictions but capable, under the right circumstances, of a different kind of negation and sublation.

The notion of alternative hegemony is not without its potential problems, especially in view of the ways in which Gramsci's work has been appropriated by various neo- and post-Marxist theorists who weaken the connection between ideology and class struggle (Mouffe 2014). Gramsci's focus upon the "subaltern classes," for instance, can be interpreted as a negation—or at least a minimization—of the central role of the proletariat in the revolutionary process. Gramsci's call for a "new hegemonic attitude" associated with a "new way of feeling and seeing reality" can be taken to mean that subversive developments occur in the realms of culture and consciousness alone. A recognition of the relative autonomy of certain features of superstructural change can be extended to the notion that the "historical bloc" of forces opposed to capital, gradually asserting its influence throughout a population, is capable of superseding the ruling class and its state without violent confrontation. Engagement in what Gramsci designated as the "war of position"—that is, the left's long-term struggle for popular influence—becomes a kind of burrowing from within that defers, indefinitely if not permanently, the need for a "war of maneuver"—that is, open class conflict (Gramsci 1971, 229–39; Egan 2016, 108–22). Particularly as it has been taken up by various practitioners in the field of cultural studies, neo-Gramscian theory stresses the ways in which popular culture, infused as it may be with dominant ideologies, can supply subversive pockets of resistance to the hegemony of the ruling class, enabling participants in the cultural war of position to encroach bit by bit upon the ideological terrain of the bourgeoisie (Hebdige 1979; Halberstam 2011).

To view alternative hegemony as a pathway to gradual social transformation, or of subalternity as in itself a privileged political vantage point (Brennan 2007), entails a serious misreading of Gramsci's project. Preoccupied with figuring out how and why Fascism had prevailed over proletarian revolution in 1920s Italy, Gramsci intensively studied how and why the Italian Communist Party (PCI) had not managed to mobilize and unify the country's exploited industrial and agrarian populations. His investigation into the ways in which dominant ideology creates and maintains consent was unsparing, as was his search for modes of cultural expression possessing the potential for enacting the "practical transformation of the real world." Accordingly, Gramsci viewed subalternity as a status to be negated and superseded, not enshrined; nor did he conceive of the project of fostering an alternative common sense as a means of bypassing proletarian revolution. Indeed, albeit along a winding path, it would pave the way.

An alertness to the dialectical relationship between opposed forces in the war of position, however, reminds us that the ideological class struggle is situational, shaped by continual mutual readjustment; we should recall the statement by the ruling-class Prince in Tomasi di Lampedusa's *The Leopard* that "If we want things to stay as they are, things will have to change." Hegemony cannot perform its tasks if it is not open to accommodation. Changing arguments for women's participation in the workforce during and after World War II, for instance, ranged from the feminism accompanying Rosie the Riveter's "We can do it!" of the wartime years to the conservative return to family values and the cult of domesticity epitomized in *McCall's Magazine* in the early 1950s (Honey 1984). While Martin Luther King was lambasted in the last year of his life for his opposition to the Vietnam War, this stance has been conveniently forgotten in his subsequent enshrinement as a believer in the American Dream (W.J. Miller 2015). Rather than undermining the British monarchy, the marriage of Prince Harry to the previously divorced biracial movie and television star Meghan Markle—unimaginable in the days of Rudyard Kipling—has given the Crown a new lease on life. The flexibility of ruling-class responses to changing social circumstances can shore up its hegemony as much as signal its accession to pressures from below.

The reason for placing the notions of hegemony and alternative hegemony at the center of the inquiry undertaken in this book is not that they offer a kind of "Marxism lite" but that these terms stress the ways in which Marxism is at once a body of theory and a critical practice embedded in lived contradictions. As the standpoint of the proletariat in its concrete and uneven process of growth and development, alternative hegemony does not sit above the fray; instead, it is itself generated by, and thus bears the marks of, its own origin in the ideological class struggle. It is, in a sense, the historically conditioned self-knowledge of the working class. As Gramsci wrote:

> The philosophy of praxis [his coded term for Marxism] is consciousness full of contradictions in which the philosopher himself, understood

both individually and as an entire social group, not merely grasps the contradictions, but posits himself as an element of the contradictions and elevates this element to a principle of knowledge and therefore of action. (Gramsci 1971, 405)

At times of sharpened class struggle and capitalist crisis, such as occurred globally during the Great Depression, alternative hegemony can become openly oppositional (R. Williams 1977, ch. 6), enabling the emergence of a revolutionary proletarian consciousness reflected in a revolutionary proletarian literature. At times of relative stability, alternative hegemony is largely limited by the horizon available to its proponents. It is precisely in this capacity to encompass a range of modes of resistance to ruling-class hegemony, however, that the concept's usefulness consists. Alternative hegemony acknowledges the role played by ideological consensus in reinforcing bourgeois class rule while continually reminding us of the ongoing class struggle in the realm of ideas and beliefs, emotions and behaviors. It reminds us that, for many in the world's proletariat, past and present, there has always been a foot that remains stuck in the ideological door, preventing it from shutting entirely.

As Bertolt Brecht wrote in this excerpt from "From a German War Primer":

GENERAL, YOUR TANK IS A POWERFUL VEHICLE,
It smashes down forests and crushes a hundred men.
But it has one defect:
It needs a driver.

General, your bomber is powerful.
It flies faster than a storm and carries more than an elephant.
But it has one defect:
It needs a mechanic.

General, man is very useful.
He can fly and he can kill.
But he has one defect:
He can think.

(Brecht 1976, 289)

PART II

Literature

4

Literature and Literary Criticism

> What we have to accomplish at present [is] the ruthless criticism of all that exists …
>
> — Karl Marx to Arnold Ruge, 1843, *MEC*

What is literature? What is literary criticism? What principles are distinctive to the project of Marxist literary criticism? Drawing upon the basic principles of Marxism set forth in the previous three chapters, our discussion will now examine the ways in which historical materialism, political economy, and ideology critique can be mobilized in the study of literary texts and traditions. We shall consider the ways in which a critical approach to the connections between literature and society can help us understand how things that we think of as being beyond politics—like novels and poems, as well as how we are trained to read them—are in fact profoundly political. It is precisely because literature is often seen as sealed off from the domain of politics that it is important to undertake this scrutiny; ideology is often most influential when it is most invisible. Accordingly, before we examine some of the key concerns of Marxist literary criticism and Marxist pedagogy, we shall interrogate several of the conceptions of literature and literary study—many of them ideologically saturated—that, functioning as common sense, prevail in capitalist society, especially in the literature classroom.

Before we begin, one proviso. A persistent but mistaken assumption guiding the construction of various introductory textbooks used in high school and college classrooms over the past several decades is that literary criticism comprises a series of approaches corresponding to various perspectives and disciplines—New Criticism, psychoanalysis, myth and symbol criticism, feminism, critical race theory, postcolonialism, post-structuralism, New Historicism, reader-response theory, affect theory, ecocriticism, queer theory, and of course Marxism—that can then be "applied" to various texts. This methodological assumption is frequently accompanied by the idea that these approaches are best deployed in connection with texts whose explicit subject matters clearly relate to the chosen perspective or discipline. Thus feminist theory is seen to match up best with a novel by Virginia Woolf or a poem by Adrienne Rich; postcolonialism with a novel by Chinua Achebe or a memoir by Arundhati Roy; and Marxism with an industrial novel by Elizabeth Gaskell or a play by Bertolt Brecht. While delimiting any kind of critical inquiry by mechanically aligning it with a set of texts assumed in advance to be its appropriate testing ground, the "applications" approach to literary criticism is, I propose, especially constraining when imposed upon Marxist literary criticism. For Marxism is often held to be relevant only to texts produced during the capitalist era and directly reflecting economic relationships and class conflicts.

As has been argued in Part I, Marxism lays claim to a far wider explanatory framework. Although its concern with totality emerges from its confrontation with the fragmentation and reification generated by capitalist social relations, Marxism's analytical domain comprises much more than the critique of economic relationships: its analysis of political economy is a means to the end of creating a world in which "economics"—capital's reduction of productive human activity to jobs, markets, and profits—ceases to dictate the course of human events and the breadth of human experience. As regards the study of literature, Marxism proposes that, in the words of the critic and theorist Fredric Jameson, the "political interpretation of literary texts ... conceives of the political perspective not as some supplementary method, not as an optional auxiliary to other interpretive methods current today ... but rather as the absolute horizon of all reading and all interpretation" (Jameson 1981, 17). The premise guiding the discussion of literary criticism in this chapter and the one that follows, as well as the range of readings offered in chapter 6, is that Marxism offers not just another angle of perception, but a lens through which one can view, analyze and interpret the representation of reality in works that are deemed "literary." Marxism draws upon and completes the insights made available through other lenses; but it proposes itself as a "meta"-theory, that is, one possessing overarching explanatory power. Needless to say, the hubris accompanying this claim will need to be justified.

Defining Literature

For starters, we need to examine some of our taken-for-granted assumptions about what literature, and its study, involve. Most of us feel that we have a working definition of literature. While we know that the term can be used to describe any kind of writing—as in references to "the medical literature" on such and such a topic—we usually associate the notion of literature with the plays, poems, short stories, autobiographies, and novels assigned in an English (or other language) class. Moreover, literature consists primarily of texts in print: teachers may occasionally assign graphic novels, popular songs, journalistic texts, or videos to their students, but these usually figure as supplements to the core literature curriculum. Most of the texts examined in chapter 6 belong to genres studied in classrooms; a number of these, considered "classics," have been chosen precisely because their broad familiarity will be helpful in highlighting the distinctive features of a Marxist approach to literary study. But the concept of literature is itself by no means self-evident, timeless, or neutral; it needs to be historicized and interrogated if we are to understand what we do when we read. Even before we pick up a book, how are our expectations shaped by what we know, or think we know, about the nature of literature?

The meaning of the word "literature" has changed significantly over time. As the cultural historian Raymond Williams points out, "In its modern form the concept of 'literature' did not emerge earlier than the eighteenth century and was not fully developed until the nineteenth century" (Williams 1977, 46). Originally designating class-based notions of educational attainment—a refined person could be said to "have literature"—and signifying books on a broad range of topics, literature gradually became associated exclusively with imaginative and creative works. That is, literature migrated from being a stand-alone category to a dialectical one, implicitly counterposed to the category of "not-literature" (often construed as in some way inferior). This altered definition, Williams notes, marked "a shift from 'learning' to 'taste' or 'sensibility' as a criterion defining literary quality" (Williams 1977, 48). Bourgeois revolutions extended the ranks of those potentially able to exercise "taste" and "sensibility," thereby rescuing literature from the domain of aristocratic patronage and enabling the emergence of new poetic, dramatic, and novelistic voices. At the same time, this redefinition was premised upon a binary opposition between emotion and reason, beauty and science, that articulated a growing antipathy to the "socially repressive and intellectually mechanical forms of a new social order: that of capitalism and especially industrial capitalism" (Williams 1977, 50). Literature's claim to invoke a realm of rich inner experience was symptomatic testimony to the incursions of capital upon the experiencing self; the text's implied resistance to alienation revealed the increasing prevalence of commodified social relations. The ensuing institutionalization of literary study as a discipline to be studied in specialized academic departments by scholars with finely honed analytical skills further reinforced the relegation of literature to a zone elevated above—yet sealed off from—the commercial realm of "getting and spending" decried in William Wordsworth's famous sonnet beginning, "The world is too much with us" (1807, in Wordsworth 1965, 206). What we think of as "literature" is, in short, a product of both history and ideology. As we seek to devise a set of criteria for determining what should be included and excluded from the definition of literature, we need to bear in mind the extent to which our query has been shaped in advance by forces far beyond the classroom or the weekly book review section of the *New York Times* or the *Times Literary Supplement*.

Just as the notion of what constitutes literature has changed over time, the activity designated by the term "criticism" has also undergone significant alteration. Originally signifying substantive commentary on affairs of the day, criticism was narrowed over the nineteenth century to pertain to commentary on the domain of the arts and to emphasize matters of aesthetic judgment (Eagleton 1984, 9–27). Over the past century or so, literary criticism—which focuses upon the study and interpretation of particular texts and traditions—has traversed the various schools aligned with the "approaches" noted above; moreover, it has often been hard to distinguish from literary theory, which focuses more generally on the philosophical bases of different types of literary criticism. The influential *Johns Hopkins Guide to Literary Theory and Criticism* in fact makes no qualitative distinction between the two activities (Groden et al. 2012). There is clearly no single methodology that constitutes literary criticism, past or present. Nonetheless, over the past century or so most literary critics, of whatever inclination, have tended in practice to agree upon some, if not all, of the features that commonly define their object of inquiry. This means, among other things, that what counts as literary criticism—for Marxists and non-Marxists alike—cannot be readily disentangled from the definitions of literature and literariness (that is, the formal qualities that define literature as literature) that have exerted dominance in the modern capitalist epoch.

The problems involved in defining literature are complicated by the fact that the criteria often advanced constitute a veritable congeries of linguistic, experiential, and aesthetic considerations drawn from a variety of sources—some theoretical, some simply reflective of assumptions about art and culture that guide everyday life. Based upon the several decades I have spent teaching literary works, reading literary criticism, and ascertaining the assumptions about literature that have shaped my students' understanding of what they do when they put on their literary-critical hats, I have concluded that the criteria most frequently invoked, whether in literature classrooms or the culture at large, can be summarized as follows. Literariness consists in some combination of: (1) fictionality (in literary works, characters, situations and voices are invented and do not refer directly to the world beyond the text); (2) density of language (literary language is characteristically concentrated and complex, inviting attention to language as such); (3) depth (meaning is usually not self-evident and must be probed out through interpretation); (4) concreteness and particularity (literary works focus on the details of lived experience); (5) showing, not telling (literature demonstrates, it does not teach or preach); (6) defamiliarization (the literary text enables us to see through and past what we take for granted, to view reality afresh); (7) universality (literature conveys important truths about experiences and emotions common to all humanity); (8) extension of experience (literature puts us in someone else's shoes and expands our capacity for empathy); (9) exploration of the inner self (literature enables us to plumb the subjective dimension of experience); (10) confirmation of group affiliation (the text connects individual selfhood with particular social identities); (11) formal unity (the literary text coheres around a synthesizing principle of order); (12) autonomy (the text's reference to the world beyond the text is mediated through its reference to itself); (13) beauty (the text's formal structure is aesthetically pleasing); (14) greatness (the category of literature consists of works of agreed-upon merit).

Not only do a number of these criteria presuppose all kinds of assumptions about the contexts in which writing and reading occur; in addition, several overlap with one another (those dealing with literary language, for instance), while others are mutually contradictory (those laying claim to the literary text's superior truth and those denying its capacity to convey truth, for instance, or those positing its affirmation of identities that are at once universal, individual, and group-based). Even as a common-sense category, then, literature would seem to display some significant internal inconsistencies. Moreover, different schools of interpretation—biographical versus reader-response, postcolonial versus New Critical, for instance—will clearly emphasize different features. We therefore need to address the logical problem entailed by this proliferation of grounds upon which literature can be defined. Does it possess a qualitative essence? If so, in what does this consist? Does a text need to possess a certain number of agreed-upon traits to be considered literary?

A useful paradigm for responding to these questions is contained in the approach to definition embodied in the notion of "family resemblance." Developed by the philosopher Ludwig Wittgenstein, this logical tool proposes that some entities should be defined as clusters of empirically identifiable traits, rather than as abstract essences (Wittgenstein 1953, 66–71; Foley 1986, 30–33). In any biological family, Wittgenstein observes, no single member possesses all the physical traits of any other; nonetheless, there can be found a common set of traits generally identifying the family as a group: height, body type, nose length, complexion, mouth shape, pitch of voice, etc. When you meet a member of the Williams family, you often (though not always) know she is a Williams. While it is not failsafe, this approach to definition has the advantage of being somewhat fuzzy around the edges; it is qualitative without insisting on the quantitative presence of any given trait. Moreover, it allows for differential weighting of different traits. While most Williamses are tall, narrow-shouldered, big-nosed, and inclined to chubbiness, a Williams who is short, broad-shouldered, and slim, but has a particularly prominent nose, might be recognizable as part of the tribe, even if she otherwise stood out oddly in a family photo.

Analogously, works of literature can be said to possess several—but not all—members of a set of agreed-upon features to qualify as literary. On the basis of a family resemblance calculus, any number of texts can also be reasonably excluded from the category of literature. A recipe for preparing applesauce might possess the qualities of concreteness and formal unity, for instance, but most readers and critics would probably agree that it meets these criteria in a fairly trivial way, and certainly does not meet enough other significant criteria to qualify as literary. Or, a bare-bones diary entry in which you recorded each day's sequence of events (what you ate and when, how much you slept and exercised) would be of little interest to anyone other than yourself or perhaps the doctor monitoring your health. But even in these extreme (and, admittedly, somewhat absurd) instances, there are no absolute principles excluding these texts from the category of literature. If the recipe were arranged on the page as a poem, for instance—and thus announced through its formal features to be "literary"—we might pause over the possible symbolic implications of words like "pinch," "stir," "boil," or "serve," newly associated with linguistic density and defamiliarization. If the diary entry were discovered in a basement excavated five centuries from now and read as a set of instructions for self-improvement—rather like the youthful diary produced at the end of F. Scott Fitzgerald's *The Great Gatsby* (1925)—then, for its latter-day readers, this historical re-visioning of your mundane reminders to yourself might constitute a poignant symbolic commentary on your abiding belief in individual discipline as the key to the Good Life. (And if these readers were inhabiting a then centuries-old communist society, we can anticipate that they'd get an ironic chuckle out of your naïveté.)

Whether or how a text is read as literature thus depends largely, but not exclusively, on its possession (or non-possession) of a number of agreed-upon traits, which are themselves subject to alteration as literary conventions and cultural pressures undergo change. An instance of such a shift was recently signaled in the controversy over the awarding of the 2016 Nobel Prize for Literature to the singer and songwriter Bob Dylan: many critics asked whether "Like a Rolling Stone" (Dylan 2016, 167–68) qualifies as a "literary" text.[1] Current debates over what constitutes "world literature" (or, more precisely, "literatures of the world"), as well as over the role of translation in shaping the body of texts considered central to this category, further challenge the boundaries between the literary and the non-literary inherited from a Eurocentric critical canon (Shankar 2012; Warwick Research Collective 2015). The family resemblance approach has the advantage of flexibility and openness, for it invites consideration of a broad range of texts, varying geographically as well as historically, for possible membership in the category designated as literature. This approach requires critics of all political stripes to acknowledge the existence of commonly accepted features of literariness that they may themselves not especially value, as well as to grant the extent to which their own chosen criteria may in fact overlap with those favored by critics of other schools. Viewing literature through the lenses of a family resemblance paradigm thus enables critics to appreciate that the definition of literature is itself a zone of struggle and debate. A possible disadvantage of the family resemblance approach, however, stems from this very capaciousness and inclusiveness. For these qualities can create the impression that literature is a stand-alone, non-dialectical category: whereas in fact, as noted previously, literature is not infrequently constituted by its implied opposition to what it is not, to "not-literature."

A final comment on methodology. I am aware that, in designating the fourteen criteria to be explored in this chapter, I have by no means come up with an exhaustive list; various readers might reject some and substitute others. I am aware, too, that I at times bend the stick in the direction of certain formalist and abstractly humanist conceptions of literature that hail from what was called, in the 1950s and 1960s, the New Criticism. Many of the tenets of this Cold War-era school have been challenged in subsequent decades—indeed, in the view of many scholars, demolished—by competing paradigms stressing the porousness of the boundary between literature and non-literature (think deconstruction), the spuriousness of ahistorical and transcendent universals (think New Historicism), and the power relations necessarily embedded in language and representation (think cultural studies). Accompanying this turn in the realm of theory, the democratization of literary study in recent decades—especially involving the impact of gender, ethnic, and postcolonial studies upon literary curricula and disciplinary boundaries—has qualitatively altered the body of texts deemed worthy of scholarly and pedagogical attention (J. North 2017). The canon of four decades ago has undergone profound and lasting transformation; it is as likely that students will have been exposed to *The Hunger Games* (Collins 2008) or *The Hate U Give* (Thomas 2017) as to *Wuthering Heights* (Brontë 2009 [1847]) or *The Scarlet Letter* (Hawthorne 2017 [1850]) in middle or high school. All the same, it bears noting that the more recent approaches to literary study insisting upon the embeddedness of literature in politics and history have managed quite readily to coexist with older and more conservative paradigms shaping the hodgepodge of literary interpretation that is actually practiced in high school and undergraduate college classrooms. Although I am aware that electronic sources are hardly stable or lasting entities, in the coming discussion I cite a number of websites for literature instructors that remind us of the limited reach of some of the ideas that have been passionately disputed and debated in the graduate seminar room. These pedagogical instruments also testify to the conceptual capaciousness and ideological flexibility of what Althusser has termed the Educational State Apparatus.

Fictionality

Because fictionality has been invoked in definitions of literature extending back many centuries—it is often what people have in mind when they refer to literature as "imaginative"—we shall devote a bit more attention to it than to the other thirteen criteria. The Renaissance poet and essayist Sir Philip Sidney wrote in the late sixteenth century that "The poet nothing affirmeth, and therefore never lieth" (Sidney, 1970 [1595], 57). Since then, a good deal of ink has been spilled (or keys have been clacked) by literary theorists arguing that what is distinctive about literary works is their limited power of reference to historical actuality (Foley 1986, 42–63). The criterion of fictionality clearly cannot be taken as a baseline requirement for determining whether a text should be considered literary. While the language deployed in most imaginative texts does not refer to "real" people and events—the words "Scarlett O'Hara" or "Jane Eyre" do not have referents in historical actuality—the criterion of fictionality fails to describe many texts routinely included in literary anthologies. One thinks of political documents like the Preamble to the US Constitution (1789) or Martin Luther King's *Letter from Birmingham Jail* (King 2018 [1963]), as well as any number of lyric poems: Emily Dickinson's "I Heard a Fly Buzz When I Died" (1890; Dickinson 1976, 223–24) evidently features a made-up speaker, but Wordsworth's "The World Is Too Much with Us" (1807; Wordsworth 1965, 206) would seem to be a fairly direct declaration of authorial standpoint. Determining fictionality is further complicated by the fact that the line between fact and fiction is often blurred. Daniel Defoe's *A Journal of the Plague Year* (2003 [1722]), like many eighteenth-century narratives, unabashedly blends journalism with techniques of representation subsequently identified with the novel (L. Davis 1983; Foley 1986); while Norman Mailer's *The Armies of the Night* (1968), a "nonfiction novel" treating the 1967 anti-war march on the Pentagon, directs critical attention to the ostensible objectivity of conventional journalistic reports.

The limited usefulness of the criterion of fictionality in defining literature should not bother us unduly, however, if we bear in mind the family resemblance model, which reminds us that no single criterion, however widely prevalent, is in itself indispensable to a determination of literariness. From a Marxist standpoint, more important to an assessment of the criterion of fictionality is what it can be taken to imply about the relationship between text and truth. When Sidney wrote that poets cannot lie because they make no claim to tell the truth, he hardly meant that works of the imagination are just entertainment, incapable of conveying important generalizations about people and societies. As teachers know when the relationship between truth and fictionality comes up on their classrooms, this is where things can become dicey. What is just a story for some readers is, for others, a call for curricular change. While some readers may accept fictional representations that accord with their own common-sense notions of what is true, others may reject fictional generalizations—about people, about the way the world works—that their own understanding of history has shown to be not just invalid, but an incitement to continuing injustice. Readers who refuse to be interpellated by the representation of antebellum plantation life in Margaret Mitchell's *Gone with the Wind*, for instance, are not likely to be consoled by the argument that this 1936 blockbuster novel—made into a 1939 blockbuster movie—is just a story. Nor are they likely to be persuaded that their negative reactions can be attributed to their own lack of readerly sophistication. Nor again will they be readily convinced that, because Mitchell's novel has been taken as an accurate rendition of life in the Civil War-era US South by generations of readers, the text's truth-value is up for grabs; indeed, antiracist readers may assert that the novel is a tissue of lies. Nonetheless, the persistent appearance of the novel in high school curricula, even when accompanied by the concession that it contains a certain amount of race- and gender-based stereotyping, suggests that the novel's fictionality enables some readers—including some teachers—to subordinate these unfortunate defects to the "epic" reach of this "coming-of-age tale [and] sweeping historical drama" set on a plantation "affectionately known as 'Tara'".[2] Affectionately by whom?

The main problem with the "nothing affirmeth ... never lieth" conception of fictionality is its implicitly positivist approach to the relationship between language and knowledge. (Positivism is a branch of philosophy that rejects speculation and confines truth to what can be demonstrated empirically.) Taking truth to consist only in the verifiable correspondence between a word and an isolable thing or process, this approach, while useful in any number of everyday contexts (the words "garbage can" refer truthfully to the object in my kitchen), ends up confining all kinds of claims about reality to a relatively narrow domain. If, however, truth is seen also to consist in generalizations about how the world works, and not just discrete nuggets of information, then the made-up quality of the characters, situations and voices we encounter in many literary works need not prevent these texts from making all kinds of assertions laying claim to extra-textual validity. As we shall see, the concept of typicality—the notion that fictional characters and events embody in microcosm the dialectics of the historical moment portrayed in a given text—has functioned centrally in Marxist analyses of the truth-telling capacities of works of fiction. Often closely correlated with the notion of realism, the notion that fiction contains truths of a general nature—actually predating Marxism by millennia, going back at least as far as Aristotle's *Poetics* (Aristotle 2013)—enables the critic to argue that the relative freedom of many literary texts from the obligation to refer directly to actually existing persons and situations need not mean that these works possess a diminished relationship to reality. Indeed, because of its broad powers of reference, the literary work can, in this light, be seen as a source of knowledge—one that is different from the kinds of cognition available to science, but not for that reason any less useful as an aid to understanding the world beyond the text.

What the literary work will help us understand, of course, is not just the world, but the various perspectives from which various people have seen, and attempted to understand, the world. Representation is re-presentation, rendering a portrait of reality as it has been processed in the mind of the writer, who has herself been shaped by the historically conditioned categories of perception and comprehension available to her, as well as the literary genres familiar to her audience. That these categories are mediated by ideologies of various kinds goes without saying; Marxist critics, we shall see, debate the role played by ideologies of various kinds in a determination of the nature and extent of a given text's ability to reflect reality (Metscher 1979; Balibar and Macherey 1996). Some emphasize the ability of even the most ideologically charged texts—*Gone with the Wind* being a case in point—to register key features of historical actuality; while others stress the extent to which such a text's mediating procedures distort both the act and the object of representation, so that the novel ends up conveying far more about the racism undergirding Mitchell's nostalgic apologia than about the "actual" US South. Whether stressing the text's capacity for reflection or its tendency toward obfuscation, though, Marxist critics generally agree that fictionality entails assertion: Mitchell's novel can be seen as a source of truth without, strictly speaking, telling the truth.

Density

If by density is meant simply the fact that literary works often compel us to slow down and be aware of language as language, as a criterion for defining literature it is certainly compatible with Marxist concerns. Language is, after all, largely (if not exclusively) what distinguishes humans as socially cooperative creatures; literature's directing attention to this fundamental feature of our species being can remind us of a potentially universal human essence (Eagleton 2006, 9). As it has been invoked in the study of literature, however—particularly the twentieth-century movement called high modernism—the stipulation that literature is characterized by its linguistic density can end up taking us in the opposite direction, away from what we all share as humans and toward our alienated state in a stratified capitalist society. For works seen to exemplify this tradition— one thinks of Ezra Pound's *Cantos* (1986), for instance, or, as an extreme case, of James Joyce's *Finnegans Wake* (1999 [1939])—contain concentrated and often tangled linguistic formulations that require intensive decoding and interpretation on the part of the reader. While the analysis of such texts can yield provocative insights into their symptomatic connection to politics and history, critical engagement with a good deal of high modernism requires specialist skills reflective of the academic professionalization of literary criticism by Raymond Williams that was noted above. The view that such skills are the prerequisite to serious literary study can also encourage a bias toward, for instance, viewing Yeats's "The Second Coming," with its arcane cosmological symbolism, as truly literary literature, while assessing Langston Hughes's "Always the Same," with its clear interpellation of a working-class reader and its readily grasped symbolism of blood and money, as less deserving of this designation. (Both texts are discussed in chapter 6.) Indeed, one might instead observe that a text's lack of comprehensibility by the average reader reinforces class divisions in the cultural domain, and that the text's opacity—even if intended as a protest against the banality of language geared to the marketplace—ends up reproducing the reification of perception prevailing in capitalist society.

This is not to say, of course, that all hard-to-interpret texts are intrinsically elitist, or that all texts written from a standpoint critical of capitalism are straightforward and broadly accessible. The lyrics of Kendrick Lamarr's Pulitzer Prize-winning *Damn* (2018) are not readily comprehensible—at least on a first hearing—to listeners unfamiliar with the conventions of hip-hop. Urayóan Noel's *Hi-Density Politics* (2010), besides teasing the reader about whose voices are being heard, ironically deploys inaccurate translations between English and Spanish to call attention to the linguistic politics involved in assessing whether a given text is doing a good job of representing social reality. To insist upon linguistic density as an intrinsic feature of literature is, however, an ideologically loaded proposition; for it presupposes a pact between author and audience in which many readers, unfamiliar with the linguistic conventions being invoked, may decline to participate—even if in so doing they run the risk of being considered uncultured or just plain "out of it."

Depth

The related criterion of depth—if taken to mean that special surgical skills are needed to get at what a text is "really" doing or saying—can raise comparable concerns about the academic domain of literary study. The critical premise that a text cannot mean what it seems to mean can give rise to the kind of fevered symbol-hunting that is an all too common practice in literature classrooms—especially those classrooms where so-called "depth and complexity" icons (aggressively marketed to teachers on the internet) are used to differentiate so-called "gifted and talented" students from their peers (S. Kaplan 2017). Besides resulting in often strained and implausible readings, the pursuit of a great white symbolic whale in every literary work can indicate a more troubling assumption, namely, that reality—both the reality in the text and the reality inhabited by the reader—consists of a polarity between surfaces and depths, appearances and essences, and that the former cannot supply a way of getting at the latter. Reacting against reification by positing a more fundamental reality lurking below what fictional characters appear to be saying and doing, this designation of depth as the zone of "real" truth, with all else being merely the foam on the sea, ends up affirming a disconnection between lived experience and some shadowy realm of ultimate meaning.

While excessively privileging the criterion of density can maroon the literary critic in an idealist linguistic realm, however, the opposition of appearance and essence implied in the criterion of linguistic depth poses a more robust challenge to Marxist criticism. For, as Marx is at pains to point out in *Capital*, appearance rarely coincides with essence. Capital does not announce its existence, let alone its meaning, through a sign on its forehead; it is, while omnipresent, invisible, a real abstraction, manifested only in its effects. Yet, as Marx is equally at pains to show, capital's appearances are not simply false; they possess a partial truth. We can "strike through the mask"—Captain Ahab's cry to the universe in *Moby-Dick* (1956c [1851])—to the extent that we recognize the mask as a necessary component of what it hides (Melville 1956c [1851], 139). Read as cues to an unseen totality, appearances—surfaces—can yield up knowledge of what lies beneath. Recent calls for "surface reading" do not address the dialectical relationship between appearance and essence; instead, in their attack on interpretive strategies premised on the notion that there is more going on in a text than meets the eye, they simply fetishize the realm of appearance (Best and Marcus 2009). The criterion of linguistic depth, when demystified, can prove essential to the materialist analysis of literary texts and traditions; indeed, as we shall see, some kind of opposition between surface and depth is indispensable to an understanding of the workings of what some Marxist critics have termed the political unconscious.

Concreteness and Particularity

The proposition that literary language is distinctly characterized by concreteness and particularity is, like the criterion of depth, ideologically flexible, depending on how these terms are understood. If each term is construed in opposition to its implied counterpart—that is, concreteness *versus* abstraction, particularity *versus* generality—then these markers of literariness render a text incapable of supplying cognition. Indeed, the text is valued precisely for its refusal of thematization, its disdain for being read as a gesture toward some kind of larger meaning. Would-be writers are reminded of T.S. Eliot's praise of the novelist Henry James for having "a mind so fine that an idea could not violate it" (Eliot 2014, 650). As we shall see in our discussion of Archibald MacLeish's "Ars Poetica" (in MacLeish 1952) in chapter 6, the concrete and the particular, when severed from their connection to history and society, reinforce the fragmented perception and understanding accompanying reification.

If, however, the categories of concreteness and particularity are viewed dialectically—that is, as sites where abstraction and generality are concentrated and embodied—then this dualism largely dissolves. "The concrete is concrete," wrote Marx, "because it is the concentration of many determinations, hence unity of the diverse" (*GR*, Introduction). Rather than treating raw experience as the sole basis of cognition, concrete and particular images and characterizations often point to larger conclusions that the reader is invited to infer about the world beyond the text. Indeed, much of the power of literary realism derives from precisely this inherence of the general in the particular. Jane Austen's rigidly judgmental Lady Catherine de Bourgh can be the object of satiric commentary in *Pride and Prejudice* (1961 [1813]) precisely because she embodies more general traits of an aristocracy impervious to change. The "'weep! 'weep! 'weep! 'weep!" of William Blake's "The Chimney Sweeper" (1794, in Blake 1953) voices the despair of "thousands of sweepers, Dick, Joe, Ned, & Jack," legions of child laborers crippled and dying in the chimneys of England's thriving metropolises (Blake 1953, 26).

Showing Not Telling

When students in creative writing classes are warned "to show, not tell," however, the debilitating aspects of the dualistic approach to concreteness and particularity come to the fore. According to this mantra, generalizations about social causality, let alone calls for social change, are beyond the proper province of the literary text. If writers wish to create literature deserving of the name, they must steer away from didacticism (that is, programmatic teaching); if they do not confine themselves to image, description, dialogue, and free indirect discourse, their works run the risk of being dismissed as propaganda. (Free indirect discourse refers to third-person narration that closely adheres to the consciousness of a character, with very little commentary by an omniscient narrator.) To be sure, writers can overdo their efforts to be didactic: the long passages in *The Ragged-Trousered Philanthropists* where Frank Owen, the central mentor character, lays out the mathematics of exploitation make for some pretty dry reading; sometimes less is more (Tressell 2012 [1914], ch. 25). But the "show not tell" argument is full of fallacies. For one thing, teachers who purport to be allergic to didacticism often blank out on literary history and geography. They forget that any number of pre-capitalist writers—John Dryden, Jonathan Swift, and John Bunyan, for starters—not yet acquainted with the modern notion that reason and emotion operate along different axes, saw no conflict between art and didacticism. More crucially, the "showing not telling" dogma ignores the "telling" power of texts that do not necessarily engage in any kind of overtly didactic procedures. *Gone with the Wind* may not contain long preacherly passages about racial hierarchy, but—through action and char-acterization—the novel reinforces all kinds of generalized ideas about racial superiority and inferiority that its readers are simply assumed to possess. The fact that Mitchell feels under no obligation to inject didactic passages conveying her attitudes speaks volumes about her expectations about the ideologies prevailing in the consciousness of those readers who are readily interpellated by the novel. It is this capacity of literary works to confirm the unspoken biases of their different audiences that led W.E.B. Du Bois to remark in 1926 that "all art is propaganda and ever must be, despite the wailing of the purists." African American writers, he urged, needed to counter the racism too frequently encountered in white-authored texts with an affirmative "propaganda" of their own (Du Bois 1926, 22). Along similar lines, the communist literary critic Joseph Freeman castigated the class bias of the liberal "Man in White," who, posing as an "'impartial' critic," in fact "drips the bitter gall of partisan hatred" when encountering literary works depicting working-class life, which he can only view as "propaganda" (Freeman 1935, 9).

The principal fallacy guiding negative assessments of texts that "tell" rather than "show" is that it conflates the common sense of dominant ideology with the absence of ideology. Proponents of "showing not telling" can readily overlook the fact that Frederick Douglass's 1852 oration, "What to the Slave is the Fourth of July?," is, effectively, one long harangue (in Douglass 1996). Douglass's brilliant jeremiad, discussed in chapter 6, is now welcomed into the literary fold not because it shuns didacticism, but because its ideological standpoint has assumed the status of mainstream liberal doctrine. (Whether this doctrine corresponds to present-day practice is another question entirely.) His proposition that the nation, in practicing slavery, has betrayed the principles articulated in its founding documents—an assertion that carried significant oppositional force in Douglass's time—is now, in a classic dialectical reversal, widely accepted in the twenty-first century, at least by those invoking an idealized vision of the Founding Fathers (as expressed, for instance, in the highly popular musical *Hamilton*) to counter ongoing racial inequality. This belief is reflected in the laudatory teaching guides for the speech that are promulgated on the internet.[3] Pro-communist didacticism, however, continues to be dismissed as un-literary. George Orwell's anticommunist allegory, *Animal Farm,* widely taught in public schools in the UK and the USA, is praised for its "biting satire," rather than faulted for its politically driven polemic.[4] By contrast, the courtroom speech in Richard Wright's *Native Son* (1993 [1940])—where Bigger Thomas's lawyer, Boris Max, seeks to ground his client's murderous motivations in capitalist-generated racism—is routinely dragged over the critical coals as an instance of intrusive didacticism. Max is, we are told, a "self-righteous bore" who "uses" Bigger for his own ends in a speech "heavy on Communist theorizing."[5] One writer reflects upon profound truths, it would seem, while another preaches to the red choir.

The doctrine that writers should "show not tell," it should be noted, itself has its origins in the Cold War-era writers' workshop movement, which aimed to diminish and marginalize the works of writers opposed to ruling-class ideological hegemony by charging them with violating fundamental principles of literary form (McGurl 2009). For some writers critical of the status quo, however, the command that the writer should "show not tell" has been resisted as a defining feature of literariness. As the Vietnamese-American writer Viet Thanh Nguyen, author of *The Sympathizer* (2015), has written:

> We, the barbarians at the gate, the descendants of Caliban ... come bearing the experiences and ideas the workshop suppresses. We come from the Communist countries America bombed during the Cold

War, or where it sponsored counter-Communist efforts.... We come with the desire not just to show, but to tell. (Nguyen 2017, 13)

Writers querying the capitalist status quo have often needed to draw upon a range of explicitly didactic rhetorical devices in their efforts to represent and interpret working-class life "from outside," as Lenin put it: that is, from a revolutionary standpoint beyond the limits—and fetters— imposed by everyday experience. Extraordinary formal measures are at times needed to combat the hegemony of what passes as common sense. To rule out of court didactic intent not only limits the domain of literary expression but also ignores the extent to which texts voicing values and beliefs consonant with dominant ideologies routinely engage in a substantial amount of telling. This telling is simply unrecognized as such.

Defamiliarization

Historically associated with a group of early twentieth-century critics called the Russian Formalists, defamiliarization—*ostranenie*, sometimes also translated as "estrangement"—focuses on the capacity of literary works to shake us out of our settled habits of perception and see familiar phenomena through defogged lenses (Shklovskij 1998). To a significant degree, this criterion presupposes reification: our perceptions of workaday reality are assumed to be so jaded by the pervasiveness of the exchange relation that we require an epistemological injection from the literary text—Ezra Pound's modernist call to "make it new!" (Pound 1935; M. North 2013)—to re-engage with the world. Conceived as a kind of medicinal intervention, literary defamiliarization becomes a way of countering the alienation of life under capitalism by directing attention to estrangement as such. Few poems embody modernist estrangement as effectively as T.S. Eliot's *The Waste Land* (1922; in Eliot 1971), with its whirling vision of entropy and its disorienting juxtaposition of voices and texts from the ancient to the modern worlds. Arguably, however, the poem's use of defamiliarizing techniques on one level codifies the fragmentation that it contests on another. The elevation of the criterion of defamiliarization to a defining feature of literature becomes an act of ideological legitimation when it posits a historically specific reaction to reification—itself a product of capitalist modernity—to be a constitutive, and timeless, quality of literature as such (Eagleton 2012, 91–105).

While historically rooted in capitalist reification, however, the call for defamiliarization is not necessarily confined to its ideological reproduction. Texts engaged in contesting reification can also make use of defamiliarizing literary devices to make readers think again about aspects of life that have been naturalized—not least by what Marx called "the dull compulsion of economic relations"—to the point of unquestioned acceptance. The routine assumption that adults should work and children should play is undermined in Sara Cleghorn's pithy quatrain (1916): "The golf links lie so near the mill / That almost every day / The laboring children can look out / And see the men at play" (Cleghorn 2007). In Italo Calvino's "Marcovaldo at the Supermarket" (1983 [1963]), the everyday urban experience of shopping for groceries is shown to be terrifying when viewed through the eyes of a recently migrated peasant family (Calvino 1983 [1963], 85–89). Marge Piercy's *Woman on the Edge of Time* (1976) queries the fixity of prevailing gendered categories of identity by portraying a futuristic classless world not only without money but also without clear distinctions between women and men. What counts as a defamiliarizing maneuver in one historical moment, however, can lose its force in another. Piercy's gender-free representation of the use of the pronoun "per" among the inhabitants of 2137 Mattapoisett, for instance, while provocative when the book first appeared, has considerably less impact on twenty-first century readers for whom "they"/"their" (along with cognate pronouns suggesting fluid notions of gender and sexuality) have largely replaced "he"/"his" and "she"/"her." The fact that one era's shock effect can morph into another era's normative usage reminds us that the project of social transformation entails a good deal more than filling old social bottles with defamiliarized new linguistic wine.

Universality

Let us now consider a cluster of criteria for defining literature that focus on what literary works have to say about the condition of being human. The notion that literature *qua* literature is privileged to depict emotions and experiences shared by all of humanity has for several decades now been deservedly interrogated as a bastion of elitism, Eurocentrism, white supremacy, and patriarchy—especially when the texts presumably supplying access to universality were almost all written by white men positioned fairly comfortably in social hierarchies. We may recall Frantz Fanon's contemptuous dismissal of the proposition that the "essential qualities of the West [are] eternal," as well as Du Bois's and Freeman's defenses of antiracist and proletarian literary works from the charge of being "propaganda."

While such interventions have historically been necessary and salutary, to move from the assertion that some universals are false to the claim that there are—or can be—no universals at all is problematic. After all, literary works often depict emotions like love, anger, hope, and fear that have been experienced by people from different social situations for a very long time. Although it is somewhat difficult to imagine the particular circumstances that might evoke these emotions in a future communist world based upon social relations very different from those to which we are accustomed, there is no reason to think that such feelings would just disappear in a classless society or vanish from its literature. Even though the past historical conditions giving rise to various emotions may have retreated from view, it remains possible to respond to their expression in literature. Present-day audiences need not identify with King Lear's loss of his massive retinue of soldiers and servants to appreciate his sense of betrayal by his daughters: "How sharper than a serpent's tooth it is to have a thankless child!" he laments (Act I, Scene iv). Our distance from the disintegration of patriarchal feudal property relations does not close off our ability to experience vicariously the pain of this angry and misguided old man who has "but slenderly known himself" (Act I, Scene i).

Although it would run counter to the experiences of theater audiences for hundreds of years to deny the abiding power of *Lear*, it would also be premature to conclude that the play's greatness consists in its enshrining a universally shared human experience. Rather, we should attempt to locate the appeal of this play—indeed, of any given text—in the level or levels of generalization that it implicitly invokes, as sketched by Bertell Ollman (1993; to refresh your memory, see above, chapter 1). While *Lear* has been interpreted as commenting on both the moment of its composition and the substantially earlier time when its action is set (Shapiro 2015), for most of the play's present-day readers or audience members its reference is to the level of class society broadly conceived, that is, Ollman's level four. For property, patriarchy, and power—all distinctive features of class-based society that were unknown in pre-class modes of production—drive the play's plot, operating with a tragic vengeance. Indeed, these markers of inequality are precisely what make Lear's half-crazed musings so poignant when, wandering on the heath, he belatedly understands his role in presiding over an unjust and inhumane social order. Like the soliloquy in *Timon of Athens* where the eponymous protagonist reflects bitterly on the corrosive effects of money—a great favorite of Marx's, by the way—Lear's soliloquy invites a contemplation of the roots of social inequalities that were—and are—hardly confined to his own time. In both tragedies, however, the implied historical reference is not to human nature as such, or to timeless archetypes, but to the warped human relationships characterizing social formations founded upon hierarchy and dominance—that is, the *longue durée* of class-based societies. Similarly, in Percy Bysshe Shelley's "Ozymandias," the "two vast and trunkless legs of stone" and "wrinkled lip, and sneer of cold command" of the fallen tyrant's statue remind the reader that oppression has been around for a long time; but it cannot last forever, for it breeds its own negation in the "sculptor who well those passions read" (Shelley 1951, 375). A comparably broad concern with the nature and effects of class-based social inequality is what Bertolt Brecht aims at when he sets his plays in times and places unfamiliar to inhabitants of twentieth-century Europe. The geographical and temporal displacements effected in *The Good Person of Setzuan* (1999 [1942])—which is set in a premodern China complete with gods visiting the Earth—and *Mother Courage and Her Children* (1991 [1939])—which is set in Germany and Poland during the seventeenth-century Thirty Years' War—enable him to examine earlier instances of the alienated social relations that have reached their fullest development in the modern capitalist West.

These texts by Shakespeare, Shelley, and Brecht do not refer to a universal human condition; nor, while they invoke powerful emotions, do they demonstrate that literature is intrinsically empowered to transcend the social circumstances or ideological conflicts giving rise to those emotions. By locating their critiques of the social forces constraining human freedom in class-based inequality, however, they commonly invoke the notion that there is a universal human need for freedom from alienation and oppression—a need that Marx described as realizable only under communism. These texts' critical dimension thus consists not in their embrace of an abstract, history-transcending humanism, but in their implication that class society cannot possibly meet this universal human need. Where Brecht differs from the others—mainly through his historical positioning in the communist movement of the mid-twentieth century—is in his more fully realized ability to point toward the kind of alternative ideological framework that will enable people to bring into being a social order capable of meeting universal human needs, as well as of expanding notions of human potential at present fettered by the restrictions of class society. When we analyze literary works that speak to profound and shared human emotions, we should carefully parse out the false universals of an abstract humanism that ignores issues of class from valid universals testifying to the need to transcend class society altogether.

Empathy

The empathy criterion—the notion that literature enables us to extend our experience through an imagined identification with people inhabiting times, places, and social positions quite unlike our own—also invites a dialectical assessment. On the one hand, the vicarious positioning made possible through the reading of literary works can make people less narrowly judgmental and more aware of the limitations of their own assumptions and beliefs. Once a present-day white reader from a relatively comfortable economic background has positioned herself in the consciousness of Bigger Thomas in *Native Son* (1993 [1940]), she will—at least one hopes—find it more difficult to reiterate the clichés about the black underclass after she has read Wright's Depression-era novel. Readers of novels of working-class struggle—whether set in the capitalist metropole, like Mike Gold's *Jews without Money* (2004 [1930]) or located in the colonized periphery, like Ousmane Sembène's *God's Bits of Wood* (1962 [1960])—can broaden a reader's understanding of the connections between alienation, exploitation, and rebellion. Moreover, exposure to literary works concretely grounded in more remote eras—such as Aphra Behn's *Oroonoko; or, The Royal Slave* (2004 [1688])—can expand our imaginations and make us aware of the transience of all historical and geographical hegemonies. For readers situated in the belly of present-day empire, such insights are salutary.

The downside to this existential decentering, however—a liability to which a pedagogy informed by the ideology of liberal multiculturalism is particularly prone—is the recognition that literary works enabling readers to feel the pleasure and pain of others can also give rise to a self-congratulatory sense that one has become a true global citizen, by education affectively attuned to difference and diversity (Berlant 2004). Especially when conjoined with a reader-response approach to texts focused upon the reader's personal feelings—how would you feel if you'd been in Anne Frank's attic (*The Diary of Anne Frank* 1995 [1947, English translation 1952]) or Harriet Jacobs's loophole of retreat (*Incidents in the Life of a Slave Girl* 2001 [1861])?—the notion that literature supplies a bridge between individuals of widely diverse backgrounds and experiences can end up re-centering the supposedly decentered reader without much difficulty. Indeed, the doctrine of empathetic connection can lead a graduating literature major—especially if she has absorbed an idealist conception of "human rights" along the way—to decide to work for the

State Department or the World Bank rather than aligning herself with the workers of the world.

Individuality

While the criteria of universality and empathy assert literature's connection to broadly shared emotions and values, other criteria emphasize its representation of the individual and demographically specific dimensions of human experience. Given the centrality of the category of identity to cultural and political analysis in recent decades, these two criteria warrant particular attention. Many literary works—especially works produced in the era of capitalist modernity—provide privileged access to individual interiority. One of the dialectical paradoxes of historical development is that, however brutal and impoverishing the effects of exploitation and reification, capitalism has also given rise to conceptions of unique individuality not readily imaginable in earlier modes of production. It is inconceivable, for instance, that Marcel Proust's *Remembrance of Times Past* (2003 [1913–27]), with its intricate exploration of the nameless narrator's stream of consciousness, could have been composed in medieval Europe or ancient Egypt; he displays a consummately bourgeois notion of introspective selfhood. The flip side of this concentration on the individual's inner reality, however, is the frequent opposition of the individual to society as such, a proposition that codifies rather than queries the psychological rifts—both within individuals and between and among them—that have been historically generated by the alienation of labor. The subjective dimension of experience emerges as the site of an ego more authentic than a selfhood shared with others: the interiority explored in the literary text inhabits a sacrosanct realm where one's true self is felt to reside. Although it is experienced individually, alienation is, Marx shows, a profoundly social phenomenon. Literary-critical categories that take as given the isolation of the individual presume an arrested historical dialectic, one that reifies solitude and diminishes the critical force of texts that target the source of human separation in historically specific social relations. For instance, Melville's "Bartleby, the Scrivener: A Story of Wall Street" (1956a [1856]) is often read not as a parable of capitalist-engendered alienation but as a commentary on the walls eternally separating man from man—as well as an inquiry into "what makes all of us who we are".[6] This enigmatic query is presumably captured in the words "Ah Bartleby! Ah humanity!" uttered at the end by the lawyer who has related the sad fate of his employee—even though

Melville has dropped multiple hints, starting with the subtitle of the story, that his bourgeois narrator is incapable of seeing his own implication in the oppressive class relations that have driven Bartleby to suicide by starvation (Melville 1956a [1856], 155; Foley 2000).

This privileging of the private over the public is often put forward in literature classrooms as "the individual's search for identity" or "the conflict of the individual versus society," themes that are then read backward into literary works emerging from very different social formations, from Sophocles' *Antigone* (1990 [c. 441 BCE]) to Thomas Hardy's *Jude the Obscure* (2009 [1895]) to Arthur Miller's *Death of a Salesman* (1996 [1949]).[7] Such formulas, while routinely presented as the ABC of literary study, enshrine the solitary ego and ignore the extent to which individuality is constituted, and not simply constrained, by social formations and historical forces. Particularly in formulations positing "the individual versus society," the social world is construed as an eternal barrier to individual fulfillment; while the self is seen either as an utterly unique being, at odds with the herd, or else a composite of all selves throughout time who have banged their heads against the fatality of human existence. Defining literature on the basis of the centrality of the individual becomes a silent affirmation of individual*ism* (the doctrine that the individual takes primacy over society) which is not the same thing at all as individual*ity* (the quality differentiating one person from others). One of the ideological mainstays of capitalism— that we are all the captains of our destinies, and that competition and loneliness are inevitable accompaniments of the human condition—is invisibly translated into a cardinal principle of literary interpretation. While one might suppose that the doctrines about the linguistic constitution of the subject that have been highly influential in graduate study and literary theory in recent decades might have made some inroads into this "individual-versus-society" analytical paradigm, it appears to have survived largely unchallenged. Ideologies so thoroughly embedded in the way we live cannot, it seems, be so readily detached from the way we read.

Group Identity

Often literary works are viewed as uniquely capable of representing the distinctive standpoints and experiences—usually described as culturally based identities—of different groups within a given social formation. One of the salutary consequences of the social movements against race- and gender-based inequality of the past several decades has been that the near-exclusive identification of literature, especially works considered to be classics, with the creations of "dead white men" has been superseded. The notion that a William Faulkner can write in mythic terms that speak directly to everyone, whereas a Toni Morrison would need to transcend her race and gender in order to achieve a wide and appreciative readership, has been buried in the graveyard of false universals. Although the emergence and popularity of both literature courses and bookstore sections that feature writers belonging to historically oppressed social groups reflect significant victories over racism and sexism, however, grouping these texts along demographic lines can end up pigeonholing female or "minority" writers—a situation lampooned in Percival Everett's *Erasure* (2001), where an African American writer's novel set in ancient Greece can be found only in the section of the bookstore where black authors are featured.

This practice of categorizing writers on the basis of their ethnicity or gender can also reify the class-based division of labor that created the exploitative and oppressive conditions giving rise to distinct group identities in the first place (Gimenez 2005; Aguilar 2015). Morrison's *A Mercy* (2008), which narrates the emergence and consolidation of conceptions of race and family in connection with property relations in colonial America, supplies imaginative insight into the overlapping experiences of a range of female characters of different geographical origins and skin colors—slave, free, and somewhere in between—before "race" became a hegemonic concept. Zora Neale Hurston's *Their Eyes Were Watching God* (2006 [1937]), by contrast, may offer a compelling representation of a protagonist achieving independent selfhood (or, in currently popular terminology, "agency"). But the novel yields relatively little insight into the larger historical forces enabling and shaping her development. Although the valorization of a shared voice emerging from a common experience contests centuries of (mis)representations of—and (mis)speaking for—the "other" in the discourses of colonialism, white supremacy, and patriarchy, moreover, the focus upon group distinctiveness can devolve into the doctrine of incommensurability. (This is the notion that each social group possesses an *episteme*, that is, a set of assumptions about reality, that cannot be readily shared with others.) Even as the capitalist classroom emerges as a site of liberal pluralism, as is indicated by the veritable cottage industry associated with the teaching of literary texts as sites of cultural identity, students from different backgrounds can end up being hesitant about exploring what they do legitimately share out of fear of being accused of "cultural appropriation."[8] Readers who in fact may have many concerns in common—not least of these being a shared class interest in understanding the truth about the world and the need to turn it upside down—are viewed as possessors of different group consciousnesses distinctive to them, and them alone. In a curious paradox, the rejection of universality and reification of particularity promulgate a new universal, namely, that particular group identities reign supreme.

Many texts that address the experiences of historically marginalized sectors of society contain a critical function, in that the standpoints from which they are written frequently register, both affectively and cognitively, the effects of hierarchy and oppression (Hartsock 2004; Moya 2002; Gonzalez and Gallego 2018). It is in practice hard to talk about "race" or gender without at the same time talking about class; it is hard to talk about racism or sexism without at the same time talking about reification (Bewes 2002). But when the category of group identity mediating between when the individual and society as a whole is a distinctly hegemonic one such as nationalism, the detrimental implications potentially embedded in viewing literature as the expression of group consciousness come to the fore. For instance, historically changing attempts to define "American" literature—from the Cold War-era formulation of the archetypal "American Adam" (Lewis 1955) to more recent multicultural treatments of "the immigrant experience" (Frosch 2007)—frequently posit an idealized national polity, one that is given voice in literary works adjudged to be authentically in the American grain. Even when the focus has moved away from the young white male coming of age on the frontier, and Natty Bumppo in James Fenimore Cooper's *The Deerslayer; or The First Warpath* (2005 [1841]) has been superseded by Barack Obama in *Dreams from my Father: A Story of Race and Inheritance* (2004 [1995]), students still routinely learn that American literature is quintessentially embodied in the narrative of ascent, wherein the individual overcomes social barriers and hardships of various kinds and finds his or her place in the national sun. Although purporting simply to describe a shared group experience, the American literary nationalism inculcated in students from middle school onward functions as a powerful ideological reinforcement of the doctrine of American Exceptionalism, which in turn plays a crucial role in justifying US foreign policy. When an identity politics based in nationalism mediates between the individual and society, the resulting false universal can end up performing some important tasks—practical as well as ideological—for imperialism (Nguyen 2016, 1–18).

Formal Unity

We now come to the final set of criteria for defining literature, those focusing on aesthetics and value. It is a cardinal principle of many approaches to literary criticism, of various political stripes, that literary texts are characterized by their formal unity. That is, however directly or obliquely they refer to an extra-textual reality, literary works are characteristically inward-directed, possessing a rule-governed coherence, one that is determined generally by the genres to which they belong and particularly by principles unique to any given text. Narratives and plays have beginnings, middles, and ends that position characters and events in meaningful, if complex, arrangements; poems weave together images and ideas in meaningful, if complex, patterns. The term "autotelic" is often used to designate a literary text's formal unity, "auto" signifying "self" and "telic" (derived from the Greek "*telos*") signifying goal. Autotelism is at times described through the metaphor of "organic form": the text's internal patterning is equivalent to the principle of energy and coherence animating a living thing. To no small degree the pleasure a reader derives from analyzing a key unifying trope in a work of literature— such as the multivalent functions of the lighthouse in Virginia Woolf's *To the Lighthouse* (2008 [1927]), from symbol of androgynous desire to testament to art's ability to suspend the flow of time—is connected to the perception and interpretation of organic form. To the extent that a text successfully adheres to its internal principles of coherence, it will be all the more successful in interpellating its readers, that is, inviting them to participate in the ideological standpoint from which it views the world.

To propose that literary works are characterized by formal unity, and that literary criticism should examine this unity, does not in itself entail an idealist methodology for literary study. Some Marxist critics, we shall see, approach the notion of organic form with suspicion, viewing the apparently seamless unity of a text as indicative of its attempts to manage or suture over unresolvable social contradictions. From the standpoint of Pierre Macherey, for instance, a text's failure to achieve formal unity may emerge as its most interesting feature (Macherey 1978). Other Marxist critics, however, have treated a text's formal unity as central to its rhetorical—and ideological—power. Ernst Bloch's notion of utopia—whether "compensatory" or "anticipatory"—hinges to a significant degree upon literature's power to evoke a sense of wholeness (Bloch 1986); Georg Lukács's defense of realism links a text's internal formal coherence to its ability to represent in microcosm the dialectic of a historical moment (Lukács 1977). Formal unity becomes a problematic criterion for defining literature only when it becomes a doctrine imposed upon a text by an interpreter bent upon detaching a text from the social contradictions from which it has emerged. Teachers and students in literature classrooms can put themselves through pretzel-like contortions to discover a principle of aesthetic coherence that will resolve a seeming ethical or thematic inconsistency, especially if the text under examination has been adjudged a classic. Ironic readings—the text doesn't really mean what it seems to be saying; it is engaged in a clever game of self-subversion—can be dragged in as a last resort to account for a text's mixed signals to its readers. Critical debates over the ending of *Adventures of Huckleberry Finn* (Graff and Phelan 1995), we shall see, illustrate some of the problems encountered when historical contradictions are excluded from the analysis of a text's formal contradictions.

In the wake of post-structuralism—a philosophical school stressing the sliding, incomplete, and power-laden relationship between language and the world, and thus the problematic nature of representation as such—organic form emerges as a category of analysis and assessment to be approached with suspicion. The critic and theorist Roland Barthes has argued that the illusion of seamless coherence guiding what he calls a "readerly" text ensnares readers in dominant ideologies supportive of existing power relations; "writerly" texts, by contrast, direct attention to the plurality of possible meanings encoded in any linguistic artifact (Barthes 1974). Along similar lines, Lennard J. Davis and Catherine Belsey have stressed the ways in which realistic novels, while seemingly positioning the reader as an agent free to judge characters and their actions, in fact strongly pressure the reader into accepting the ideological framework in which characters and actions are embedded (L. Davis 1987; Belsey 1980). When undecidability becomes the name of the game, however, and the critic abandons the quest for—or valuation of—organic form, ahistorical idealism has not necessarily been superseded; it has simply migrated to the valorization of linguistic ambiguity. The notion that meaning cannot be nailed down, but instead endlessly proliferates, emerges as an intrinsic and timeless feature of language *qua* language: by another turn of the interpretive wheel, what appears to be the confident assertion of hegemonic ideologies, even in the most "readerly" of realistic novels, can be rediscovered as fragile and provisional, readily undermined by a close reading of the text's continually failed attempts at stylistic and structural coherence. Subversion and oppositionality now lurk under every textual bush; the patterned intricacies of the literary work, once displayed in their instability, again become the focus of literary analysis. Such maneuvers suggest that, while it may be possible to dispense with organic form, it is harder to get away from formalism.

Autonomy

Autonomy, we will recall from the discussion of base and superstructure in chapter 1, signifies independence and self-regulation; relative autonomy refers to the multiply mediated relationship between economic practices, political institutions, and dominant ideologies. In relation to the study of literature, autonomy need not imply a particular politics; like autotelism, it can figure in a broad range of critical methodologies, including Marxism. When literary historians investigate the correlations between changes in literary genres and evolving social formations, for instance, the notion of relative autonomy is in fact indispensable, insofar as the relationship between literary forms and modes of production is intricate and complex. This relationship bears particular scrutiny when a genre emerging from one era, say, the sonnet, is repurposed at a later time for quite different ends. To what extent, the historical materialist critic might ask, does the inherited form bear the ideological traces of its historical origins? To what extent can the genre be deployed to convey quite different meanings and affects in a different time and place? This question has proven to be of no small importance to revolutionary writers seeking to gesture toward future forms of consciousness by means of literary forms familiar to their readers in the present. As we shall see, the question of autonomy has also entered into Marxist considerations of the ways in which (at least some) literary works can—when viewed as use values produced by the creative imagination and constituted by unique principles of wholeness—resist the commodification of the capitalist marketplace. Indeed, aesthetic autonomy is not a stand-alone concept, but has as its implied opposite the notion of instrumentalization, that is, serving as the means to an end. The whole debate over whether or not artistic works have autonomous status can be seen as a historical consequence and ideological reflection of the incursion of exchange value on nearly every aspect of life (Van Rooden 2015).

When the notion of autonomy is deployed to argue that a text's formal unity signals its independence from the world from which it arises, however—that is, when relative autonomy devolves into absolute autonomy—the text's organic quality becomes equivalent to self-nourishment. It needs no sustenance from the extra-textual world;

art exists for the sake of art. At times conjoined with arguments about fictionality as non-assertion, this narrowly formalist version of the doctrine of literary autonomy proposes that literary works are under no obligation to allude to anything beyond themselves—that, indeed, they are most literary when they are most self-reflexive, pointing to their own artificiality and lack of external reference. In its original formulation in the context of Romanticism, the doctrine of literary autonomy performed a salutary function, insofar as it signified the right of the writer to express ideas and emotions often constrained in pre-capitalist systems of literary patronage; the writer's imagination, like Shelley's West Wind, could range freely over the world. As it devolved into the notion that there exists an aesthetic realm separate from that of everyday life, however, the doctrine of literary autonomy increasingly discouraged critical attention to the referential powers of literary works. This development reached its high-water mark during the Cold War, when a group of poets and theorists calling themselves the New Critics emphasized the centrality of structure and style in both literary works and the ways they should be talked about. Attention to form gave way to the doctrine that extra-textual considerations—biography, history, economics, conditions of production and reception—are irrelevant (indeed deleterious) to textual analysis: the critic should remain focused on matters of technique (Wimsatt and Beardsley 1954; C. Brooks 1947). Somewhat ironically, for all its pretensions to being liberated from history, this aesthetic doctrine recapitulates in the realm of literary theory the fetishism of commodities in the realm of economics, insofar as both present the appearance of a given entity—whether commodity or poem—as self-generating, divorced from the social relationships from which it has arisen.

It is now widely agreed that New Critical doctrines about the self-contained nature of poetry, which yoked autotelism to autonomy and put out a ban on history, was itself a consummately historical phenomenon, fitting nicely with (indeed, at times funded directly by) contemporaneous ruling-class attempts to delegitimate the communist-influenced literary radicalism that had attained considerable popularity and influence during the previous two decades (Mueller 2013; Karanikas 1966). Indeed, in their first bid to fame as the so-called Agrarians, the New Critics were politically quite open, almost giving their opening salvo in *I'll Take My Stand* the subtitle *A Tract against Communism* (Twelve Southerners 1978 [1931]; Rubin 1978). While the New Critics represent an extreme version of the argument for literary autonomy, their premises continue to guide creative practices associated with the New Formalism (Levinson 2007) and the critical practice calling itself "surface reading" (Best and Marcus 2009; Lesjak 2013). At least at the high school and undergraduate college levels, ambiguity, paradox, irony, and ambivalence—the mainstays of New Critical formalism—are still commonly treated as indispensable guides to literary interpretation and criteria for defining literary value (Bartolini and Stephens 2010; Schmertz 2006).

It bears noting, however, that some literary works are premised on the need to dispense with autonomy altogether, preferring instead to break through the illusion that text and world inhabit different onto-logical realms. This strategy—in theater it is called "breaking down the fourth wall" and often associated with the dramaturgy of Bertolt Brecht (Brecht 1964, 179–205; Barnett 2015)—has served a variety of ideolog-ical ends. These range from Clifford Odets's enlistment of the audience in shouting "Strike!" at the end of *Waiting for Lefty* (1979 [1935]) to Kurt Vonnegut's challenge to government-sanctioned versions of truth in *Breakfast of Champions* (1973) (Waugh 1984). Abandoning the illusion of autonomy has at times proven especially effective in works of anti-capitalist literature seeking to jolt readers out of their armchairs and into action. For instance, at the ending of "Merrie England—No More!" (1995 [1845]), the Chartist writer Thomas Cooper refuses to supply closure, much less a happy ending, to his narrative of the miserable lives of his working-class characters. "There is no 'tale' to finish," he writes. "They went on starving, – begging, – receiving threats of imprisonment … and they are still going the same miserable round, like thousands in 'merrie England.' What are your thoughts, reader?" (T. Cooper 1995 [1845], 59).

Beauty

We have almost reached the end of our list. As the basis of the emotional and cognitive response routinely accompanying the perception of formal unity, the criterion of beauty focuses the discussion of literature around the category of aesthetics, wherein judgments of beauty versus ugliness, the sublime versus the mundane, come to the fore. The grounds for such judgments are, of course, notoriously hard to pin down. While experienced subjectively—someone has to experience the sensation that something is beautiful in order for it to be considered beautiful— this sensation has to be socially shared if it is to qualify as something other than an anomalous response of a single individual. The standards for adjudging beauty are, however, hardly universal. As the sociologist

Pierre Bourdieu has proposed, social class fundamentally shapes aesthetic response: the detached "pure gaze" of more privileged readers is epistemo-logically and politically anchored in a "life of ease" reflective of "an active distance from necessity" that is largely unavailable to many working-class readers (Bourdieu 1990, 5, 41). Not only do class hierarchies spill over into the different experiences of beauty of different demographic groups; in a capitalist society where advertising sets all kinds of aesthetic norms, racism, sexism, and heteronormativity strongly influence hegemonic notions of beauty. These create false universals that, when internalized, can have profoundly damaging psychological consequences. Any father who has tried to dissuade his 10-year-old daughter from thinking that she needs to look like a Barbie doll knows how powerful and pervasive such standards can be.

Resistance to hegemonic aesthetic norms can at times constitute a sig-nificant political act, as was shown when in the 1960s and 1970s many people of African descent proclaimed that "black is beautiful" and chose to wear their hair in a natural Afro style (A. Davis 1994). When signaled through works of art, moreover, challenges to conventional binary opposi-tions of beauty and ugliness can challenge dominant ideologies of various kinds. When a shark suspended in formaldehyde is displayed in an art museum—as was the case with the 2007 display at New York's Metro-politan Museum of Art of Damien's Hirst's *The Physical Impossibility of Death in the Mind of Someone Living* (1991)—clearly the standards used in choosing the works featured in the rest of the museum's galleries are put in relativistic perspective, no longer taken as given. When N.W.A.'s "Fuck tha Police" appeared on the hip-hop scene in the mid-1980s, the song's shock value stemmed not just from its angry condemnation of racist police violence but also from the ways in which its obscenity-laced language transgressed norms of propriety prevailing in popular music. Although in quite different ways, such instances—the hairstyle, the artwork, most popular music—implicitly suggest that affirmations of familiar notions of beauty lull people into an acceptance of the world as it is. To interpellate the viewer—or, listener, or reader—in defamil-iarized terms is to dislodge a complacency that is at once aesthetic and political. It remains questionable, however, whether such acts of aesthetic rebellion alter the boundaries that they aim to violate—or, if they do, whether they manage to resist being reincorporated into a new kind of aesthetic hegemony in which transgression becomes part of the fun. Marcel Duchamp's toilet sculptures provide the template for normative representatives of modernism at New York's Museum of Modern Art;

while the once-raw diction of early rap has been largely absorbed into a set of stylistic conventions possessing mainstream aesthetic status, both for the well-heeled descendants of N.W.A. and for the millions who consume their songs. Like many other phenomena and processes, ugliness and beauty can turn into their opposites, undergoing dialectical inversion over time (Ngai 2012).

To assert that standards for adjudging beauty are historically and geographically relative does not mean that certain works of art have not been widely held to be beautiful, instilling in many readers a thrilled response at what the Roman philosopher Longinus termed "the sublime" (Longinus 1957). We should bear in mind, however, that the sublime is sublime largely because of its difference from, and superiority to, the everyday world. The problem is not that there is no such thing as beauty, if we consider its historically and socially variable definitions. The problem is that beauty is not a stand-alone, undialectical concept, for it has as its dialectical counterpart non-beauty. And non-beauty is not only an aesthetic category, the ugly; it is instead irretrievably social, the cause of the "'weep!' weep!'" of Blake's chimney-sweeper. Even such a resonantly beautiful poem as Dylan Thomas's "Fern Hill"—with its extraordinary closing lines, "Time held me green and dying / Though I sang in my chains like the sea" (D. Thomas 1957, 180—implicitly contrasts the "lamb-white days" of an idealized farm childhood with the decisively non-Edenic character of rural life in impoverished Wales represented in such proletarian novels as Gwyn Thomas's *Sorrow for Thy Sons* (written in 1936, first published in 1986), or Jack Jones's *Rhondda Roundabout* (1934). Many students and teachers of literature have some notion of beauty in mind when we say that we love literature; it is for this reason that we labor in the groves of the humanities for what are, generally speaking, such puny rewards. As Nguyen warns, however, lurking in these groves are the "*in*-humanities" of a world where beauty is largely inaccessible to the impoverished millions (Nguyen 2016, 71–102).

Greatness

Finally, the criterion of greatness as the differentia between literature and non-literature has continuing influence in discussions of literature and literariness. Indeed, when all is said and done, the notion that literature is simply superior writing may be the basis on which it is most frequently defined. The notion of superiority begs the question, of course, of how this judgment is to be determined. For one thing, the category of greatness remains circularly defined, insofar as a given critic's preference for a given cluster of defining traits of literariness constitutes the basis for determining a given text's membership in the club. Clearly, moreover, the category has been historically constituted. Under the influence of multiculturalism and postcolonial and gender studies—which have produced both pressures from below and accessions from above—the canon has been significantly expanded. Elie Wiesel's *Night* (1960 [1954]), Maya Angelou's *I Know Why the Caged Bird Sings* (1969) and Rigoberta Menchú's *I, Rigoberta Menchú* (2010 [1983]) are now placed alongside Benjamin Franklin's *Autobiography* (2016 [1793]) and Jean-Jacques Rousseau's *Confessions* (1953 [1782–89]) as instances of great autobiographies.

While the boundaries separating the great from the not-great have been to a degree reconfigured, still routinely tied up in judgments of literary value is the assignation of lesser merit to what is known variously as mass, popular, or commercial culture. The grounds for assessing literary greatness often contrast texts and genres enjoyed by millions of readers (murder mysteries, romance novels, chicklit, street fiction) with those appealing to a narrower—and presumably more sophisticated—demographic. Indeed, while some authors and critics have objected to the distinction, the term "literary fiction" is widely used, by booksellers and writers alike, to distinguish between "serious" novels on the one hand and "genre" or "commercial" novels on the other (Saricks 2009). The hard-and-fast distinction between elite (high) and mass/popular (low) works of art has been eroded to a degree by the postmodernist challenge to traditional cultural categories, as well as by the emergence of cultural studies as an academic discipline. Over the past couple of decades, university presses—which are a reliable gauge to what is considered the acceptable province of scholarship in the humanities—have been publishing critical commentaries on television, cinema, comics, popular music, and social media. Especially in connection with texts designated as the classics with which every high school or college student needs to be acquainted if he or she is to be considered cultured, however, the category of literary greatness generally places commercially successful genres beyond the pale. The immense success of Suzanne Collins's *The Hunger Games* trilogy—which as of 2015 had sold over 50 million copies in the US alone and spawned scores of teachers' guides and learning apps—is the exception that proves the rule. "Even students not usually interested in reading" gravitate toward the exciting narrative, remarks one relieved middle school teacher.[9]

To point up the elitist bias implicit in many designations of literary value is not to make the counter-claim that, because of their popularity, mass-market texts are intrinsically liberatory. One would be hard-pressed to argue that Helen Fielding's *Bridget Jones's Diary* (1996), while enabling ordinary-looking young female readers to identify with an ordinary-looking protagonist who nonetheless gets her good-looking (and rich) man, offers a compelling critique of sexism. E.L. James's *Fifty Shades of Grey* (2011; discussed in chapter 6) participates quite energetically and unabashedly—and, it would seem, effectively—in the dissemination of dominant ideologies of various kinds. To dismiss commercially successful literary works as not-literature, however—and those readers who enjoy them as philistines incapable of entering the shrine of the real thing—simply reifies literature and reinforces the class divide already prevailing in the cultural apparatus of capitalist society.

Finally, a consideration of the politics of literary greatness requires that we frontally address the relationship between politics and aesthetics. In particular, can a text that embodies reactionary attitudes, but that does so in formally persuasive ways, ever be said to be beautiful? To be great? Going back to the time of Plato, these questions have retained their urgency over the years. They surfaced, for instance, in the 1949 controversy surrounding whether or not the prestigious new Bollingen Prize in literature should be awarded by the Library of Congress to the modernist poet Ezra Pound, whose works were riddled with anti-Semitic stereotypes and who had, moreover, done radio broadcasting in behalf of the Italian Fascist regime during World War II. That the judges acted in Pound's favor spoke volumes about the temper of the times (the early days of the Cold War) and the growing ideological hegemony of formalist definitions of literary greatness. To this day, however, teachers of film courses need to consider whether—and if so, how—to screen such early twentieth-century racist classics as D.W. Griffith's *The Birth of a Nation* (1915), which glorifies the origins of the Ku Klux Klan, or Leni Riefenstahl's *The Triumph of the Will* (1935), which celebrates the Nazi regime. While both films have played significant historical roles in bolstering reactionary regimes, both also display expertise in avant-garde cinematic techniques and have significantly influenced modern film-making. What would it mean to call either or both of them "great"? Does one person's refusal to be interpellated by such films make him an obtuse viewer, politically dogmatic and formally insensitive? Or, conversely, is he just someone who is unwilling to separate appreciation of aesthetics from assessments of political effects? Conversely, does his ideological counterpart, by insisting on making a distinction between films' formal qualities and their reprehensible politics, yield ground to white supremacy and fascism, past and present? Or, conversely, is she just unwilling to conflate assessments of aesthetic value with judgments of political stance? The questions surrounding these notorious movies from the past century apply with equal force to more recent controversial works, such as the debate over whether racialized and gendered stereotypes of poor black women are reinforced or challenged in Sapphire's *Push* (1996), which was later made into the movie *Precious: Based on the Novel "Push" by Sapphire"* (Daniels 2009).

Clearly different writers, critics, readers, and teachers will respond differently to continuing disputes over the criteria for determining whether or not a given text should be considered great. Truth and beauty are more intricately intertwined than many a critic would like to suppose. The social positioning of the person making this judgment frequently enters into the equation: Du Bois, aware as he was of the racist "propaganda" embedded in much mainstream writing, would probably have been less generous in his criteria for admission to the halls of greatness of any number of texts that Margaret Mitchell, for instance, might have found beautiful and compelling. But while groups of differentially positioned readers will often reach varying value judgments, aesthetic and political, about particular texts and traditions, they may also disagree about the extent to which it is legitimate to mix aesthetic and political judgments in the first place. Even if such disagreements cannot be resolved by debate, let alone by fiat, simply to rule out of court the question of whether or not politics can or should enter into an assessment of artistic value is itself a political act.

This consideration of the necessary imbrication of politics and ideology in the reading, study, and teaching of literature brings us to the domain of Marxist literary criticism. We may now step over the threshold.

5

Marxist Literary Criticism

The social revolution cannot take its poetry from the past but only from the future.

— Karl Marx, *The Eighteenth Brumaire of Louis Bonaparte*

We shall now examine the ways in which key concepts associated with the study of historical materialism, political economy, and ideology shape the kinds of questions that Marxist critics characteristically bring to bear upon their study of literary texts and traditions. A number of these concerns were implicit in the previous chapter's critical examination of the definitions of literature and literariness that underpin a good deal of the literary criticism that is taught and practiced today. We can now incorporate these somewhat scattered insights into a more comprehensive discussion of the principal strategies of literary criticism that have been advanced under the banner of Marxism. While this analysis will feature concerns broadly shared by Marxist literary critics—the rhetorical positioning of readers, the role of ideology critique, the function of symptomatic reading—we shall also highlight a few issues that have been the subject of considerable debate and disagreement ever since the time of Marx. These include the status of the text as commodity; the nature of humanism and realism; and the place of explicitly proletarian or revolutionary texts and traditions within the larger literary field. Marxism, we shall see, does not prescribe a single focus for literary criticism; rather, it opens up for investigation a range of possible questions.

First, however, it bears noting that some Marxist critics have given up entirely on the project of defining literature. Given the ideological bias built into so many of the commonly agreed-upon traits of literature and literariness—especially the aesthetic formalism and abstract humanism that guide a good deal of institutionalized literary study—these critics have concluded that literature has no constitutive principles, whether described by a family resemblance model or by any other paradigm (T. Bennett 1990; J. Williams 2015). Literature can only be defined according to the ideological practices performed in its name; it is what people *do*. While I have sympathy with the impulse to pull literature down from its pedestal, it is (to mix metaphors dramatically) premature to throw the literary baby out with the sociological bathwater. Too much has been written—not least by Marxist critics—in efforts to grapple with what is distinctive about literature to conclude that there is no such thing, or that its study cannot yield up valuable insights into the pressures and limitations shaping the historical actuality in which literature is produced and received. Moreover, to concede the entire terrain of defining literature to the conceptual framework supplied by mainstream modes of literary criticism is to confuse what something is with the way that it is talked about. The literature that has been produced during the span of literate human civilizations has largely reflected the worldviews and ideological proclivities of ruling elites: how could it be otherwise? It should therefore come as no surprise that the prevailing categories of literary criticism should also reflect dominant ideologies of various kinds.

But just as class-based societies are riven by conflict, however visible or submerged, so too are the literary texts and critical practices emerging from these societies. Bearing in mind that we should never underestimate the power of contradiction, we can view both literature and literary criticism as contested domains where the ideological class struggle is continually being fought out. To clarify the purposes of Marxist literary criticism is to contribute to the project of constructing what Antonio Gramsci called an alternative hegemony: an oppositional common-sense understanding of the ways in which artistic production and reception can either foster or fetter revolutionary change.

Rhetoric and Interpellation

Let's start by considering a tool of literary analysis routinely used by Marxist critics engaging in ideology critique: the study of rhetoric, that is, the persuasive power of literary texts. Central to a Marxist understanding of the mechanisms of class rule, you will recall, is the analysis of interpellation, that is, the procedures by which individuals are hailed in such a way as to make them feel recognized as the possessors of distinct social identities. Yet this recognition usually involves a degree of misrecognition, insofar as the available categories of selfhood have been constructed in advance—and linguistically validated—through the requirements of dominant ideology. To grasp the ways in which a text at once creates and reproduces a reading subject—a process largely enabled, we have seen, by the ways in which the reader has been socialized to read—the Marxist critic needs to analyze the means of persuasion embodied in the text. Examination of the different techniques by which a literary work makes compelling its vision of reality, thereby creating, or attempting to create, assent in the reader—what the mid-twentieth-century Marxist critic Kenneth Burke called the "dancing of an attitude" (Burke 1941, 9), or what speech-act theorists call the text's "perlocutionary effects" (Ohmann 1971)—is central to an understanding of the text's procedures of inter- pellation. This investigation includes, but also goes beyond, the ideas, attitudes, or beliefs explicitly encoded in the text; form—meaning here both the conventions embedded in genres and the techniques practiced by individual writers—can in fact be a principal carrier of ideology.

In examining the rhetoric of literary form, literary critics of all political stripes deploy many of the same analytical tools. In the study of poetry, they all pay close attention to word choice, repetition, syntax, rhyme, image, metaphor, metonymy, rhythm, voice, you name it: the ensemble of stylistic devices that supply the poem with its power to move the reader toward acceptance of a given set of ideas or emotions, which in turn entail various ideologically coded assumptions about social causality and human possibility. In the study of narrative fiction, most literary critics are interested in how plot arouses expectations and desires and then resolves (or fails to resolve) conflicts of various kinds (P. Brooks 1984); how a writer's decision to summarize some events and dramatize others shapes the reader's sympathies (Genette 1980; Moya 2002); how tropes (that is, interconnected images and symbols) point to important themes and patterns (Burke 1941); how narrative point of view gives the reader access to certain standpoints while marginalizing or silencing others (Chatman 1978); how characterization and character systems—that is, the alignment of the narrative's created people into moral opposi- tions and comparisons—sketch the ethical pattern underlying the text (Woloch 2005).

The analysis of rhetoric enables readers to view the text not as a reified linguistic artifact, but as a process by which they are being urged to embrace certain feelings and beliefs and reject others. Raymond Williams has introduced the useful term "structures of feeling" to stress the often unformulated and precognitive nature of the matrix of emotions and attitudes summoned up in the act of reading (R. Williams 1977, 128–35). Peter J. Rabinowitz refers to the rhetorical work performed by the literary work as the creation of an "authorial audience": readers may or may not wish to identify with the values encoded in the text, but they can either agree or refuse to do so only if they recognize what these values are by at least temporarily joining the audience interpellated by the text in the first place (Rabinowitz and Smith 1998).

In and of itself, rhetorical analysis is not political; it is practiced by critics of all kinds. Nor, however, while it focuses on matters of technique, is it necessarily formal*ist*, in the sense of valuing "form" over "content"; indeed, the rhetorical analysis carried out by Marxists attempts to display the inevitable conjunction of the two. In what ways, for instance, does a given instance of metonymy—that is, the proposition that a part stands for a whole—implicitly designate what is most distinctive about that whole? In a particular metaphor, why has the author chosen to describe the tenor (the entity being reimagined) attributing to it the qualities of the chosen vehicle (descriptive image) and not some other (Richards 1930)? How do the gaps and silences in a text testify to what the author is excluding from consideration? In a narrative, how do proximate (that is, short-term and contingent) causes of events signal ultimate (that is, long-term and structural) causes? Without being eclectic—that is, drawing from so many sources that it becomes theoretically incoherent—Marxist literary criticism absorbs into its methodological field a wide range of tools and strategies also deployed in other analytical paradigms; this is in part what Fredric Jameson means when he calls Marxism a mode of "metacommentary" (Jameson 2008, 5–19).

What distinguishes Marxist rhetorical criticism from that practiced by non-Marxist critics—especially those working in fields concerned with power relations and social inequality, such as gender and sexuality studies, ethnic and critical race studies, and postcolonial studies—is not that the Marxists are more passionate or more political. But the Marxists' commitment to the explanatory framework supplied by the base–superstructure paradigm leads them above all to inquire, how does a given text interpellate its reader in relation to dominant ideologies and modes of class rule, past and present—or, for that matter, in relation to ideologies and social movements opposed to ruling-class hegemony? This does not mean that every instance of Marxist literary criticism, in its attempt to be materialist, has to circle on back to the extraction of surplus value; that would be a fairly predictable and boring procedure. But it does mean that, if the critic is to heed the imperative "Always historicize!" (Jameson 1981, 9), the many mediations linking the text to the social totality from which it emerged need to be laid bare, or at least gestured toward. Attention to ideology figures centrally in this attempt to avoid mid-level analytics. To what extent does the text function as apologia? As critique? As a contradictory blend of the two? To address such questions is to explore how Marxist criticism "conceives of the political perspective [as] ... the absolute horizon of all reading and all interpretation" (Jameson 1981, 17).

Ideology Critique

One of the key tasks of Marxist criticism is, accordingly, to examine literary works through the lens of ideology critique, especially in connection with dominant ideologies. This line of inquiry often focuses not so much upon explicit declarations of political or philosophical doctrine as upon the implicit assumptions about individual and social being—the often preconceptual structures of feeling—upon which the texts are premised. Marxism here functions as a kind of "hermeneutic of suspicion," a phrase coined by the philosopher Paul Ricoeur (2008, 32). (The word "hermeneutic" denotes the methodology of interpretation.) That writers may well be unaware of their texts' roles in reinforcing ruling-class domination— indeed, may be in various ways protesting that very domination—only points up the ironic disparity between intention and consequence, as well as the invisible hold of the second-order ideological mediations in which their writings are enmeshed. Using the term "maneuver" to designate ideological strategies that are both purposive and inadvertent, I offer a brief (and hardly complete) sketch of some key ideological maneuvers of which the Marxist critic is routinely "suspicious."

One such maneuver is dehistoricization, that is, the portrayal of phenomena specific to a given social formation not as the products of historical forces, but as features of a timeless human condition and a changeless human essence. The notion of original sin serves this causal function in many Western texts emerging from premodern societies dominated by Christianity: without original sin, there would be no "The Pearl" (late fourteenth century), no *Pilgrim's Progress* (Bunyan 2008 [1678]), no *Paradise Lost* (Milton 2003 [1674]). In texts produced in the capitalist era, original sin is more often portrayed as an illusory belief linked with sexual repression, as in James Joyce's *Portrait of the Artist as a Young Man* (2003 [1916]), or conditioned passivity, as in Helena Maria Viramontes's *Under the Feet of Jesus* (1995).

As an ideological premise, original sin has largely been supplanted by the more modern conception of human nature as intrinsically greedy, brutal, and individualistic—a doctrine that, in a deft equation of appearance with essence, takes behaviors fostered by the capitalist marketplace and reframes them as impulses hardwired into the human DNA. For instance, in William Golding's (2003 [1954]) novel *Lord of the Flies*—a Cold War-era polemic still widely taught at the secondary school level—this premise is embedded in allegory: the brutal selfishness manifested by schoolboys stranded on a desert island reflects what human beings are really like, beneath the veneer of civilization. Along similar lines, Ayn Rand's 1957 novel *Atlas Shrugged* portrays capitalism as a reflection of essential human energies and needs, fettered only by ill-conceived liberal policies and programs that shield vulnerable (read, lazy and undeserving) social groups from the fates that they deserve. While Rand's turgid novels are not usually taught in high school, they have experienced an immense revival in popularity in the context of the post-2016 Republican resurgence in the United States.[1] In these novels by Golding and Rand, the assertion of timelessness serves highly timely ideological functions.

Another rhetorical maneuver calling for Marxist suspicion, one closely related to dehistoricization, is naturalization, that is, the depiction of behaviors and beliefs fostered in specific social formations as products of processes beyond human creation or intervention. The examples of the Great Chain of Being and the analogy between monarchy and the solar system, both mentioned in chapter 3, are premodern instances of naturalization, in that hierarchical social relations are posited as inherent in the natural world. In the capitalist era, the perversion of Darwinian natural selection into the Social Darwinist doctrine of "survival of the fittest," justifying the rapaciousness of the robber barons, supplies a quintessential instance. The ideological effect of this doctrine is neatly encapsulated in Theodore Dreiser's *The Financier* (1912), where the young Frank Cowperwood, viewing a lobster attacking and consuming a squid, concludes that he will identify with the former rather than the latter in a world where only the strong survive (Dreiser 1967 [1912], ch. 1). That lobster aggression continues to supply an analogy with presumably innate hierarchical tendencies is illustrated in the recent assertion by Jordan Peterson that there is an "unspeakably primordial calculator, deep within you, at the very foundation of your brain, far below your thoughts and feelings, [which] monitors exactly where you are positioned in society" (Peterson 2018, 15). Metaphors that naturalize social inequality are not restricted, however, to novels and pseudoscientific treatises; they also figure in present-day popular journalistic discourse, as in frequent references to "a perfect storm." Alluding to the devastating confluence of meteorological phenomena portrayed in Sebastian Junger's 1997 novel (and the 2000 movie) of that name, this metaphor was frequently invoked during the 2008 financial crisis to portray as beyond human responsibility a situation that was most assuredly the creation of human actors. Indeed, while Junger coupled his scientific analysis of the confluence of natural forces with close attention to the class-based pressures motivating the fishermen to risk their lives, the financial press's use of the metaphor of natural disaster often served to legitimate the escapades of hedge fund CEOs by describing their untrammeled lust for profits as something beyond human decision-making (Stackhouse 2017).

When we approach literary works that contain both naturalizing images and images of nature, we should note that all metaphors linking the human and the nonhuman—whether flowers or singing birds, hurricanes or quicksand—need not engage in the kind of legitimating allegory noted above; sometimes a bird is just a bird, quicksand is just quicksand. Indeed, such metaphors can function as powerful means of social criticism, as in Nella Larsen's novel *Quicksand* (1971 [1928]), which portrays an African American woman's entrapment within sexist and racist commodification that drags her down to symbolic death. Some literary works engage in a direct critique of naturalization as an ideological maneuver. Herman Melville's ironic portrayal of *Benito Cereno*'s Captain Amasa Delano—who cannot envision an African woman nursing her child as anything other than a doe with a fawn, an embodiment of "pure Nature," when actually she is a rebelling slave—supplies a case in point (Melville 1956b, 42).

Naturalization involves not just the invocation of "nature," however; more generally, it signifies the process of ideological mystification accompanying any representation that adheres to the surface of things, arresting the dialectic of history and freezing phenomena into an eternal present in which cause and effect are one. Marx had this mystifying procedure in mind, we will recall, when he asserted that the fetishism of commodities creates "an enchanted, perverted, topsy-turvy world," in which "the personification of things and conversion of production relations into entities" constitute "a religion of everyday life." This "religion of everyday life," in turn, allowed the "vulgar economists" to treat the laws of capital accumulation as "overwhelming natural laws that irresistibly enforce their will," and had to be "confront[ed] ... as blind necessity" (*C* III, ch. 48). That naturalized mystification can serve more directly propagandistic ends is displayed in wartime visual propaganda, ranging from the apelike figures of "Huns" in World War I Allied recruiting posters to the famous image—described by Roland Barthes—of the "young Negro in a French uniform ... saluting, with his eyes uplifted, probably fixed on a fold of the tricolour [flag]" (Barthes 1972, 116) that appeared on the cover of the popular magazine *Paris-Match* in 1955 during the Algerian War. The image assured the magazine's readers that, as Roland Barthes wrote, "France is a great Empire ... and that there is no better answer to the detractors of an alleged colonialism than the zeal shown by this Negro in serving his so-called oppressors" (Barthes 1972, 116). The childishness of the soldier emphasizes the naturalness of his allegiance; the nation, a stand-in for the family, is his parent. Portraying as natural phenomena that have come into being in history mystifies social causality and routinely legitimates ruling-class hegemony. Indeed, naturalization is, arguably, the principal ideological expression of reification.

That the expressions of dominant ideology noted above are often enshrined in literary works of considerable rhetorical power—from T.S. Eliot's *The Waste Land* to Margaret Mitchell's *Gone with the Wind*—only makes more formidable the challenge these texts pose to the Marxist critic. It bears noting, however, that many literary works aiming at critiques of oppression and inequality, and of the doctrines and structures of feeling by which these are sustained, do not themselves escape the snares of dominant ideology. In Suzanne Collins's *The Hunger Games*, for instance, the character system assigning personal integrity to the rebels against the rapacious Capitol, and craven selfishness to its supporters, is undermined by rhetorical appeals that simultaneously reinforce values familiar to the contemporary inhabitant of the world of Capital. The protagonist, Katniss Everdeen—of whose markedly Anglo-Saxon-sounding name we take note—may eschew high-heeled shoes and gem-encrusted gowns; but she wows her audience with a graceful twirl that would have won her a perfect score on *American Idol*. She detests competition but overwhelms the judges with her archery skills. Although it takes the death of an ally to commit Katniss to winning the Hunger Games—which pit young people against one another in a blend of gladiatorial combat and the reality show "Survivor"—win she does, along the way killing several other "tributes" (coerced participants in the games). Collins's young adult readers of the trilogy can thus comfortably admire this rebel against the status quo even as her tale affirms meritocracy and competition as intrinsic to success.

Although such ideological maneuvers are fairly easy to spot in popular genre fiction, more oblique affirmations of dominant ideologies can also crop up in works of literature that engage in more searching critiques of capitalist social relations. For instance, in Viramontes' *Under the Feet of Jesus*, a novel foregrounding the reactionary role played by religion in the lives of brutally exploited migrant farmworkers, the adolescent protagonist, Estrella (in Spanish, "star"), embodies the spirit of feminist self-assertion and working-class resistance. Yet at the novel's finale she ascends to a rooftop where, communing with the stars above, she resembles "an angel standing on the verge of faith" (Viramontes 1995, 176); militant materialism dissolves into—or at least discovers an affinity with—mystical revelation. Even in a novel written from an explicitly Marxist standpoint during the Depression-era heyday of revolutionary proletarian literature, Mike Gold's *Jews without Money* (2004 [1930]), calling itself "A Truthful Book about Poverty," the central character's conversion to communism is figured in quasi-religious terms. Having encountered a soapbox orator advocating "world revolution to abolish poverty," the protagonist proclaims: "O workers' Revolution ... You are the true Messiah" (Gold 2004 [1930], 309). While the trope of religious conversion offers a convenient means of interpellating readers who are accustomed to associating a change in outlook with a change in faith, the use of this trope to assert an alternative hegemony for some readers significantly weakens the text's otherwise radical critique of the religious dogmatism that helps to maintain the proletariat in its subordinated position. It is easier to reject dominant ideology in theory than to transcend its limits in practice.

Symptomatic Reading

This recognition that many texts send out mixed ideological signals to their readers brings us to a consideration of the role played by ideological contradiction and symptomatic reading in Marxist criticism. When they focus upon ideology critique, Marxist critics often emphasize the ways in which literary works serve an apologetic function that sustains ruling-class hegemony. When they examine texts symptomatically, however—that is, as reflections, however inadvertent, of the social reality that they would deny or transcend—Marxist critics can also discover an objectively critical dimension in the texts they read. For just as society is riven by contradictions, so too are the literary works emerging from it; a given text's failure fully to control the rhetorical signals it sends out to its readers can be taken as testimony to the irreconcilability of the social contradictions that have generated the text in the first place. Marxist critics can adopt this seemingly inconsistent interpretive stance—that is, viewing the text as signaling at once apology and critique—not because they have decided to bend the stick back in the direction of abstract humanism, now proposing that literary works, qua literature, somehow manage to transcend the limits of ideology and speak the truth about the human condition. Rather, this recovery of the text's critical dimension hinges upon the proposition that the text's relationship to its origins is oblique. The text does not wear its politics on its sleeve, so to speak; its relationship to what Marx called the "real foundation" needs to be ferreted out and brought to light. But when this is done, the recovery of origins enables an unmasking of the reasons for the masking.

These origins are, of course, in history: the project of symptomatic reading is premised upon the notion that history supplies the ground— the "untranscendable horizon," as Jameson puts it—that enables critique in the first place. This ground is not just the historical context that helps the reader grasp the literary conventions relevant to a text or its references to contemporaneous sociological realities; much mainstream criticism also pays heed to such matters. Instead, for the Marxist, the literary work is *constituted* by its embeddedness in history; it cannot be understood apart from the ways in which it is shaped and constrained by material existence. The proposition that readers should "always histori-cize" does not require them to engage in extensive historical research in order to affix a given text in the circumstances of its production (although such grounding in the concrete particularities of the historical moment is indeed necessary at times). Rather, we are called upon to view a given text as a mediation—indeed, a series of mediations—of the contradic-tions shaping the world from which it has emerged. Even if the text eschews direct representation of that world, it is a response to that world, an answer to a question posed by that world. *Lord of the Flies* can thus be read, at least in part, as a reaction to the imagined threat of communism in the wake of World War II; *The Hunger Games* symptomatically voices anxieties about the untrammeled hegemony of the 1% in the wake of the 2007–08 financial meltdown. What might be described in formalist criticism as "ambivalence" or "complexity" is historically generated; the text's unique insertion in a given time and place does not preclude inves-tigating the larger historical forces at once confronted and eluded in the text's act of representation.

This proposition brings us to what has been called the "political unconscious" and the activist role it assigns to the Marxist critic. Primarily associated with the work of Jameson, the term denotes the process by which a literary work symptomatically registers extra-literary situations and conflicts. Such apologetic functions as dehistoricization, naturalization, and the like, while remaining targets of critique, become of interest for the Marxist critic primarily for the ways in which these ideological maneuvers mediate historical contradictions that cannot be directly represented. Recalling Althusser's definition of ideology as "the imaginary relationship of individuals to their real conditions of existence" (Althusser 2014, 256), the political unconscious of a text testifies to the ways in which both the form and the explicit propositions embedded in it function strategically to contain—that is, encompass and control—social contradictions that defy reconciliation in the world beyond the text. "History is what hurts," writes Jameson; the text takes shape as an ensemble of elements that at once acknowledge and obscure their origins in the class struggle and its accompanying modes of oppression and domination (Jameson 1981, 102). And while truth is not directly accessible, but is known only through its various textual mediations, it objectively exists; it is the extra-textual rock that the eighteenth-century philosopher Dr. Samuel Johnson famously kicked to refute the idealist doctrine that reality is not real, but only a matter of perception (Boswell 1964 [1791], vol. I, 471).

As the term "unconscious" suggests, this model of analysis incorporates elements of psychoanalysis into its conception of causality. Just as, in the Freudian model, the neuroses plaguing a patient are sometimes too anxiety-provoking to achieve direct articulation, but instead manifest themselves indirectly through dreams, irrational acts, and other symptomatic modes of expression, the fetters to human development in a given social formation, as well as the ideological maneuvers by which such fetters are legitimated, often cannot be directly confronted. While some literary works overtly affirm the status quo—and function, in effect, as straightforward ruling-class propaganda, as in case of *Atlas Shrugged*—in many others the existence of exploitation, alienation, and oppression is granted but then, to one degree or another, papered over. In its baffled attempts to confront contradictions that appear insoluble—the history that hurts—the literary work engages in procedures of repression, displacement, and sublimation that are analogous to the operations by which a psychiatric patient attempts to cope with emotions and ideas whose sources cannot be granted on a conscious level. Like the patient, the text continually gestures toward what it cannot directly reveal: that is, the ways in which the class struggle, while often expelled from the text's explicit object of representation, generates insurgent doubts and undermines settled assumptions about the nature—and legitimacy—of existing social reality. The task of the Marxist critic examining the political unconscious of a text is to bring to light its various strategies of repression.

Some methodological caveats are in order. The analogy between psychoanalysis and Marxist symptomatic reading can clearly be overdrawn, insofar as the goal of psychoanalysis is to enable patients to align themselves more successfully with existing social realities, whereas that of the Marxist critic is to expose the ultimate grounding of such realities in class-based exploitation and, if anything, to encourage nonacceptance of the world as it is. Moreover, symptomatic reading does not usually entail psychoanalysis of the author: the writer may be grappling with personal demons, but the unconscious of the text is broadly social, not individual. Nor does symptomatic reading call for psychoanalysis of individual characters. Indeed, texts often represent a character's psychic repression as part of a problem for the reader to untangle: the sexual past that haunts Florence Ponting in Ian McEwan's *On Chesil Beach* (2007), for instance, or the political past that requires a full confession in Viet Thanh Nguyen's *The Sympathizer* (2015). The analogy between the psychoanalyst and the Marxist critic consists primarily in their use of theory to penetrate through surface to depth, examining those moments when the patient's guard is down and the text's formal stability is disrupted, revealing the roots of repression in history.

To bring to light the text's political unconscious, the critic involved in symptomatic reading thus looks not for declarations but for symptoms. The hermeneutic of suspicion is directed not primarily at the ways in which various modes of reification are present in the text as explicit beliefs or ideas but instead at the ways in which ideologically driven mystifications—producing moments of stammering, inconsistency, or reticence—simultaneously determine and impede the text's attempts to achieve organic form (Macherey 1978, 85–95; Rose 2006). Indeed, it is often at the level of form—implausible narrative closure in novels, disrupted imagistic patterning in poems—that literary works most fully display their origin in extra-textual historical contradiction. At the end of Elizabeth Gaskell's *Mary Barton* (1997 [1848]), for instance, the abandonment of the political assassination plot surrounding the character of the working-class John Barton, conjoined with the anomalous conversion of the factory owner John Carson into an enlightened philanthropist, indicates the repressive role played in the text by Gaskell's accession to Thomas Carlyle's worship of the beneficent "captain of industry." The inhumanity of the "cash nexus" that Carlyle elsewhere condemned, and that the novel has portrayed in all its brutality, is transcended through acts of paternalistic kindness (Carlyle 1970 [1843]; Loose 2014, 7; Gardner 2005). At its moment of choosing sides, as it were, the text cannot break with dominant paradigms for describing class relationships: pro-capitalist liberalism rather than pro-Chartist radicalism supplies the set of second-order mediations linking the text to the class struggle, even though the murmurings of class antagonism have hardly been silenced.

In Carlos Bulosan's autobiographical novel *America Is in the Heart* (1946), by contrast, the repressive gesture inviting symptomatic reading consists not so much in the plot as in the disparity between the text and its title. The heartfelt yearning for patriotic belonging suggested by the text's title conflicts dramatically with the accompanying narrative's unremitting portrait of the racist exploitation and violence faced by Filipino workers in the American heartland, as well as its implied call for proletarian internationalism. By contrast again, in Dylan Thomas's "Fern Hill," a single word appearing at the poem's very end shifts the dominant imagistic patterning, signaling an eruption from the political unconscious. The poem's famous final lines—"Time held me green and dying / Though I sang in my chains like the sea"—remove the reader from the compensatory utopia of the farm, now "forever fled / from the childless land," and turn to the sea as the only possible site of freedom from mortality. Although the poem has celebrated the solitary joys of the child "under the apple boughs / About the lilting house," as well as the seemingly eternal quality of childhood ("in the sun born over and over / I ran my heedless ways"), the farm is irretrievably social, too much bound to the history that hurts, and must be abandoned at the poem's end (D. Thomas 1957, 178–80). Whether readily discernible, as in the case of *Mary Barton*; discernible as inadvertent irony, as in *America Is in the Heart*; or subtly encoded in a single disruptive word, as in the case of "Fern Hill," anomalous formal maneuvers suture over unresolvable historical contradictions in the world beyond the text.

The usefulness of the notion of the political unconscious to the project of Marxist literary criticism has been subjected to a good deal of interrogation. Some critics have objected that seeking out evidence of a political unconscious proves far more productive in encounters with texts permeated by dominant ideology—thus having a good deal to repress—than in analysis of literary works that seek to unmask hegemonic ideas and beliefs (Warwick Research Collective 2015, 10–15). Other skeptics have argued that the emphasis upon the causal role played by impersonal social forces in this analytical model can too readily pass over the role of the individual author, who, after all, sat down and wrote the text under examination. How are authors, in possession of their own sets of ideological contradictions—their own "political unconsciousnesses," if you will—individually inserted into the matrix of these larger historical processes? Still other critics have argued that the model of the Marxist as unmasker positions the critic peering into a text's murky interior as somehow superior to both the work and its creator. Positioning the Marxist critic as the privileged possessor of a refined set of tools for poking and prodding, these skeptics complain, the notion of the political unconscious implies a claim to specialist expertise that seems peculiarly at odds with the stated democratic goals of the Marxist critical project (Best and Marcus 2009). Still another group of critics, rebelling against what they view as the "nay-saying" premises and "predictable" readings accompanying approaches that "whittl[e] ... texts ... down to the bare bones of political and ideological function," have recently sought to recover the awe-inspiring humanism—indeed, the "joy, hope, love, optimism"—embedded in great works of literature (Felski 2008, 7, 2015, 130, 152; Fuss 2017).

The first of these objections carries some weight: texts that aim to subvert the existing social order—or at least call its legitimacy fundamentally into question—do indeed require a good deal less unpacking than do texts more or less wedded to the status quo. While texts that are deeply critical of capitalism are not without their own zones of unease, the rhetorical and political problems endemic to such works generally arise, we shall see, not so much from the repression of a history that hurts as from their inability fully to shrug off ideologies enjoying hegemony in the moments of their creation—as well as from the formidable challenge of representing in plausible terms the possible seeds of a communist future within the class-bound present. The second objection noted above also has some validity, but only in relation to explorations of the political unconscious undertaken by critics who opt to overlook the role of authorial biography in the production of the particular text under consideration. As I have attempted to argue in my own analyses of works by individual writers, there need be no contradiction between focusing one's attention on the matrix of capitalist social relations, both short- and long-term, as well as the *longue durée* of class society (Bertell Ollman's levels two, three, and four) and considering any given writer's unique insertion in a particular time and a place (Ollman's level one) (Foley 2000, 2010, 2013, 2014; Foley and Gardner 2017). To view the author as an intermediary between the text and the world is simply to acknowledge the particularity as well as the generality of contradiction; after all, as the designation suggests, an intermediary engages in mediation.

The last two of the objections listed above cannot, however, be sustained; a given critic's decision to investigate a text's political unconscious need not bespeak an assumption of superiority, in relation either to the author or to other readers. When they engage in interpretation, all critics mediate between texts and their readers; the desire on the part of Marxist critics to view a text's contradictions from the standpoint of totality does not necessarily mean that they believe themselves to be privileged to go where others fear to tread. One need not embrace a fetishized, undialectical notion of complexity—that is, the notion that the world is so multifarious and ambiguous that it defies rational analysis— to assert that reality is indeed complex, and that, while appearance points toward essence, the two rarely coincide. Just as there was nothing elitist in Marx's decision to inquire into the workings of capital—and to write up his discoveries in thousands of pages, many of them quite challenging—there is nothing elitist in the goal of probing out the ways in which many literary works point only indirectly toward their repressed historical origins. Nor—here I respond to the fourth and final objection—is there something drab and joyless in the project of analyzing the ways in which texts come to us trailing the mists of ideology. Some texts speak to deeply human impulses and needs, but in so doing they often mystify the situations in which these impulses and needs gain expression. Still other texts embody these human yearnings in discourses that are not only mystifying but also reactionary: millions of people have thrilled to the beat of hooves of horses ridden by Klansmen in *The Birth of a Nation*. The objection that "suspicious" critics are missing out on the pleasures of reading by constantly focusing on ideology simply obscures the ideologically charged assumptions involved in calling upon readers to relish the "joy, hope, love, optimism" presumably encoded in great literature. Indeed, this accusation constitutes little more than an updating of Cold War-era formalism, extending the radical-baiting historically directed at specifically Marxist criticism to the entire domain of politically charged cultural critique (Robbins 2017).

If we wish to avoid the pitfalls of mid-level analytics by connecting the formal and ideological complexities of a text with its material grounding in productive human activity and the historical division of labor, analysis focused on the political unconscious frequently supplies a very useful way of getting at the multiple mediations connecting text and world.

Humanism

While the notion of the political unconscious enables the Marxist critic to discover a critical function even in texts that in various ways shore up ruling-class hegemony, this approach is premised upon the assumption that most literary works produced in the crucible of class society—and especially of capitalism in its phase of full-fledged reification—are constituted by ideologies that, to one degree or another, they need to evade or repress. The literary work is, whatever its contradictions, contaminated to its core; Marxism supplies the suspicion-laden hermeneutic enabling the critic to dig out and bring to light the ways in which the text ends up legitimating existing social relations. From this critical perspective, humanism—if it is taken to mean that human beings share a common moral essence and common moral needs, and that there is such a thing as "humanity" in the abstract (Althusser 1971, 21–22)—can be seen as one more false universal, occluding the social contradictions lying at the root of the very alienation that the literary work often aspires to contest. Whether embraced by the author as a standpoint from which to view life, or by the literary critic as a constitutive feature of literariness, humanism entails an ideological strategy enabling its adherent to bypass levels two through four in Ollman's schema (the class-based historical matrices from which causes arise) and settle upon level five (what all people have shared, as people, throughout time) as the ground upon which literary works should be interpreted and assessed.

There is, however, another school of thought within the Marxist tradition, one that approaches the relationship of literature to humanism quite differently and requires some rethinking—or at least qualification—of the somewhat accusatory critique of humanism just stated. This alternative approach views the literary text, like other artworks, as a use value, a product of concrete labor that refuses commodification in the capitalist marketplace. The writer who creates the text is, by virtue of its repudiation of exchange value, occupying a position inherently hostile to the reigning social order. This judgment applies not only to works that, like Wordsworth's sonnet "The World Is Too Much with Us" (in Wordsworth 1965)—which forthrightly opposes the world of "getting and spending" to that of art and myth—but also to works that would appear to accede to existential alienation, such as Eliot's "The Love Song of J. Alfred Prufrock" (Eliot 1971, 3–7). Even if it underwrites dominant ideologies, the text, as a unique creation of purposive human activity, points toward the universal human need to engage in unalienated labor. Literary works, viewed from this standpoint, do not so much evade confrontation with class antagonisms as express a universal human yearning to transcend those antagonisms. The autotelism of the work of literature or art testifies to its being a product of labor that has no end other than itself. In this analytical approach, labor is not the antithesis to art but the basis of aesthetics: the inward directedness of a work of art, its pursuit of organic form, does not result in a disempowering doctrine of art for art's sake, or the assertion of an autonomy legitimating the separation of the text from the world. Instead, the text's autotelism constitutes a rebellion against the hegemony of the market and its ultimate fetish, money.

This notion that literature is intrinsically at odds with capitalism finds its advocates in quite a few Marxist commentators on the relationship between literature and society—starting, we should note, with Marx himself. Throughout his life Marx stressed the writer's alienation from the marketplace: "The writer in no wise considers his work a *means*. It is *an end in itself*, so little is it a means for him and for others that he sacrifices *his* existence to *its* existence, when necessary" (*RZ*, ch. 6). The conception of "species being" explored in the *Economic and Philosophic Manuscripts of 1844* features unrestrained creativity, manifested under communism as un-estranged labor, as one of "man's essential powers" ("Private Property and Communism," *EPM*). While some scholars—most notably Althusser (1969, 51–86)—have argued that the mature Marx abandoned the philosophical humanism of his youth, it bears noting that in *Theories of Surplus Value* (ch. 4), Marx opined that "[c]apitalist production is hostile to certain branches of spiritual production, for example, art and poetry." Linking the antagonism between the artist and the market to the distinction between productive and unproductive labor—that is, between work that generates surplus value and work that does not—he contrasted John Milton, an "unproductive" worker, with "the writer who delivers hackwork for his publisher.... Milton produced *Paradise Lost* in the way that a silkworm produces silk, as the expression of *his own* nature" (italics in original). It was only "later on," Marx wrote, that Milton "sold the product for £5 and to that extent became a dealer in a commodity" (*TSV*, ch. 2). Marx's hostility to the impact of the market on artistic production was accompanied by a deep and passionate appreciation of classic—and especially pre-capitalist—art and literature. He admired Greek sculpture for its "eternal charm," which he linked to the "unripe social conditions from which it arose" in the "historic childhood of humanity" (*GR*, Introduction). Throughout his life, moreover, Marx expressed his admiration for Aeschylus and Ovid, Cervantes and Goethe, and above all Shakespeare, for whom, according to his son-in-law Paul Lafargue, Marx had "boundless ... respect," making a "detailed study of [Shakespeare']s works" and knowing "even the least important of his characters" (Reminiscences of Marx, in *MELA*).

It may appear that, in his valuation of the classics of Western art and literature, as well as his view that artists and writers are antagonistically opposed to the capitalist status quo, Marx evinced a set of attitudes somewhat at odds with his otherwise rigorous adherence to historical materialism. To be sure, Marx was very much a man of his time in his elevation of the aesthetic realm (and in his youth authored a good deal of quite romantic—and, it is generally agreed, not especially good—poetry) (Lifshitz 1973 [1938], 12). His predilection for viewing starving artists as social rebels was enhanced by his friendships, particularly in his youth, with an impoverished circle of bohemian writers and artists sympathetic with the embryonic workers' movement (Gabriel 2011, 78–85). Moreover, Marx wrote at a time when literature and art had not yet undergone the large-scale commodification accompanying their absorption into the productive processes of what Walter Benjamin would in the next century call "the age of mechanical reproduction" (Benjamin 1969, 217–52; Eagleton 1990, 196–223).

Even if we take such historical particularities into account, however, it bears noting that Marx's opinions about art and literature were largely consistent with the historical materialist principles informing the body of his work as a whole. In proclaiming "capitalist production" to be "hostile to ... art and poetry," Marx was not idealizing a timeless aesthetic sphere apart from the everyday world. Rather, he was insisting that the species being of humanity is premised upon the existence of universal human needs, needs that are thwarted in social formations where exchange value reigns supreme: on the very first page of *Capital*, in fact, he writes of the "human needs ... whether their origin is in the stomach or in the fancy" (*C* I, ch. 1). The notion of "fettering" does not pertain only to property relations constraining the development of productive forces; it is also relevant to constraints operative in the realm of ideas and emotions, inhibitions and blockages that prevent the expansion of human potential. Communism entails the dis-alienation of labor; the emergence of the kingdom of freedom from the kingdom of necessity will have little meaning if it does not also signal the emergence of liberated human beings increasingly capable of self-realization, of enlarging the limits of what it means to be human.

In his valuation of literary and artistic works produced in prior phases of human development, moreover, Marx frequently linked these works' enduring power not to timeless archetypes, but to the relations of production informing the social formations from which the works arose. He viewed the literary genres and characterizations prevailing in pre-capitalist modes of production in this light. "What chance has ... Jupiter against the lightning rod and Hermes against the Crédit Mobilier? ... [I]s Achilles possible with powder and lead?" (*GR*, Introduction). This materialist approach to the links between "spiritual production" and production in general underpins his (frequently misunderstood) comment on Greek sculpture. Although ancient Greek civilization was premised upon slavery, its economic arrangements were largely exempt from the working of the law of value—that is, the exchange of the products of labor on the basis of their embodiment of socially necessary labor time— that penetrates every sphere of capitalist society. The freedom from market-based alienation in the ancient world, and not some notion that earlier forms of class society possessed less sophistication than modern social formations, is what is meant by "the historical childhood of humanity" (Morawski 1970, 190; Lifshitz 1973 [1938]). Marx's valuation of such features as harmony and symmetry as the basis of the "eternal charm" may be geographically and historically bound; asymmetry, for instance, was and is a cardinal feature of much Asian art (Chung 2004). Moreover, in the historical wake of the racialized Nazi worship of Greek sculpture as an embodiment of so-called "Aryan" beauty, exemplified in Leni Riefenstahl's *Olympia* (1938), it is more difficult still to separate out historically bound politics from any assertions about the timelessness of aesthetics. But Marx's connection between what he called "immature social conditions" and the capacity of ancient art to "still give us aesthetic pleasure" is not confined to a specifically Western set of aesthetic values; his point is that different possibilities for artistic expression are opened up (or for that matter closed off) in different modes of production. His admiration for Cervantes and Shakespeare is similarly based in historical materialist premises. These writers could represent certain enduring features of human behavior to the extent that they wrote at a time when the formal subsumption of labor had not yet been supplanted by the real subsumption of labor in societies based upon universal commodifica- tion. "Don Quixote long ago paid the penalty for wrongly imagining that knight errantry was compatible with all economic forms of society" (*C* I, ch. 1): Cervantes' positioning on the cusp of modernity to no small degree accounts for his protagonist's ability to embody the more general comic dilemma of the individual out of step with his time.

In considering the literature of their own era, moreover, Marx and Engels tended to voice a broader range of judgments about the relation- ship between politics and ideology. On the one hand, Engels admired Honoré de Balzac not for possessing a progressive political vision (the novelist was in fact a conservative, favoring the restoration of monarchy), but for encapsulating in his characters and their destinies the fundamental contradictions driving social development in his time. Engels wrote:

> Realism, to my mind, implies, besides truth of detail, the truthful reproduction of typical characters under typical circumstances.... That Balzac thus was compelled to go against his own class sympathies and political prejudices, that he saw the necessity of the downfall of his favorite nobles, and described them as people deserving no better fate; and that he saw the real men of the future where, for the time being, they alone were to be found—that I consider one of the greatest triumphs of Realism. (FE to Harkness, April 1888, *MEC*)

Similarly, Marx admired Charlotte Brontë, Elizabeth Gaskell, and Charles Dickens for uttering in their "graphic and eloquent pages ... more political and social truths than have been uttered by all the professional politicians, publicists and moralists put together" *(New-York Tribune*, 1 August 1854, *MEC*). Neither Marx nor Engels, it bears noting, viewed a writer's class background as in itself a barrier to representing reality. Engels offered constructive critical commentaries, of both formal technique and political perspective, to writers of the "socialist problem novel" like Minna Kautsky and Margaret Harkness (a.k.a. John Law). While praising Kautsky's characterizations and acknowledging the "partisan" character of all literary works, he warned of the dangers of excessive didacticism. "The purpose must become manifest from the situation and the action themselves without being expressly pointed out," he wrote. "The author does not have to serve the reader on a platter ... the future historical resolution of the social conflicts which he describes" (FE to MK, 26 November 1885, *MEC*). The characters in Harkness's *City Girl*, he opined, were "typical enough," but "the working class figures as a passive mass, unable to help itself." Rather than declaring Harkness incapable of representing the class struggle by virtue of her class background, however—that is, of inhabiting a standpoint incommensurable with that of her fictional creations, as some present-day critics of writers "speaking for the other" might opine—he advised that she examine more closely the workers' "rebellious reaction" and "attempts at recovering their status as human beings, [which] belong to history and must therefore lay claim to a place in the domain of realism" (FE to Harkness, April 1888, *MEC*). The dialectic of history was objective; some writers might have to work harder than others to discern its lineaments, but these were there for all to see.

Finally, despite their admiration of the classic writers, Marx and Engels viewed politically radical literature as essential to the growth and development of the workers' movement. Engels, referring to Heinrich Heine as "the most eminent of all living German poets," viewed his "Song of the Silesian Weavers" as "one of the most powerful poems I know of" (*NMW*, 13 December 1844). (The 1844 revolt of the Silesian weavers was one of the earliest mass uprisings of German workers against the regime of factory labor.) Marx defended the "modern prose and poetry emanating in England and France from the lower classes of the people" from the high-minded critics—that is, the Young Hegelians—voicing the "*Holy Spirit of critical criticism*" (*HF*, ch. 6; italics in original). Engels commented on the revolutionary tragedy *Franz von Sickengen* composed by their (at the time) fellow leftist, Ferdinand Lassalle; Engels's critique of the aesthetic and historical issues raised by the play was undertaken "for the interests of the Party itself" (FE to Lassalle, 18 May 1859, *MEC*). Marx and Engels engaged in literary criticism as members, indeed leaders, of "the Party"; their appreciation of the cultural monuments of the past did not substitute for the need to abolish the conditions that mutilated human potential and blocked the present movement toward communism. "The weapon of criticism cannot, of course, replace criticism of the weapon, material force must be overthrown by material force; but theory also becomes a material force as soon as it has gripped the masses" (*CHPR*, Introduction). Only in a society based upon the fulfillment of universal human needs could art be universally liberated from the constraints of class-bound necessity; the social movement seeking to transform social reality in the here and now must "draw its poetry from the future" (*18 B*, ch. 1).

Marx once noted his fondness for a maxim by the Roman playwright Terence: *humani nihil a me alienum puto* ("Nothing human is alien to me") (*Confession*). Although this statement can be interpreted to mean that Marx embraced a transcendent notion of human-ness, it only asserts that he felt able to understand whatever another person might write or say, might have written or might have said. It certainly did not prevent him from castigating the vulgar economists of his time for their propagandistic mystifications of the workings of capital. Marx's proclamations about the alienation of the artist or the enduring power of classic great literature, while situating him in his time, can be taken as evidence of a covert bourgeois humanism only if they are cherrypicked and read in isolation from the rest of his writings.

Subsequent theorists in the Marxist tradition have insisted that the creation and enjoyment of art and literature constitute fundamental human requirements: proletarian revolution should entail not the destruction or abandonment but instead the repossession of a cultural heritage previously available only to the exploiting class and its minions. Although Lenin was an astute critic of the novels of Leo Tolstoy, which he saw as reflective of "both the strength and the weakness, the might and the limitations ... of the peasant mass movement," these novels' ruling-class ideological origins did not mean, Lenin wrote, that the revolutionary proletariat should relinquish this legacy, any more than it should abandon the technological advances bringing modernity into being. "Marxism has won its historic significance as the ideology of the revolutionary proletariat," wrote Lenin, "because, far from rejecting the most valuable achievements of the bourgeois epoch, it has, on the contrary, assimilated and refashioned everything of value in the more than two thousand years of the development of human thought and culture" (Lenin 1975, 61, 143). For the socialist and artist William Morris, aesthetic pleasure was central to life; when his time traveler visits the classless world of the future, one of the things that delights him the most is the design and fine craftsmanship of the clothes people wear. Gramsci argued that "while the slavery of wages and work cuts [workers] off from a world that integrates man's life, that makes it worth living," the "reign of beauty and grace" is essential to communism (Gramsci 1985, 38). "Bread and Roses," an early anthem of the labor movement in the United States, put the point succinctly: "The worker must have bread, but she must have roses too" (Ross 2013).

Despite such efforts to clarify the relationship between human need and artistic enjoyment, however, a fundamental ambiguity about the position of writers and artists in capitalist society has dogged a good deal of Marxist literary and cultural criticism over the years. The English critic Christopher Caudwell, for instance, while authoring a rigorously materialist study of the origins of poetry (Caudwell 1937) as well as devastating critiques of the petty-bourgeois limitations of such writers as George Bernard Shaw and H.G. Wells (Caudwell 1971, 1–19, 73–95), also maintained, however contradictorily, that "the artist continually discovers new kingdoms of the heart" and "new seas of feeling." Caudwell wrote, because "there is no firm ground of cognitive reality beneath his feet, [the artist] becomes dizzy and tormented" (Caudwell 1971, 109). The Spanish philosopher and aesthetician Adolfo Sánchez Vázquez, while acknowledging the existence of a class struggle in the realm of artistic production, wrote that, for Marxist critics, the main contradiction to consider is "not one between capitalism and an art which poses an ideological challenge to the dominant ideology," but one "between capitalism and art as such." He continued, "A critique of bourgeois social relations should not lead to a rejection of the great art that has been created within the framework of those relations, namely, art that transcends the class interests to which it responded" (Sánchez Vázquez 1973 [1965], 103, 106). Caudwell's and Sánchez Vásquez's broad generalizations about art *qua* art—its intrinsic antagonism to capitalism, its transcendence of its class origins—have been reiterated in various forms over the years; a recent iteration is Tony McKenna's claim that "art is the medium in which history dreams" (McKenna 2015, 8).

The notion that there is something inherently liberatory in art and literature acknowledges the ways in which many texts invoke, and many readers yearn for, universal conceptions of human need and human potentiality. But to move from the insight that many writers and artists perform their "exceptional" work outside the regime of wage labor and commodity production (Beech 2015) to the conclusion that their creations are for that reason intrinsically hostile to capital is an unwarranted leap. Writers and artists excluded from the halls of power may be a "dominated" group, as Pierre Bourdieu suggests, but they remain perfectly capable of reproducing dominant ideologies all the same (Bourdieu 1990, 145–46). The idealist assertion that art and literature gesture toward a realm beyond alienation blurs the necessity for a materialist transformation, through class struggle, of the social conditions that cause alienation. Marx loved Shakespeare, and Gramsci loved Dante; yet both also knew that it is only by fighting through the political that humanity can negate and sublate the political. When Marx wrote that "communism ... equals humanism ... the riddle of history solved," he placed the solution to the riddle in the practice of revolutionary social transformation. Gramsci made a distinction between works of literature that moved him aesthetically and those that, instilling in him a "moral enthusiasm," made him a "willing participant in the artist's ideological world." What Gramsci longed for was creative expression where "both factors were included" (Gramsci 1985, 108), and he would not have to choose between formal appreciation and political affirmation.

Even as we may be moved by the beauty—or, what we experience as the beauty—of aesthetically powerful works of literature and art, past and present, we do well to remember Walter Benjamin's caution that "[t]here is no document of civilization that is not at the same time a document of barbarism" (Benjamin 1969, 256). This statement pertains as much to a poem by Dylan Thomas or a novel by Jane Austen as it does to the Great Pyramid of Giza. Humanism never makes its way to us in a pure state; it inevitably bears the marks of the history that hurts.

Realism

While some debates among Marxist critics have focused upon literature's contradictory capacity at once to reinforce dominant ideologies and to anticipate a space beyond them, others—frequently citing Marx's admiration for Gaskell, Brontë, and Dickens—have focused upon its capacity to render insight and cognition. A key concept here is realism, which Engels, in his writings on Balzac, defined as "the truthful reproduction of typical characters under typical circumstances." The most prominent theorist of realism in the Marxist tradition is Georg Lukács, for whom the categories of typicality and totality furnish the key concepts upon which realism is grounded. In a realist text (Lukács deals almost exclusively with the genre of the novel), the typical protagonist is the focus of attention not because he (in these discussions it is usually "he") is an extraordinary person, but precisely because his very "mediocre" or "middling" quality enables him to embody in microcosm the pressures and possibilities of his time and place (Lukács 1962 [1937], 34). "The central category and criterion of realist literature is the type, a peculiar synthesis which organically binds together the general and the particular both in characters and situations," writes Lukács. "[W]hat makes it a type is that in it all the humanly and socially essential determinants are present on their highest level of development ... rendering concrete the peaks and limits of men and epochs" (Lukács 1964, 6). For Lukács— whose formulation of typicality was strongly influenced by Hegel—the capacity of writers to penetrate from appearance to essence hinged not so much upon individual genius as upon the epistemological framework either made available or foreclosed by the social relations of production in a given historical moment.

Reinforcing Engels's valuation of Balzac's realism, Lukács argued that the transparency of such relations in early nineteenth-century France derived in large part from the still-progressive historical role being performed by the rising bourgeois class: bent upon vanquishing the remnants of aristocracy, the bourgeoisie, as "the ideological leader of social development," had no interest in camouflaging its own beliefs and motives (Lukács 1962 [1937], 173). After the revolutions of 1848, however, when the main contradiction in European society was rearticulated as the class struggle between the bourgeoisie and the proletariat, dominant ideologies increasingly functioned to legitimate bourgeois class rule, thereby obfuscating class contradictions and rendering it more difficult for writers to compose realist texts, no matter what their espoused political orientations. "[T]he idea of progress undergoes a regression," he writes. No longer viewed as "the prehistory of the present ... history is conceived as a smooth, straightforward evolution" (Lukács 1962 [1937], 174, 176). Abandoning realism, he argued, many writers turned to naturalism—which emphasized the helplessness of individuals buffeted about by forces beyond their control, as in the works of Émile Zola— or to modernism, which enshrined fragmentation and anomie, as in the works of Franz Kafka. Indeed, for Lukács, naturalism and modernism were, however paradoxically, two sides of the same epistemological coin, in that both substituted appearance for essence and viewed change as a function of external determinism rather than internal contradiction. In the twentieth century, only "critical realism"—a paradigm increasingly difficult, though not impossible, to achieve, exemplified in the works of Thomas Mann—could, in Lukács's view, contest the mystifying effects of the "contemplative consciousness" fostered by reification. Only critical realism could convey knowledge of the fundamental dialectic of historical process (Lukács 1963).

Lukács's approach to realism has been widely influential among literary critics bent upon analyzing the truth-value they find embedded in literary works, even works written from standpoints seemingly remote from expressly Marxist concerns. Annette Rubinstein draws upon a Lukácsian conception of realism when she locates the greatness of Shakespeare in his ability to "sense 'the future in the instant'" by discerning "the vital current which moves steadily beneath the immediate eddies and confusing cross-currents of life's surface" (Rubinstein 1969 [1953], v). Julian Markels makes the notions of typicality and totality central to his designation of what he calls the "Marxian imagination" at work in texts by patently non-Marxist writers (Shakespeare, Dickens, William Faulkner, Henry James) who intuitively grasp the "class processes" at work in stratified social worlds (Markels 2003, 11–30). But Lukács's theorization of realism has hardly gone uncontested, by both non-Marxists and Marxists alike. Certain criticisms—such as the charge that Lukács's "reflectionist" view of literature as the representation of a knowable reality is episte-mologically naïve—erroneously conflate reflectionism with positivism (Thompson 2011). From a Marxist standpoint, there may not be such a thing as a literary work that transparently conveys a "Truth" that can be fully known; but there is no question that some texts, such as Wright's *Native Son*, come much closer to conveying objectively valid propositions about society and history than do those that reify race and mystify historical processes, such as Mitchell's *Gone with the Wind*. The charge that Lukács's later writings on realism betray the revolutionary vision of the earlier *History and Class Consciousness*, showing him kow-towing to aesthetic programs emanating from Moscow, misrepresents the international history of socialist realism and ignores Lukács's continuing contribution to a critical tradition extending back to Marx and Engels (Stasi 2015). But other criticisms of Lukács's theory of realism—and its accompanying across-the-board condemnation of modernism—bear careful consideration.

The most important of these criticisms was posed by the communist poet and playwright Bertolt Brecht. Faulting Lukács for nostalgically favoring the mode of realism embodied in the nineteenth-century novel, with its focus on the historical significance of typical individual destinies, Brecht argued that the literary forms needed in the present are "not linked to the good old days but to the bad new ones.... Man does not become man again by stepping forth from the masses but by sinking deeper into them." For Brecht, the realism called for by "the dehumanization of capitalism in its fascist phase" requires the development of new artistic forms that "uncover the causal complexes of society" and "unmask the prevailing view of things as the view of those who are in power" (Brecht 1977, 69, 81). In this alternative conception of realism, a text's organic form does not necessarily provide access to totality; rather, its autotelic quality can function not as an antidote to, but instead as an evasion of, the disunity and alienation experienced in the world beyond the text. While preoccupied with the definition of "man" (in German, *mensch*)—indeed, no other word receives more attention in his poetry and plays—Brecht concludes that, in a world dominated by market relations where only selfish behavior is rewarded, there is no "essence" to "man" (Squiers 2014, 99–110). Rather, for Brecht, "man" consists of a set of possibilities that can develop in one direction or another. Communist humanism can supersede the obscurantism of bourgeois humanism only through a process of unremitting ideological critique; literature's principal role is not to offer coherent representations of reality—however persuasive and moving these may be—but to encourage critical questioning about why that reality exists. Brecht's famous "V-Effect"—a series of acting and scene-setting strategies designed to invite theater audiences consciously to examine the assumptions guiding the play in process—embodied his attempt to find a form appropriate to this political vision (Brecht 1964, 179–205). While Brecht did not view the disruption of conventional forms as an intrinsically radical act—some experimental artists sought to "free themselves from grammar, not from capitalism," he sardonically observed—the political wine of revolutionary proletarian conscious-ness could not be poured from the old ideological bottles of bourgeois humanism (Brecht 1977, 73). In his formulation, then, the purpose of realism is to dislodge static and idealist notions of what it means to be human—to undo the suturing supplied by dominant ideologies. Where for Lukács the goal of realist literary representation is to embody the dialectics of totality, for Brecht realism requires first and foremost an assault upon the dominant ideologies producing false notions of totality.

The theories of realism advanced by both Lukács and Brecht, it bears noting, were formulated in the crucible of the mid-twentieth-century struggle against Fascism. In this context, the debate among Marxists over revolutionary strategy—could residual liberal democratic traditions be mobilized to support the workers' movement, or was a more revo-lutionary approach to class struggle the order of the day?—was, to say the least, of more than merely literary importance. Lukács's and Brecht's conceptions of realism and humanism, both based in Marxist principles and commitments, outlined two possible responses to this situation. The welcoming reception of such dramatically new narrative forms as the so-called "collective" or "choral" novel—embodied in such texts as Ignazio Silone's *Fontamara* (1933; English trans. 1934) and John Dos Passos's *U.S.A.* trilogy (1937)—indicates that many critics and writers were rising to the challenges, political and aesthetic, of the time (Hicks 1974; Foley 1993).

A third position in the so-called realism–modernism debate of the last century was articulated by the philosopher Theodor Adorno, a leading figure in the Frankfurt School of Critical Theory. (This was a group of philosophers who, while critical of capitalism, focused more on reifica-tion than on exploitation and were skeptical about the desirability of proletarian revolution [Kellner 2002].) Where Lukács and Brecht, albeit in very different ways, viewed both literature and criticism as essential adjuncts to revolution, Adorno expressed skepticism toward works of art or literature aspiring to lodge explicitly formulated protests against the status quo: by acceding to prevailing practices of representation, he warned, such works would end up "following the bidding of the alienated world and persisting obdurately in a state of reification" (Adorno 1977b, 160). In the wake of World War II, moreover, Adorno contended that the "mass deception" of a postwar "culture industry" had created audiences comfortably rocked into quiescence (Horkheimer and Adorno 1994, 120–67); most artworks and literary texts, swallowed up in the maw of near-universal commodification, were part of the problem rather than the solution. "Politics has migrated to autonomous art," wrote Adorno (1977a, 194). The truth-value of artistic or literary works consisted not in their attempts to portray totality, but in their capacity to reflect reification; by a curious turn of the wheel, anti-realist modernism was, for Adorno, the necessary mode of realism suited to capitalist modernity. Notably, Adorno admired above all else the works of Samuel Beckett.

The debates about humanism and realism briefly sketched above hardly exhaust the range of aesthetic and political issues that have pre-occupied Marxist critics for over a century. I have focused upon these figures' positions, however—especially with regard to the realism–modernism debate—because the larger issues they treat have not gone away. We frequently hear that neoliberalism, globalization, and the age of information technology have created new social conditions requiring new politics, new epistemologies, and new modes of representation, including—whether we like it or not—a "capitalist realism" premised upon the notion that, in the words of former UK Prime Minister Margaret Thatcher, "There is no alternative" (TINA) (Fisher 2009). But this conclusion risks fetishizing novelty and mistaking appearance for essence; we are still in the *longue durée* of capitalist modernity. The failure of twentieth-century efforts to bring into being a "post"-capitalist world does not mean that we inhabit a "post"-political "post"-modernity, or that there have emerged "alternative modernities" irrevocably shifting the terrain of cultural production and analysis (Wood 1995; Warwick Research Collective 2015, 1–48). In the twenty-first century, the pressures of reification have if anything multiplied and intensified beyond what Lukács, Brecht or Adorno could have imagined; indeed, these are not so much pressures as an unmarked given of our world, as seemingly natural as the unnatural air breathed by a larger and larger number—and proportion—of the planet's inhabitants. The global extension of the real subsumption of capital has not meant, however, that social contradictions have eased. The gap between the haves and the have-nots has if anything drastically widened; imperialist-fostered uneven development takes increasingly vicious forms; the fascist threat that energized the realism–modernism debate in the last century has, by all appearances, taken a new and frighteningly energized lease on life. Grappling with this still-capitalist reality, writers work with a wider range of representational modes than ever before—from a realism that Lukács would have recognized to irrealist and hyper-realist modes of fiction, poetry and other genres of writing, increasingly appearing on computer screens rather than between book covers—which would have had even Adorno scratching his head (Damon 2011). Although the long detour through post-structuralism, discourse theory, and their ideological spin-offs over the past several decades has created an academic literary establishment still leery of traditional modes of realism, this predilection has not necessarily won the day in the actual practice of writers around the world (Maerhofer 2009; Warwick Research Collective 2015, 49–80). The question of what counts as a realistic portrayal of reality abides, as does the question of whether certain forms and techniques are more likely to obfuscate or reveal, mystify or expose, the contradictions of capitalism—the bad new days—in the twenty-first century. Many of the issues confronting Marxist critics constitute a changing same, even as their responses continue to evolve.

Proletarian Literature and Alternative Hegemony

Finally, we shall address the status in Marxist criticism of literary works that have expressly attempted to articulate a revolutionary outlook, the "standpoint of the proletariat." Besides asking us to consider texts and traditions routinely overlooked in literary history and canon formation, these texts raise a number of important theoretical questions about the nature of literature and the goals of Marxist literary criticism. Do these works exhibit the same kinds of rhetorical procedures as do those mediating ideological standpoints more readily assimilable to ruling-class interests? If these purposively leftist texts aim, as Mao Zedong put it, to "fit well into the whole revolutionary machine as ... component part[s] [and] operate as powerful weapons for uniting and educating the people and for attacking and destroying the enemy" (Mao 1943, 251), does this unabashedly instrumentalist assertion of purpose mean that Marxist critics adopt different standards and criteria for assessing these works' value, including their "greatness"? What, moreover, is the relationship between literary works that engage in anti-capitalist critique by halts and starts, querying without negating the legitimacy of the status quo, and those texts that more directly call for revolutionary social transformation? How do we characterize the texts and traditions that have kept hope alive during the dark night of oppression—containing what Amilcar Cabral calls the cultural "seed of opposition" to colonial degradation and domination (Cabral 1970, 42), what the US historian Robin Kelley calls the "freedom dreams" of the enslaved and their Jim Crow-era successors (Kelley 2002, 36–59)? If texts aspiring to raise the reader's class consciousness are committed to cultivating what Gramsci theorized as an alternative common sense, do texts produced when the revolutionary tide is at a low ebb figure any less prominently in defining the function and features of politically radical literature than do those produced when class struggle is at—or approaching—its crest?

The currently available terms for describing different variants within this oppositional literary tradition are many: literature of social protest; resistance literature; leftist literature; radical literature; partisan literature; literature of commitment; revolutionary literature; literature of alternative hegemony; proletarian literature. Of these, the last, with its explicit allusion to Marxist categories of analysis, would seem to be the most useful because it alludes to the class whose self-abolition opens the door to human universality. Moreover—if we bear in mind the broadened conception of the proletariat discussed in chapter 1—the notion of proletarian literature can be linked to a domain extended both temporally as well as geographically. It need not be confined to the communist-aligned literature of class struggle that achieved status as a recognized genre during middle decades of the twentieth century—a genre internationally ranging from Richard Wright's *Uncle Tom's Children* (1965 [1940]) to Myra Page's *Moscow Yankee* (1996 [1935]); from Jorge Amado's *The Violent Land* (1943; English trans. 1945) to Ousmane Sembène's *God's Bits of Wood* (1960; English trans. 1962). Proletarian literature can be seen to comprise literary traditions ranging from the poetry and prose of the Chartist movement in early nineteenth-century England to the slave narrative in the antebellum United States; from memoirs recording the dispossession of Latin American peasants to testimonials of prisoners from Johannesburg to Baghdad to Detroit; from apocalyptic anti-capitalist dystopias to speculative imaginings of communalist societies on other planets. Repurposed spatially and temporally, proletarian literature need not be a dated concept, one to be buried along with the notion of class struggle in a presumably post-industrial world (Holstun 2017; Mullen 2013).

How, then, can we describe the body of literature that goes against the capitalist grain? The geographical and historical extensions of the definition of proletarian literature noted above are welcome, for they not only enable a rethinking and rewriting of past literary traditions but also make room for the emergence of an oppositional body of literature reflecting the altered forms taken by class struggles in the twenty-first century. Yet, especially when the main form of class struggle appears to be ruling-class attack rather than proletarian resistance—much less a revolutionary challenge for state power—this choice of a name for the body of literature in question runs the risk of sounding curiously nostalgic, bound to a nineteenth-century vocabulary possessing little relevance to the present. The term "proletariat" can be viewed not as a dialectical category, defined in opposition to its counterpart, that is, "bourgeoisie," but as a stand-alone category signifying not structural location but group experience defined by identity. The designation of "working-class literature"—along with "working-class studies"—as a field of teaching and research often reproduces this ideologically saturated recodification: rather than calling for the abolition of class, this terminology solidifies class as a demographic category, a positivist given (Foley 1992). By contrast, the somewhat awkward term "literature of alternative hegemony" has the advantage of focusing on the struggle over ideology and power; moreover, it invites consideration of the proletarian qualities often embedded in literary and cultural forms that do not name themselves as such—hip-hop and spoken-word poetry being obvious candidates (Abrams 1995). The signal disadvantage of "literature of alternative hegemony," however, is its lack of explicit reference to class, thereby entailing the risk of reducing class to one identity among many, an "alternative" that by no means possesses particular explanatory power or revolutionary potentiality. In addition, the designation of "hegemony," absent the context of class struggle, raises the problem of culturalism, including a reformist politics of "boring from within," noted in the critique of neo-Gramscianism in chapter 3. There would seem to be no single term that encompasses the full range of political and historical concerns at stake in defining the body of literature under consideration.

The notion of family resemblance—this time in connection with the body of anti-capitalist literature in question—may once again prove useful. Giving the name "literature of alternative hegemony" to this grouping as a whole, we can stipulate that at its core are works of pro-communist revolutionary literature that—like Langston Hughes's "Good Morning, Revolution!" (1994, 162–63) or Brecht's "Praise of Communism" (Brecht 1965, 73)—have historically urged readers to join an authorial audience—a "we"—posing a frontal challenge to ruling-class state power. Such core works have for the most part been produced during periods of capitalist crisis when social revolution appeared to be a real possibility—not least because examples of anticipated and ongoing socialist construction suggested that another world was not only possible but coming into being. For this core group of revolutionary works, utopia was—if in still imperfect form—somewhere, not nowhere. Moving outward from the center we find works of proletarian literature that are class-conscious but not necessarily revolutionary: they imply the possibility of dialectical negation without calling for a new world order in so many words. Still further toward the fuzzy outer fringes of this family resemblance model are those texts and traditions, past and present—and, one hopes, future—that, without necessarily addressing class and class consciousness as such, suggest the need for a world beyond exploitation. One advantage of this model is that, while it avoids liberal pluralism, it includes a significant range of oppositional political perspectives. Another advantage is that it is constituted not by a checklist of traits but by a shared affinity. Each text included in the model either obliquely or directly gestures toward the need for the world to rise on new foundations but invites analysis in its own terms: no one size fits all.

Whatever we decide to call this corpus of texts and traditions is, however, less important than considering some of the challenges it poses to the theory and practice of literary criticism. One such challenge involves the standards for evaluation that Marxist critics, recognizing the importance of nurturing an emergent radical literary culture, bring to bear in their assessment of works exploring this terrain. Despite their profound acquaintance with classic literary and artistic traditions, Marx and Engels, we will recall, responded enthusiastically to the "modern prose and poetry emanating in England and France from the lower classes of people," defending this literature from its elitist Young Hegelian critics. Mike Gold, when serving as the literary editor of the *New Masses* in the late 1920s and early 1930s, welcomed to its pages "worker-correspondents" who would let the magazine's readers "know the heart and mind of the workers." He advised, "Don't worry about grammar or syntax," he wrote. "Write as you talk" (Gold 1929, 4). Such initiatives did not, however, position leftist critics as uncritical cheerleaders. Engels, while supporting the project of the "new socialist novel," faulted both Kautsky and Harkness for an incomplete grasp of the realism required to treat working-class life; while the *New Masses'* sponsorship of interchanges like the 1934 "Author's Field Day" enabled authors and critics alike to comment frankly—and at times acerbically—on one another's writings ("Author's Field Day" 1934; Foley 1993, 129–69). At the same time, critics defending literature that violates mainstream assumptions about the relationship of art to politics, then and now, have been aware of fighting an uphill battle. Hence W.E.B. Du Bois's insistence that "all literature is propaganda, and ever will be"; hence Joseph Freeman's critique of the pseudo-objectivity of the liberal "Man in White"; and hence, in our time, Viet Thanh Nguyen's declaration that "We, the barbarians at the gate, the descendants of Caliban … come with the desire not just to show, but to tell." In literary criticism as elsewhere, while there are indeed standards for assessing value, these are not neutral; taking sides involves both political and aesthetic considerations.

A second challenge to Marxist criticism posed by the literature of alternative hegemony entails an assessment of the extent to which the notion of the political unconscious remains a useful tool in connection with this corpus of texts and traditions. After all, the strategies of suspicious reading enabling Marxist critics to destabilize dominant ideologies would seem to be a good deal less germane to the interpretation of literary works aiming to destabilize the worlds giving rise to those ideologies. In works like Thomas Cooper's "Merrie England—No More!" and Langston Hughes's "Goodbye, Christ," the gap between surface and depth that generates the need for symptomatic reading is largely absent. But if we bear in mind that ideology entails not only distortion but also limitation of vision, we should be alert to ways in which otherwise revolutionary texts can bear residual traces of the hegemony that they contest. At times these traces testify to the historical and political constraints upon the social movements with which an author has been—either directly or indirectly—aligned. In Viramontes' *Under the Feet of Jesus*, for instance, the retreat from class struggle in the novel's final pages acknowledges the retreat from militant confrontation in the contemporaneous farmworkers' movement (Garcia 2012)—with which Viramontes was well acquainted (López 2014)—as well as, arguably, the more general disorientation of leftist politics around the world in the years following the break-up of the USSR. The text's ambiguous standpoint with regard to religious idealism can thus be read symptomatically as a register to this larger historical arc. At times the political unconscious reflects contradictions in the line and practice of the leftist movement with which a writer was aligned. The discordance between the title of Bulosan's *America Is in the Heart* and the narrative that it precedes, for example, invites interpretation as a confused—and confusing—response to the contradiction between nationalism and internationalism in the strategy embraced by the communist-led left in the era of the Popular Front Against Fascism and World War II, during which the text was largely composed (Foley 1993, 126–28). Even as radical and revolutionary social movements have inspired writers to imagine their way through and past current fetters on human potentiality, these writers' works have often played out the limits and constraints of the parties and organizations with which they have been aligned. Ideology may not be eternal, as Althusser proposed; but its period of radioactive decay promises to be prolonged—persisting, we may conjecture, long after many features of capitalist social organization have been negated and sublated in what Marx termed the "first phase" of communism.

A third challenge posed to Marxist criticism by the literature of alternative hegemony involves its relationship to "utopia." The conception of utopia relevant here is, in Ernst Bloch's useful distinction, not the "compensatory" utopia embodied in any number of literary works that bypass the harshness of the here and now in their search for transcendence—"Fern Hill" supplying a case in point—but the "anticipatory" utopia heralded in texts that point the way, however hesitantly, toward the real possibility of a better world. The alternative common sense encoded in this body of texts is clearly future-oriented, in that it implies the need for, and possibility of, the dialectical negation and sublation of the existing social order. It is this version of utopian potentiality that Tillie Olsen had in mind when she wrote of the need to recognize the "not-yet in the now"; that Langston Hughes explored throughout his life in representations of the "dream" of liberation; that Sol Funaroff spoke about when he referred to himself as an "exile / from a future time, / from shores of freedom I may never know," whose task as a writer was to convey the "tidings" of that future time which were "sounding in the surf" of today (Funaroff 1938, 9). Radical writers committed to representing the seeds of a better world buried in the soil of the capitalist present have sought to invoke that present in all its concreteness—while at the same time indicating its possible negation in a world that, having not yet come into being, is of necessity abstract. These writers have needed to feel dialectics in their bones as they strive to create literary forms capable of encompassing this contradiction; some have been more successful than others. Marxist critics committed to supporting this literary project have equally needed to feel dialectics in their bones as they devise frameworks for interpreting and assessing texts and traditions that have been obliged to "draw their poetry from the future." The utopian leap at the end of Gold's *Jews without Money* signals a phenomenon—at once a problem and a promise—intrinsic to the literature of alternative hegemony, especially, perhaps, of those core texts of proletarian literature informed by an explicitly revolutionary outlook. Such texts at once tease and trouble the

Marxist critic. Severe constraints are placed upon the ability of politically radical literary works to leap beyond the limits of capital; yet without confronting the contradiction between what is and what can be, they cannot aspire to represent the dialectics of the history that hurts.

The literature of alternative hegemony thus poses questions that invite the practitioner of Marxist criticism to reconsider the nature of literature itself. For the notion that literary works should be what Mao called "powerful weapons for uniting and educating the people and for attacking and destroying the enemy" entails a view of literature that is, to say the least, unmistakably functional. While the proposition that literature is in some sense useful is non-controversial, except perhaps for the most formalist of critics, a Marxist approach to the functionality of proletarian literature—and, more broadly, the literature of alternative hegemony—entails a more focused conception of what "useful" can mean. For if politically radical literature aspires to represent the "not-yet in the now," the potential for becoming inherent in being, it goes against the grain of the now; it transgresses assumptions about what it means to be human that enjoy the ideological shelter and comfort of familiarity. If a literary text interpellates its readers as participants in the process of changing the world, to one degree or another it has to come "from outside" everyday life, in a manner analogous to Lenin's view that a revolutionary party must address the class struggle "from outside" the limits imposed by the everyday experience of the oppressed masses. There is a quotation, widely attributed to Brecht, often seen on posters and T-shirts at left-wing cultural gatherings: "Art is not a mirror to reflect reality, but a hammer with which to shape it." Mirror versus hammer; reflection versus trans-formation; portrayal of what is versus anticipation of what may be: the notion that literature can be a practical tool for transforming the world is an essential tenet of Marxist criticism. Literature has been, is now, and can be many things; we will bear this range of possibilities in mind as we turn to a practical exploration of the domain of Marxist pedagogy.

6

Marxist Pedagogy

The weapon of criticism cannot, of course, replace criticism of the weapon, material force must be overthrown by material force; but theory also becomes a material force as soon as it has gripped the masses.

— Karl Marx, *Critique of Hegel's Philosophy of Right*

Through a closer examination of a range of individual texts, we will now test out various ways in which Marxism enables us to deepen and extend our comprehension of literature—as a reflection of historical pressures and limits, a site of ideological reproduction, a space of political struggle. The discussion is organized with pedagogical practice foremost in mind: hence the grouping of texts in clusters potentially useful in the high school or college literature classroom: Alienation; Rebellion; Nation; War; Money; Race; Gender and Sexuality; Nature; Mortality; Art. These topics are chosen not because they constitute an exhaustive list—one can imagine any number of other possibilities—but because they correspond to concerns commonly viewed as central to an education in the humanities. Within each category, however, the featured texts are intended to highlight debates—over ideology, over history, over interpretation—that demonstrate how each cluster represents not a self-evident theme but a problem, or series of problems. More than just a procedure of "putting in conversation," this methodology explores the dialectics involved in the time-honored practice of "compare and contrast." What mediations are needed to establish significant similarities and differences between and among the texts? How do these clusters enable us to think about totality? To "think totality"?

The concepts outlined in preceding chapters—both basic concerns of Marxist theory (historical materialism, political economy, and ideology) as well as fundamental principles of Marxist approaches to literature and literary criticism—will supply a toolkit for our investigations here. At the same time, the categories chosen for discussion will enable us to test out the adequacy of Marxism as an approach to literary criticism, especially its claim to be a "metatheory," capable of absorbing findings and insights from other methodologies while keeping its own principles centrally in view. What is its legitimate domain? Does Marxist criticism address certain genres, subject matters, and historical periods more effectively than others? Clearly a category like alienation—which invites historicization within the era of capitalism and theorization by means of a specifically Marxist set of concepts—is going to pose quite different questions than does a category like mortality, which addresses experiences and concerns that people can be said to have in common regardless of the era they inhabit or social status they possess. What kinds of generalizations about humanity—and the humanities—do these clusters of texts invite, or conversely, discourage?

Two final points about methodology. First, the texts I have chosen for exploration in each category have the status of examples, but they function more as illustrations than as specimens held to be definitively typical. As the many allusions to literary works in preceding chapters have indicated, any number of alternative texts could have served here equally well. Second, the works discussed in each cluster inevitably reflect my own interests, but also limitations, as a scholar and teacher of US (and to a lesser extent UK) literature of the nineteenth and twentieth centuries, with particular emphasis on African American literature and US literary radicalism. This restriction does not mean that Marxist literary criticism is less relevant to the study of literature produced in other periods and other places: there are Marxist scholars of classical antiquity (Thomson 1968 [1940]; Rose 2012), the Middle Ages (Schlauch 1956; Delany 1990), and contemporary literatures of the world (Shankar 2012; Lazarus 2011). Nonetheless, I regret that I have been able only to gesture toward those parts of the immense literary field where I have relatively little expertise. I hope that this limitation is at least partially offset by my decision to discuss some indisputably classic literary works probably familiar to many readers and teachers. These discussions of well-known works will enable me to highlight some of the emphases that distinguish Marxist from non-Marxist critical approaches.

The textual commentaries offered here vary in depth and detail, and the mode of presentation will vary. When entire poems are under discussion, we shall reproduce them all at once and then discuss them sequentially (unless copyright restrictions require that certain poems not be reproduced in their entirety). When shorter and longer texts are combined within a single thematic cluster, they will be juxtaposed as best suits the goals of our analysis. When longer prose works are under discussion, our approach will be more schematic, dealing with general matters of plot, character, and point of view, with occasional glimpses at specific passages. Whether our inquiry is focused or broad, however, and directed toward poetry or prose, we shall be examining not just the rhetoric of the work in question—that is, the formal means by which the text interpellates its reader—but also those moments when the text reveals, either purposively or inadvertently, its embeddedness in politics and history. Given the inevitable impact of dominant ideologies on both individual writers and the literary conventions they deploy, a good deal of our attention will be devoted to ideology critique. Most important, however, will be our exploration of how historically driven ideological contradictions work themselves out in individual literary works: why "always historicize" is a necessary imperative if we wish to understand what a text is saying to us. The Marxist critic is not a scold, seeking out political shortcomings for exposure and punishment. Rather, the goal of Marxist criticism—and pedagogy—is the development of a fuller dialectical understanding of the social totality giving rise to both doctrines and structures of feeling, whether these clarify or obfuscate the "real foundation." After all, as Marx well knew, the main object of critique is not bad thinking, or even people who think badly, but the social arrangements generating bad thinking— and badly thinking people—in the first place.

Alienation

Consider the following cluster of three poems. The first, by the English poet and critic Matthew Arnold, was published in 1852:

To Marguerite—Continued

Yes! in the sea of life enisled,
With echoing straits between us thrown,
Dotting the shoreless watery wild,
We mortal millions live *alone*.
The islands feel the enclasping flow,
And then their endless bounds they know.

But when the moon their hollows lights,
And they are swept by balms of spring,
And in their glens, on starry nights,
The nightingales divinely sing;
And lovely notes, from shore to shore,
Across the sounds and channels pour—

Oh! then a longing like despair
Is to their farthest caverns sent;
For surely once, they feel, we were
Parts of a single continent!
Now round us spreads the watery plain—
Oh might our marges meet again!

Who order'd, that their longing's fire
Should be, as soon as kindled, cool'd?
Who renders vain their deep desire?—
A God, a God their severance ruled!
And bade betwixt their shores to be
The unplumb'd, salt, estranging sea.

(Arnold 1965, 123–25)

The second, by the US poet Muriel Rukeyser, was published in 1938:

Boy with His Hair Cut Short

SUNDAY shuts down on this twentieth-century evening.
The L passes. Twilight and bulb define
the brown room, the overstuffed plum sofa,
the boy, and the girl's thin hands above his head.
A neighbor radio sings stocks, news, serenade.

He sits at the table, head down, the young clear neck exposed,
watching the drugstore sign from the tail of his eye;
tattoo, neon, until the eye blears, while his
solicitous tall sister, simple in blue, bending
behind him, cuts his hair with her cheap shears.

The arrow's electric red always reaches its mark,
successful neon! He coughs, impressed by that precision.
His child's forehead, forever protected by his cap,
is bleached against the lamplight as he turns head
and steadies to let the snippets drop.

Erasing the failure of weeks with level fingers,
she sleeks the fine hair, combing: 'You'll look fine tomorrow!
You'll surely find something, they can't keep turning you down;
the finest gentleman's not so trim as you!' Smiling, he raises
the adolescent forehead wrinkling ironic now.

He sees his decent suit laid out, new-pressed,
his carfare on the shelf. He lets his head fall, meeting
her earnest hopeless look, seeing the sharp blades splitting,
the darkened room, the impersonal sign, her motion,
the blue vein, bright on her temple, pitifully beating.

(in Rukeyser 1978, 114–15)

The third is Xu Lizhi's "I Swallowed an Iron Moon," which was published (in Chinese) shortly before Xu's death in 2014, and in English print translation in 2017:

I swallowed an iron moon
they called it a screw
I swallowed industrial wastewater and unemployment forms
bent over machines, our youth died young
I swallowed labor, I swallowed poverty
swallowed pedestrian bridges, swallowed this rusted-out life
I can't swallow any more
everything I've swallowed roils up in my throat
I spread across my country
a poem of shame.

(Xu 2017, 198)

These poems ostensibly treat very different situations. How can it be said that they all contend centrally with the phenomenon of alienation?

The Arnold poem, while not alluding directly to its moment of creation, invites historical contextualization. The trope comparing humanity to isolated islands that were "once part of a single continent" invokes a famous statement made more than two centuries previously by the poet John Donne: "No man is an island, entire of itself; every man is a piece of the continent, a part of the main" (Donne 1959, 108–9). That this now-universal state of individual isolation—"we mortal millions live alone"—came into being in time is suggested by the poem's reference to the theory of continental drift (that is, the notion that the continents once were a continuous land-mass, pushed apart by the shifting of earth's tectonic plates—a geological theory gaining increasing currency in the mid-nineteenth century). The poem's allusion to contemporaneous science further links it to the associated crisis of religious faith in Victorian England, a crisis also registered in the image of the receding "Sea of Faith" in Arnold's famous "Dover Beach," a companion poem of this text. That "a God" is charged with responsibility for creating this "severance" of one human being from another reveals the speaker's antipathy toward conventional religion, even as the designation of "*a* God" indicates a crisis in monotheism. Although the title raises the expectation that the poem addresses his lover, the speaker's "we"—its implied authorial audience—comprises the "mortal millions" who individually "dot" the sea of modernity.

The poem's rhetoric interpellates a reader who identifies with its outcry of pain but is also capable of taking a certain melancholy pleasure in contemplating the unchangeable loneliness of the human condition. The speaker's sense of urgency is conveyed through frequent exclamations—"Yes," "Oh!"—as well the repetition of "a God" and the piled-up questions in the final stanza. His deployment of archaic-sounding words—"enisled," "marges"—hints at his longing for a bygone era of human solidarity. The metaphor of people as islands and the sea as fate is ably conveyed through paradox: the islands are "enclasped" not by one another, but by the determining forces that keep them apart. The songs of the nightingales, which "pour across the sounds and channels," suggest the role played by the aesthetic realm in supplying a compensatory utopia by affirming a universal human connection. (The nightingale figures prominently in Romantic and post-Romantic poetry as a conventional symbol of artistic inspiration.) But Beauty is, almost by definition, impotent; it can at most evoke nostalgia for an unspecified past. The fire of hope briefly "kindled" by the birds' song only enhances the mood of helplessness when the poem shifts back to the prevailing trope of the "estranging sea," whose salt is at once the chemical compound of the extra-textual Real and the concentrated tears of millions.

It is difficult to read this poem without being moved by its testimony to the sense of atomization and loneliness accompanying the experience of modernity. At the same time, the terms in which the problem is formulated obfuscate its causality, linking the present to a geologically distant past (Ollman's level 7) precluding the possibility that human intervention might create an imaginably different future. The genesis of estrangement in the increasingly reified social relations of mid-nineteenth-century England—and reflected, it bears noting, in "Estranged Labor," the translated title to Marx's essay on the alienation of labor in his *1844 Economic and Philosophic Manuscripts*—is portrayed through metaphors that naturalize and dehistoricize the experience of alienation that the poem acknowledges came into being in time. This is not to say, of course, that the poet, in order to explore the genesis of

the "severance" among people who "once" felt conjoined, was obligated
to refer to the crowded streets of London or the fetid factories of
Manchester: Ollman's level two. Yet the guiding metaphor of continental drift, a geological process occurring over millions of years, deflects
attention from anything resembling a historically specific inquiry into
the period during which estrangement took hold and differentiated
Arnold's world from Donne's—namely, the (comparatively) short two
centuries in which merchant and industrial capitalism came into being.
Arnold's invocation of science fails to supply a materialist explanation of
the origin of the history that hurts; it is no wonder, then, that the speaker
reverts to idealism at the end, proclaiming that "a God" is the locus of
causality. In its contradictory rejection of and accession to alienation, "To
Marguerite—Continued" invites symptomatic interpretation as at once
reacting against and reinforcing the reification increasingly prevailing
throughout capitalist society in Arnold's time.

"Boy with His Hair Cut Short" would seem, at first glance, to have
little to do with the issues raised in Arnold's poem. The mention of a
"twentieth-century evening," coupled with the poem's publication in
1938, locates the poem in the Great Depression. The absence of parental
figures remains unexplained; these young siblings are on their own, with
the boy thrust prematurely into the role of family wage-earner and the
sister tasked with the emotional and physical work involved in the daily
reproduction of labor power. The furniture, as well as the boy's possession
of a "decent suit," indicate that the family was once better off; his sister's
joking comment that "the finest gentleman's not so trim as you" suggests
that he has been seeking to sell his labor power in a white-collar office
setting. While the characters' whiteness is apparent—his forehead is
"bleached," while her throbbing vein is visible through the pallor of her
skin—their racial identity has hardly rescued them from the general fate
of the working class. Even as the radio next door, through its broadcast
of "stocks, news, serenade," urges its listeners to ignore the gravity of the
economic crisis, the girl's hands are "thin," suggesting that malnourish-
ment has contributed to the carefully saved carfare. In its simple depiction
of a brother and a sister in a shabby room on a Sunday evening, the poem
represents in microcosm the hunger and desperation—and fettering
of human potential—widely experienced by those forced into capitalism's reserve army of labor. As in Arnold's poem, the situation described
pertains to millions.

The poem's imagery and syntax reinforce its implied commentary
on reification. The "impersonal" neon arrow on the drugstore sign

indicates the prevalence of advertising and exchange value in the forces, material and ideological, ruling the siblings' lives. The fact that the boy is "impressed by the precision" of the "successful neon [that] always reaches its mark" suggests his having internalized the dominant ideology that, since upward mobility is available to all, he is somehow responsible for his own lack of success. The "cheap shears" with which his sister carefully clips the hair above his "young clear neck" further signal his vulnerability: one missed stroke, and he will bleed. "Sunday shuts down" and "twilight and bulb define": the present-tense verbs delineate the situation over which the siblings have no control; their impotence is further signaled by the present participles in the final stanza—"meeting," "seeing," "splitting," "beating"—especially the juxtaposition of the "sharp blades splitting" and the "blue vein ... beating." This final image, whose steady motion recalls the automatic movement of the drugstore arrow, underlines the domination of the neon sign over the human body, signaling their common reification in an "impersonal" regime of capital accumulation.

In "Boy with His Hair Cut Short," we see how the poem's characters are being interpellated, that is, how they misrecognize their situation. They cannot see beyond their brown room; what Marx called the "dull compulsion of economic relations" confines them within the limits of dominant ideology. But how is the reader being interpellated? By supplying the means to connect the dots and defetishize what appears to be given, the poem invites the reader to "think totality," to see through and past appearances to the essential capitalist social relations that structure the characters' lives. The poem's closing image of the red sign and the shears reminds us that capital can kill. But the arrow is mechanical, while the girl is human; the pulsing vein has the potential to contest and resist the power of the pulsing arrow. The arrow has created the conditions making for the thin hands and pulsing vein; but the history that hurts can move ahead via its bad side. Hands and blood—images that allude to conventions in proletarian literature signaling the potential for dialectical reversal—obliquely allude to the class struggle that can negate and sublate the present situation. The boy and girl may never think beyond the limits of their room; but readers may be inspired to put their shoulders to the wheel of revolutionary social transformation. Despite its confinement to a bulb-lit twentieth-century room, the poem rejects the notion that there is no alternative (TINA); alienation implies the possibility for dis-alienation. The poem draws its poetry from the future.

In connection with Xu Lizhi's "I Swallowed an Iron Moon," which addresses the situation of hi-tech factory workers in twenty-first-century

China, the mandate to "always historicize" carries particular poignancy. Sometimes called "the Foxconn poet," Xu published the poem first on the internet; it appeared in an anthology of migrant worker poetry after he committed suicide in 2014 by jumping from a seventeenth floor. In 2010 there was a spate of such worker suicides at Foxconn's plant in Shenzhen, China, the largest factory in the world where Apple's electronic components are assembled; in response, the company set up nets around the factory buildings.[1] In 2011, Apple earned an average profit of $400,000 per employee, most of them in China.[2] As of this writing in 2018, "appalling conditions" still prevail at Foxconn, where precarious workers, in order to keep their jobs, are forced to work 100 hours a week producing the Amazon Kindle during peak season.[3]

Bitterly reversing the association of the moon with serenity and love in classical Chinese poetry, Xu's speaker repeatedly "swallows" the entities and processes—"industrial wastewater ... unemployment forms ... labor, poverty, pedestrian bridges"—that have mapped out his "rusted-out life"; notably, his catalogue renders equivalent the abstract ("labor, poverty") and the concrete ("unemployment forms ... pedestrian bridges") in a blur of alienated experience. The lack of end punctuation implies that living labor has now been completely absorbed into the dead labor embodied in the machine, to be then regurgitated in the form of an iPhone. While his individual body revolts against what he has ingested, the speaker is well aware that his situation is widely shared: "our youth died young ... I spread across my country / a poem of shame." Moreover, the poem testifies to the conditions of its own production: "I swallowed" leads to "I can't swallow" to "I spread." The poem dramatically refutes any illusions we may have that the age of IT has led to enhanced human communication and greater democracy: ironically, it is the production of the very electronic devices enabling the publication of the poem on the internet that has driven the speaker to despair.

"I Swallowed an Iron Moon" brutally registers the effects of the restoration and expansion of capitalist relations of production in China, where the nationalist proclamation to be building "socialism with special Chinese characteristics" has served to paper over the growing class contradictions in a society dominated by markets and spiraling inequality (Foley 2002). While Xu's poem, like those by Arnold and Rukeyser, displays the effects of reification on millions, his contains a qualitatively heightened register to the ways in which, under conditions of real subsumption, estranged labor annihilates species being in the age of globalized capital accumulation. For Xu, alienation is not, as for Arnold, a matter of anomie essentially ungrounded in historical processes. Nor, however, is it, as for Rukeyser, a phenomenon capable of generating its dialectical negation. Xu's speaker has been lied to by a "they"—presumably the Chinese state, in conjunction with US-based capital—who promised him a job ("iron screw") but crammed an entire reified existence ("iron moon") down his throat. Evidently, he has not thought through and past the nationalism implied in the accusation that "our youth" and "my country" have been betrayed; class struggle is not in the purview of the poem. The rash of strikes in Foxconn since 2014 reveals, however, that the contradictions generating the text have by no means disappeared.

If we choose to teach these poems as a cluster treating the problem of alienation, we are challenged to come up with analytical categories that enable us to discern where the texts converge—as reactions to the *longue durée* of capitalism that they encompass in different parts of the world—and where, conversely, they require analysis specific to their moments of creation. Comparison and contrast need not entail a mechanical listing of shared and divergent traits; embedded in this pedagogical strategy is a dialectical understanding of the mediations enabling us to think totality in materialist terms.

Rebellion

We now consider the phenomenon of rebellion in connection with two famous poems that both appeared in 1919, a year of worldwide revolutionary upsurge in the wake of the Russian Revolution. The first text, William Butler Yeats's "The Second Coming," is a key text in the canon of modernism:

> Turning and turning in the widening gyre
> The falcon cannot hear the falconer;
> Things fall apart; the centre cannot hold;
> Mere anarchy is loosed upon the world,
> The blood-dimmed tide is loosed, and everywhere
> The ceremony of innocence is drowned;
> The best lack all conviction, while the worst
> Are full of passionate intensity.
>
> Surely some revelation is at hand;
> Surely the Second Coming is at hand.
> The Second Coming! Hardly are those words out

When a vast image out of *Spiritus Mundi*
Troubles my sight: somewhere in sands of the desert
A shape with lion body and the head of a man,
A gaze blank and pitiless as the sun,
Is moving its slow thighs, while all about it
Reel shadows of the indignant desert birds.
The darkness drops again; but now I know
That twenty centuries of stony sleep
Were vexed to nightmare by a rocking cradle,
And what rough beast, its hour come round at last,
Slouches towards Bethlehem to be born?

(in Yeats 1956, 184–85)

The second, Claude McKay's sonnet "If We Must Die," is a Harlem Renaissance classic:

If we must die, let it not be like hogs
Hunted and penned in an inglorious spot,
While round us bark the mad and hungry dogs,
Making their mock at our accursèd lot.
If we must die, O let us nobly die,
So that our precious blood may not be shed
In vain; then even the monsters we defy
Shall be constrained to honor us though dead!
O kinsmen! we must meet the common foe!
Though far outnumbered let us show us brave,
And for their thousand blows deal one death-blow!
What though before us lies the open grave?
Like men we'll face the murderous, cowardly pack,
Pressed to the wall, dying, but fighting back!

(in McKay 2004, 177–78)

Whereas the texts in our cluster on alienation spanned over one hundred and fifty years, those chosen here respond to the same historical matrix, albeit in profoundly different ways.

Yeats's famous poem has been the source of repeated borrowings: how often have you heard variants on "widening gyre," "things fall apart," "the centre cannot hold," and the "rough beast / Slouching toward Bethlehem" in literary works or popular culture? For the poem's speaker, everything is out of control. The "widening gyre"—referencing a key concept in Yeats's personal cosmology (Yeats 2013 [1925])—describes a spiraling centripetal movement toward generalized chaos when the gravitational force exerted by the traditional "centre" of social order has dissolved. The reference to the medieval aristocratic sport of falconry ("the falcon cannot hear the falconer") alludes nostalgically to the hierarchical order associated with feudalism, contrasted with the "indignant desert birds" occupying the skies of the present. The "best" (presumably those responsible for maintaining order) have not risen to the occasion, while the "worst" (presumably those responsible for the "anarchy") have taken command, "loos[ing] the blood-dimmed tide" and drowning the innocent. Indeed, the conjoining of "mere anarchy" with the "blood-dimmed tide" as forces that have been "loosed" links the purposiveness of destructive human agents with the uncontrollability of natural forces; naturalization bypasses the necessity for historical analysis. The poem's speaker tries to convince himself that, in the second coming predicted in the biblical Book of Revelations, Christ will return and raise the dead for the Final Judgment. But instead of mythic redemption the speaker envisions a future in which a monstrous Anti-Christ will rule, and two millennia of Western civilization will be wiped out by an atavistic reversion to unthinking bestiality.

The dominant images in Yeats's poem contain no specific references to the Russian Revolution, the contemporaneous anticolonial upsurge in Ireland, or the intense class struggles that erupted in 1919 around the world. Yet the very absence of such references, even though by context they are implied, suggests that, for Yeats, contemporaneous historical reality cannot supply the terms of its own analysis. There is a crisis in the hegemony of dominant ideologies; the deep structure of events has to be explained by means of the extra-historical (or supra-historical) vocabulary of myth. Although the Sphinx-like figure of the "rough beast" whose "hour [has] come round at last" lacks a specific historical referent, its emergence from a distinctly non-European zone racializes its spectral monstrosity. Its "blank and pitiless gaze," "slow thighs," and "slouching" movement suggest the mental vacuity, brute sexuality and simian posture variously attributed to inferior peoples in the writings of influential reactionary pseudoscientists like Madison Grant and Lothrop Stoddard, who viewed contemporaneous revolutionary activity on the part of the world's darker-skinned peoples as a threat to the ruling "great race" of Nordic descent (Grant 1918; Stoddard 1920). Moreover, Stoddard would choose the metaphor of a "rising tide of color" to signify the threat to the defensive "dikes" of European and US culture; Yeats's "blood-dimmed tide," drowning the "ceremony of innocence," suggests the trope's widely shared usage. Finally, Yeats's portrayal of his "rough beast" that is heading to Bethlehem to be born, thereby supplanting Christ, obliquely echoes the obstetrical trope in the writings of Marx, which influenced the representation of the Russian Revolution as a revolutionary birth in the discourse of contemporaneous literary radicalism (Foley 2014, 55–65). The central images in "The Second Coming" reflect a class struggle occurring at the level of the poetic image. The poem is often taught as a register to a general sense of angst prevailing after World War I.[4] When fully historicized, however, the poem's central metaphors and tropes invite symptomatic interpretation as rhetorical mediations that at once acknowledge and mystify the crisis of capitalist legitimacy characterizing the revolutionary moment of the poem's production.

"If We Must Die" offers a vision of revolutionary struggle that contrasts powerfully with the prediction of chaos set forth in "The Second Coming." Like Yeats, McKay does not make explicit reference to the poem's formative historical moment. Yet it matters if we know that the poem was written in response to the so-called "red summer" of 1919, when African American inhabitants of dozens of cities fought back against invasions by racist mobs; the "red" in "red summer" referred to the blood flowing in the nation's streets, as well as to the wave of postwar political radicalism inspired by the Russian Revolution. The poem was printed in the pro-communist *Liberator* in August 1919 and rapidly reprinted in the *Crusader* and the *Messenger*, both radical black journals that enthusiastically supported the working-class revolution halfway around the world (Foley 2003, 60–68). While "If We Must Die" can be read in isolation from other works by McKay, it is best historicized in connection with his entire cluster of revolutionary and antiracist sonnets from this moment of crisis and change. It is also usefully read alongside "Exhortation, Summer 1919," in which the reader is challenged to "look to the East" [Russia], where a "new birth rends the old earth" enabling "[g]hosts ... [to] turn flesh, throwing off the grave's disguise" (in McKay 2004, 176). For McKay, 1919 meant that the specter haunting the capitalist world might indeed become flesh, and that a new social order might emerge from the womb of the old.

From a pedagogical standpoint, McKay's poem invites an image-by-image comparison with "The Second Coming." Where Yeats associates revolution with a "rough beast," McKay invokes animal imagery to turn the tables on a long history of racist ideology and practice: the white attackers are compared to "mad and hungry dogs"—a trope used conventionally by slaveholders describing rebelling slaves—while the

African Americans resisting assault by the "monsters" in the "murderous, cowardly pack" are proclaimed *not* to be "like hogs / Hunted and penned in an inglorious spot." De-naturalization is essential to the assertion of humanity. The fighters are described as "kinsmen" who, willing to "nobly die," will earn "honor"; the anachronistic overtones of this language, invoking premodern notions of valor, hijack the language of gentility often deployed to rationalize the regime of racism. Where Yeats alludes to feudalism nostalgically, McKay insists that true "nobility" is shown through the affirmation of solidarity leading to a different social order. McKay's deft use of the sonnet form reinforces his revolutionary theme: the turn (the "volta") between the first eight lines (octet) and the last six (sestet) shifts the declaration from negative to positive, defensive to offensive; while the final couplet, rhyming "murderous, cowardly pack" with "fighting back," captures the dialectical emergence of resistance from oppression.

McKay's repurposing of the genre of the sonnet, conventionally associated with lyric contemplations on love, mortality, or art, is itself a radical act, asking the reader to rethink what it means to love, what it means to contemplate life and death—and what the role of poetry may be in causing this rethinking of what it means to be human. McKay's use of the sonnet form illustrates the relative autonomy of literary genres and asks us to reconsider widely accepted notions about the relationship between literary texts and political action. At once affirming present-day rebellion against racism and inspiring future resistance, the poem queries and expands the limits of familiar conceptions of literature and literariness. We are reminded of Brecht's notion that art is a hammer rather than a mirror—as well as of Marx's statement that the point of philosophy is not just to interpret the world, but to change it. While "If We Must Die" does not contain an explicit call for social revolution, its representation of humanity enhanced through "fighting back" has political implications extending beyond its immediate context of the "red summer" of 1919; the poem calls upon its authorial audience to imagine, and participate in, comparable rebellions of their own.

Nation

We will now examine a cluster of texts that address the nation and its ideological correlative, nationalism. All three texts address key events and situations in approximately the first century of US history.

The first is a work familiar to most people who have attended school in the United States: The Preamble to the US Constitution (1787):

We the People of the United States, in Order to form a more perfect Union, establish Justice, insure domestic Tranquility, provide for the common defence, promote the general Welfare, and secure the Blessings of Liberty to ourselves and our Posterity, do ordain and establish this Constitution for the United States of America.[5]

The Preamble establishes the principles presumably motivating the text that follows and claims the common interests of the "People of the United States" as its basis. The Preamble consists of a single sentence, in which a series of secondary verbs ("form … establish … insure … provide … secure") lead logically to the main action ("do ordain and establish this Constitution"). It is very rational and confident, signaling the ideological basis for the transcendence of feudalism and monarchy—including the "divine right of kings"—by a bourgeois revolution guided by Enlightenment reason and premised upon the notion that meritocracy should supplant aristocracy. Along with the Declaration of Independence and the rest of the Constitution, this text supplies an important ideological basis for the doctrine of American Exceptionalism, that is, the claim that the United States is, among the nations of the world, uniquely positioned to embody universal ideals of freedom and democracy.

Yet the Preamble raises as many questions as it appears to resolve. Who is the "we" claiming to be "the People"? Who is being interpellated here? After all, enslaved African Americans, unable to "secure the Blessings of Liberty to [them]selves or [their] Posterity," were not considered "People" (even though, to skew the apportioning of legislative representatives at the federal level to states dominated by the plantation economy, each enslaved person was considered three-fifths of a human being). The native peoples whose lands were seized to make room for incipient capitalism were not included among those enjoying the "Blessings of Liberty," much less able to pass on to "Posterity" their relationship to the earth. Women were unable to hold property or have full legal status, let alone vote, as were white men not possessing a requisite amount of wealth. Clearly, then, the "we" possessing metonymic status in "We the People" consists of those white men possessing enough property to qualify them to participate in the founding Constitutional Convention of 1789 (Beard 1957 [1913]). The text calls to mind Marx and Engels's observation, in *The*

German Ideology, that every ruling class, while promoting and articulating its own interests, proclaims its outlook to be a universal one.

The phrases involving some of the secondary verbs suggest, however, that certain conflicts are being sutured over in the text's assertion of its capacity to speak for the nation. "To form a more perfect Union" implies that the existing "union" of social forces needs shoring up; "insure domestic Tranquility" suggests that, in the wake of the recent victory over the British, there persist revolts of the less privileged like the recent Shays's Rebellion; "provide for the common defence" leaves it to the "deciders" to determine who is to be defended and who—especially among the despoiled native peoples—is to be attacked, indeed eliminated; "promote the general Welfare" is premised on the notion that there *is* a general welfare, and that the writers of this text know what that is. Even as the document announces a series of certainties, it implicitly acknowledges the shadowy presence of those demographic sectors whose claims to inclusion in "the people" would require a different set of social arrangements. It bears noting, finally, that the word "establish" occurs twice in a single sentence. One meaning of this word—to create something of permanence—is "stable," meaning fixed; another meaning—to cause something to be widely known and accepted—proposes that this fixity is to be seen as legitimate. This odd redundancy in the framers' otherwise spare discourse suggests that, like other expressions of dominant ideology, the text masks the provisional—even precarious—nature of the hegemony it is attempting to bring into being.

Our second text, describing the mid-to-late nineteenth-century "settling" of the West, is a 1987 poem by Gloria Anzaldúa titled "We Call Them Greasers":

> I found them here when I came.
>
> They were growing corn on their small ranchos
> raising cattle, horses
> smelling of woodsmoke and sweat.
> They knew their betters:
> took off their hats
> placed them over their hearts,
> lowered their eyes in my presence.
>
> Weren't interested in bettering themselves,
> why they didn't even own the land but shared it.

Wasn't hard to drive them off,
cowards they were, no backbone.
I showed 'em a piece of paper with some writing
tole 'em they owed taxes
had to pay right away or be gone by mañana.
By the time me and my men had waved
that same piece of paper to all the families
it was all frayed at the ends.

Some loaded their chickens children wives and pigs
into rickety wagons, pans and tools dangling
clanging from all sides.
Couldn't take their cattle—
during the night my boys had frightened them off.
Oh, there were a few troublemakers
who claimed we were the intruders.
Some even had land grants
and appealed to the courts.
It was a laughing stock
them not even knowing English.
Still some refused to budge,
even after we burned them out.

And the women—well I remember one in particular.

She lay under me whimpering.
I plowed into her hard
kept thrusting and thrusting
felt him watching from the mesquite tree
heard him keening like a wild animal
in that instant I felt such contempt for her
round face and beady black eyes like an Indian's.
Afterwards I sat on her face until
her arms stopped flailing,
didn't want to waste a bullet on her.
The boys wouldn't look me in the eyes.
I walked up to where I had tied her man to the tree
and spat in his face. Lynch him, I told the boys.

(Anzaldúa 1999 [1987], 156–57)

In its portrayal of an unnamed speaker who evidently considers himself entitled to steal, rape, and murder at will, Anzaldúa's poem displays the monstrous potential encoded in the Founders' "we." American Exceptionalism has here morphed into Manifest Destiny—that is, the doctrine that the United States was mandated by God and fate to extend west and south across North America, eliminating as needed any non-European peoples inhabiting pre-class societies. While an individual reminiscence, the poem encapsulates a genocidal narrative in which sexism, racism, and contempt for indigenous peoples are shored up by nationalist dogmas proclaiming the supremacy of individualism and private property. Identifying himself with the spirit of Columbus ("I found them here when I came"), the speaker justifies the subjugation of the people he calls "greasers" by the fact that they "didn't even own the land but shared it," and thus "weren't interested in bettering themselves." Although his claim to have the law on his side is spurious—the piece of paper he waves at them has no legal status, whereas some of the people he dispossesses have land grants—this does not matter in the wake of the Indian Removal Act of 1830 or the seizure of mestizo peasant lands after the Mexican-American War of 1846–48. In this phase of primitive accumulation called pioneering, the state is defined by the naked power of wealth; violence is the principal historical and geographical presupposition of the expansion of capital. The speaker's rape and murder of the woman, whom he "plowed into hard," and the subsequent lynching of "her man," complete his seizure of the land and its conversion into a profit-yielding asset. And while "the boys" (presumably working-class white men under his command) will not look him in the eye—and they and their descendants may never themselves be homesteaders on any of the stolen land—in carrying out his patriarchal bidding they become complicit in the racialized project of settler colonialism.

Although it may seem to be loading the dice to juxtapose the Preamble to the US Constitution with the harrowing account of theft and violence in "We Call Them Greasers," a historical materialist understanding of the role of the state in capital accumulation invites us to link the eminently civilized and rational prose of the Founding Fathers with the crude brutality evinced by the speaker in Anzaldúa's poem. The realities of slavery, class struggle, rape, and genocide are masked in the enlightened language of the Preamble: yet one "we" leads to the next "we." The framers of the Constitution claimed to be speaking in the best interests of society as a whole when they set up the rules for statecraft in the emerging bourgeois era. The speaker in Anzaldúa's poem, by contrast, is defined by an identity blatantly based upon the hate-filled "thingifi-cation" of others; for him, the term "greaser" usefully mediates between personal greed and government policy. Yet the Founding Fathers' belief in the sanctity of private property as the basis upon which the citizens of the United States might "secure the Blessings of Liberty" sets the stage for the rapacity of Anzaldúa's unnamed landgrabber. Readers of "We Call Them Greasers" are interpellated in such a way as to be repulsed by the poem's speaking voice—Anzaldúa's harsh irony makes it near-impossible to identify with the poem's "we." But we—"*we*"—should not become too self-congratulatory in our sense of moral distance; her speaker is, after all, a native son, offspring of the Signers of 1776 and 1789. Those in our time who persist in using the term "greaser"—or any similar slur—may not advocate rape and genocide; but they render themselves susceptible to interpellation by the anti-immigrant propaganda that entraps them in a twenty-first-century version of the class-based dilemma faced by "the boys."

The US Founding Fathers once again come to the fore in the third text in this cluster, Frederick Douglass's "What to the Slave is the Fourth of July?", a speech that he delivered on July 5, 1852, to an anti-slavery society in Rochester, NY. In this oration, Douglass castigated his listeners for abandoning the path followed by the nation's founders of the century before, men whose "denunciations of tyrants" had led to rebellion. Invoking the familiar metaphor linking a nation to a ship of state, he asserted that the Declaration of Independence "is the ring-bolt to the chain of your nation's destiny." The Constitution, moreover, is "a GLORIOUS LIBERTY DOCUMENT" (Douglass 1996, 112–13, 127). (A ringbolt is a metal bolt with a ring attached, through which a rope or a chain can be drawn; it can be used to attach a ship to a dock.) The nation's hypocrisy in abandoning the principles laid out in these documents, he asserted, was epitomized in the celebration of freedom and independence on the Fourth of July, which:

> reveals to [the slave], more than all other days in the year, the gross injustice and cruelty to which he is the constant victim. To him, your celebration is a sham; your boasted liberty, an unholy license; your national greatness, swelling vanity; your sounds of rejoicing are empty and heartless; your denunciations of tyrants, brass fronted impudence; your shouts of liberty and equality, hollow mockery.... There is not a nation on the earth guilty of practices, more shocking and bloody, than are the people of these United States. (Douglass 1996, 118–19)

Douglass's accusatory use of "you" and "your" left his audience with a stark choice: either they would accept the apostrophe that made them pro-slavery or the interpellation that recruited them to the abolitionist cause.

Douglass's 1852 speech needs to be historicized in the context of the contemporaneous debate within the abolitionist movement over the legitimacy of the Constitution, since other prominent leaders, including William Lloyd Garrison, were proclaiming that this document was pro-slavery: those committed to freeing the enslaved, they urged, should secede from the Union. Moreover, the new horrors imposed by the 1850 Fugitive Slave Law—which required all citizens, north as well as south, to turn over to legal authorities anyone suspected of being a runaway—were posing increasingly urgent moral choices on individuals and communities: what was the relationship between the people, the nation, and the law? In proclaiming the transcendent authority of the Declaration and the Constitution, Douglass asserted an originalist patriotism that gained him access to the political premises shared by the majority in his audience who were not ready to contemplate secession. Given the force of his condemnation of the nation's ongoing hypocrisy, however, it is noteworthy that Douglass's chosen metaphor of ringbolt and chain, which he deploys four times in the course of the speech with reference to the ship of state, summons up at the same time the quintessential symbol of enslavement in abolitionist rhetoric, namely, the iron shackle: "I hear the mournful wail of millions!" exclaims Douglass, "whose chains, heavy and grievous yesterday, are, to-day, rendered more intolerable by the jubilee shouts that reach them" (Douglass 1996, 116).

How are we to read Douglass's contradictory use of the image of the ringbolt and the chain? Reading suspiciously, we could view the trope as an eruption from the political unconscious, symptomatically acknowledging the impossibility of asserting that the ship of state—originally constructed, after all, by slaveholders, and inevitably linked to the ships of the middle passage—can in fact be safely brought to harbor and tied to the nation's shore. Reading strategically, we can interpret Douglass's invocation of the disparate associations of ringbolts and chains as a deft ploy aimed at focusing his listeners' attention on the impossibility of conjoining two such images in a common discourse. His listeners would have to choose which meaning of "chain" would correspond with their sense of themselves as a "people" comprising a "nation." My preference is for the latter interpretation: Douglass had a masterful control of irony. Whether we read Douglass's use of ringbolt/chain trope as evidence of an uneasy political unconscious or an ingenious exercise in dialectics, however, it clearly invokes an oppositional version of American Exceptionalism: the nation cannot be true to its stated principles so long as it permits the existence of slavery. In its day, Douglass's invocation of the founding documents of the past to blast the moral cowardice of the present was a radical act of interpellation. But one era's challenge to the status quo can become another's mainstream doctrine. Extending from Douglass's time to present-day activist calls to "take back our democracy," liberal patriotism has as long a history as does the reactionary conception of Manifest Destiny expressed by Anzaldúa's apostle of genocide. The challenge confronting Marxist critics of US literature and history—indeed, of any nationally defined literature and history—is not only to expose the role played by overtly conservative nationalist doctrines in reinforcing the hegemony of capital, past and present, but also to examine the hold that presumably progressive versions of nationalism continue to have upon both individuals and social movements seeking to counter social inequality without challenging its basis in capitalism. The need for solidarity in opposition to ruling-class ideologies and practices can devolve into a mere politics of inclusion; the nationalism that shores up imperialism can be rearticulated as the "*e pluribus unum*" (Latin for "out of many, one") that sutures over fundamental class contradictions. Even "power to the people," a chant often heard at rallies against social injustice, displays the ambiguities involved in attempts to leverage one kind of nationalism against another. Who actually is meant by "we the people"?

War

Closely linked to the representation of nation is the representation of war; all wars (at least all modern wars) have been waged in the name of the nation. Especially in the modern era, few serious writers have celebrated the carnage of the battlefield. When it comes to examining the causes and consequences of war, however, as well as the dominant ideologies invoked in its justification, writers can differ widely. We'll first consider two short poems that came out of World War I—John McCrae's "In Flanders Fields" (1919 [1915]) and Carl Sandburg's "The Grass" (1950 [1918])—and then examine a passage from a novel written some two decades later, Dalton Trumbo's *Johnny Got His Gun* (1989 [1939]). We focus here on a single war in order to enable closer historicization and avoid the cliché that all wars are fundamentally the same. Our three texts are to a degree limited by the standpoints of their writers, all North American white men; the colonial nature of World War I, for instance, is not addressed in these texts. The advantage gained from this restriction, however, is that these three works, especially when taken as a cluster for pedagogical purposes, enable us to focus upon questions of ideology often sidelined when the brutal contents of war literature—from Homer's *Iliad* (2011 [c. 700–800 BCE]) to Tim O'Brien's *The Things They Carried* (1990)—occupy the foreground of our attention.

"In Flanders Fields," by the Canadian physician and Lieutenant Colonel John McCrae, was written in mourning for a fallen comrade after McCrae visited the site of the battlefield at Ypres in Belgium, where there had been over 200,000 casualties, and chemical weapons had been used on a massive scale:

> In Flanders fields the poppies blow
> Between the crosses, row on row,
> That mark our place; and in the sky
> The larks, still bravely singing, fly
> Scarce heard amid the guns below.
>
> We are the Dead. Short days ago
> We lived, felt dawn, saw sunset glow,
> Loved and were loved, and now we lie
> In Flanders fields.
>
> Take up our quarrel with the foe:
> To you from failing hands we throw
> The torch; be yours to hold it high.
> If ye break faith with us who die
> We shall not sleep, though poppies grow
> In Flanders fields.
>
> (McCrae 1919, 1)

The contrast between life and death in McCrae's poem is wrenching: the poppies flourish, the birds sing. Men who just a short time before "loved and were loved" are now gone. The insistent rhymes with "blow"—"row," "below," "glow," "throw," "grow"—as well as the repetition of "in Flanders fields" at the beginning and the end, reinforce the funereal mood. The deployment of the first-person plural pronoun here in the text's present-tense address to the reader is chilling: "We are the Dead."

But who is this "we"? At Ypres, the casualties from all nations—the Germans on one side, the British, Belgians, French, and Canadians on the other—were immense; the reader might at first think that *all* the dead soldiers (the vast majority drafted or recruited from the ranks of the working classes of the nations involved, as well as colonies) might be included in this pronoun's universal appeal. The final stanza, however, enlists pity for the dead of only one side; the authorial audience (addressed in the biblical-sounding "ye") is urged not to protest the war, but to "take up our quarrel with the foe." The reasons for the war ("*our* quarrel") remain unexplored, however, and the "foe" remains unspecified, simply defined by its antinomic relationship to "we." The imagery of passing the torch—symbolic of heroic military continuity from the first marathon runner onward—ennobles the combat in which the young men perished. Nationalism is a matter of honor; to refuse to continue the fight is to "break faith," to allow those who died to have died in vain. The poppies that grew spontaneously over the bodies at Ypres are now institutionalized. While McCrae did not intend his poem—handwritten in a notebook at the site of the battle—for publication, it is now ritually read, and poppies ritually displayed, on days set aside for honoring dead soldiers in the United States and the former British Empire, accompanied by the singing of national anthems.

While "In Flanders Fields" appears to be a simple, stand-alone statement of patriotism, it is haunted by its negation: not the armies of other nations, but the spirit of proletarian internationalism that rendered moot the nationalism upon which the poem—and the war—was premised. For a principal dilemma faced by the general staff of all the armies involved in the war's Western front, from the fall of 1914 onward, was the passive resistance on the part of large numbers of working-class soldiers uninspired by nationalist rhetoric. This rebellion first took shape in the so-called "Christmas Truce" of December 1914, when troops from the opposed armies, calling a rolling series of unofficial ceasefires, shared food and drink and played football in the no-man's land between the trenches (M. Brown 2007). This inability of many soldiers to see the "foe" as a "foe"—manifested in escalating mutinous activity as the war continued, and contributing to the Bolshevik Revolution—is the specter that haunts the battlefield in McCrae's poem.

In "The Grass", Chicago poet Carl Sandburg, also featuring a military cemetery, lodges a searing critique of nationalist militarism and postwar ideological suturing:

Pile the bodies high at Austerlitz and Waterloo.
Shovel them under and let me work—
      I am the grass; I cover all.
And pile them high at Gettysburg
And pile them high at Ypres and Verdun.
Shovel them under and let me work.
Two years, ten years, and passengers ask the conductor:

      What place is this?
      Where are we now?

      I am the grass.
      Let me work.
                     (Sandburg 1950 [1919], 136)

Although the dating of the poem, as well as the mentions of Ypres and Verdun, suggest that Sandburg had World War I (then called the Great War) in mind, he alludes to battles from three different armed conflicts of the modern era—the Napoleonic wars of the early nineteenth century, the US Civil War, and World War I—in which the casualties were immense as generals flung huge numbers of troops into the fray. Casualties at Austerlitz numbered 35,000; over 50,000 soldiers died at Waterloo and again at Gettysburg; at Verdun the ten-month battle in the trenches took more than 300,000 lives, with the victorious French not even fully regaining the land lost in the original German offensive.[6] While the poem's use of the first person to capture the voice of the grass recalls McCrae's use of "we" to speak for the dead (or, for *some* of the dead), Sandburg's apostrophe serves quite a different end. For the grass's abrupt repeated orders to "pile the bodies high" and "shovel them under" refers not to physical burial, but to the naturalizing and dehistoricizing work performed by "conductors" of the train of dominant ideology, who blur and then efface the memories of different wars for the "passengers" on the train. Military graveyards, the poem implies, are museums laid out on turf, and therefore part of cultural apparatus of the capitalist state. Embedded in the poem's address to those who would forget is an appeal to an authorial audience who should get off the train of official memory and instead ponder, "Where are we now?"

Ironically recalling Walt Whitman's *Leaves of Grass*, where grass figures as a symbol of democracy and renewal, Sandburg's poem treats grass as a means of "covering" up historical memory through a reified invocation of nature. "I am the grass. Let me work": the poem critically reveals the labor involved in suturing over the results of wars where vast numbers of rank-and-file troops died for the greater glory of the nation. The broadside nature of Sandburg's denunciation of nationalism, however, obscures a fault line in his critique—namely, that the Union victory at Gettysburg, despite the immense toll of the dead, turned the tide of the US Civil War and hastened the demise of slavery. Who is the "we"? Where would "we" be if the South had won the Civil War? "The Grass," for all its satirical force, displays the dangers of over-generalizing, even about wars ostensibly fought in the name of the "nation." Not all wars are the same, even if the ruling-class memory factory would have us lose track of their causes and results.

Set in a hospital room in an undesignated nation at an undesignated time following the Great War, Trumbo's *Johnny Got His Gun* features a horribly injured war veteran named Joe Bonham, who, while lacking legs, arms, vision, hearing, or even a face, has remained fully conscious. He is the living dead, the quintessential unknown soldier. Ironically alluding to "In Flanders Fields," the novel is divided into sections titled "The Dead"—where Joe thinks in fragments—and "The Living," where he fuses his scattered memories into an increasingly totalized understanding of the nature of imperialist war. Gradually recalling both personal experiences and memories of the militaristic propaganda accompanying his induction into the army, Joe links his own situation of that of "little guys" over thousands of years: Roman galley slaves, builders of the Egyptian pyramids, blinded and chained Carthaginian guards of treasure. He closes with a ringing call for revolutionary proletarian internationalism.

> We will use the guns you force upon us, we will use them to defend our very lives, and the menace to our lives does not lie on the other side of a nomansland that was set apart without our consent it lies within our own boundaries here.... Give us the slogans and we will turn them into realities. Sing the battle hymns and we will take them up where you left off. Not one, not ten, not ten thousand, not a million, not ten millions, not a hundred millions but a billion, two billions of us all— the people of the world.... We will be alive and we will walk and talk and eat and sing and laugh and feel and love and bear our children in tranquility, in security, in decency, in peace. You plan the wars, you masters of men—plan the wars and point the way and we will point the gun. (Trumbo 1989 [1939], 242–43)

There is no one to hear this message in the pages of the novel; having attempted to reach out to the world by rocking his torso in Morse code, but learning that his desire to speak is in violation of regulations, Joe remains locked in the prison of his body. But the text interpellates a reader who hears Joe's summons to turn the guns around: not just on the rulers of the United States, but on all the "patriots ... spawners of slogans ... masters of men" who would use the rhetoric of nationalism to divide the "two billions of us all—the people of the world." The "boundaries" that matter are not between nations, but within them. There is no such thing as "our quarrel" defined in nationalist terms; the "foe" is those who rule the nation. The corollary of the necessity for proletarian internationalism is the necessity for class-based civil war, what Lenin called "revolutionary defeatism" (Lenin, *April Theses*). The theme of dialectical inversion is embodied in the novel's title, which ironically echoes the refrain in the highly patriotic 1917 George M. Cohan song titled "Over There": "Johnny get your gun ... Put Hun on the run" (Cohan 1917). Trumbo's Joe "got his gun"—though it remains for the novel's readers to take up their own. A ghost from an imperialist war two decades in the past, Joe Bonham is also a specter from the future, signaling the presence of the "not-yet in the now."

Money

Now we come to money, for Marx the supreme embodiment of exchange value and abstract labor; the "pimp between man and his need"; the medium at once enabling and obscuring the operations of capital; the thing that is most needed for survival and yet withheld from so many. Money figures centrally in the literary representations of societies where it reigns supreme—from Shakespeare's *The Merchant of Venice* (2011 [1596–99]) to Honoré de Balzac's *Old Goriot* (1835; English translation 1999 [1860]), from Charles Dickens's *Hard Times* (2003 [1854]) to Arthur Miller's *Death of a Salesman* (1996 [1949]). We'll start by considering the role of money in two canonical works of fiction about women in the marriage market—Jane Austen's *Pride and Prejudice* (1961 [1813]) and Edith Wharton's *The House of Mirth* (1994 [1905])—and then examine its dramatically different treatment in "Always the Same" (1994 [1932]), a forthrightly anti-imperialist poem by Langston Hughes. The rationale for constructing this unusual conceptual cluster will, I hope, become clear when we recall Walter Benjamin's observation that "every document of civilization is simultaneously a document of barbarism."

Pride and Prejudice famously begins with the narrator's tongue-in-cheek remark that "It is a truth universally acknowledged that a single man in possession of a good fortune must be in want of a wife" (Austen 1961 [1813], 5). As the novel's many admirers know, the validity of this statement is immediately called into question by the following conversation, where it becomes clear that, while the status-eager Mrs. Bennet is a firm believer in the statement's truth, her sardonic husband begs to differ. We start the novel, in other words, with what appears to be a false universal. The ensuing characterizations of the Bennet daughters further dispute its general applicability: the giddy Kitty and Lydia may be inveterate husband-hunters, but the sober-minded Jane and the witty and independent Elizabeth—with whom the reader is especially urged to identify—place integrity before money—even though when their father dies each of them stands to inherit only £40–50 per year. Yet economics does indeed constrain the choices available to the Bennet sisters, since as women they are unable to inherit the modest patrimony that instead will be passed along to their male cousin, the blowhard Mr. Collins, to whom the estate is entailed by primogeniture—that is, the sexist laws stipulating that only males could inherit land. The family is not exactly poor, but they are barely members of the landed squirearchy, with an income of merely £2,000 to support a family of seven; moreover, the fact that Mrs. Bennet's brother, Mr. Gardiner, lives in London and is "in trade"—that is, he makes his living (amount unspecified) as a merchant—associates the Bennets with the decidedly non-aristocratic urban business world. These determining circumstances are complicated by Elizabeth's refusal to marry her repulsive cousin; by the strong mutual attraction that develops between Jane and the wealthy Charles Bingley, the "single man in possession of a good fortune" (estimated by Mrs. Bennet to be £4000–5000) who has just moved into the neighborhood; and by the appearance of Bingley's best friend, the fabulously wealthy (worth at least £10,000 per year) and intolerably snooty (or so it seems) Fitzwilliam Darcy, master of Pemberley, a massive estate in Derbyshire. Fitzwilliam Darcy and Elizabeth Bennet are, of course, irresistibly drawn to each other when they meet at various teas and balls; but, as befits the conventions of a comic plot, their union is long deferred by a series of mutual misunderstandings, as well as by the need for each of them to undergo an internal process of moral chastening through the relinquishment of their varying degrees of pride and prejudice.

Pride and Prejudice is a classic—perhaps *the* classic—romantic comedy, a novel of manners in which a cross-class marital alliance serves at once to delight the reader with a satiric commentary on the habits and practices of the upper classes while ensuring that all will be well if the best representatives of all social groups, whether merchants or squires or landed aristocrats, learn to appreciate one another as individuals. The novel's clear critique of the notion of inherited aristocracy is borne out by the characterological parallels between the boorish behavior of Darcy's aptly named aunt, Lady Catherine de Bourgh, the moral crassness of Lydia Bennet, and the obtuse narcissism of Mr. Collins. By contrast, the growing friendship between Darcy, Mr. Bennet, and the Gardiners at the novel's end embodies the transcendence of artificial class barriers through the mutual recognition of honesty, intelligence, and loyalty as the markers of true gentility. The character system informing the novel's implied moral judgments thus posits that individual rectitude trumps class hierarchy. The novel's meritocratic stance is compounded by its strong feminist argument that the world will be a far healthier place if women are not treated like reified assets on the marriage market but instead valued for their moral leadership; it contains an implicit call for broadening the gendered demographic to which post-feudal bourgeois freedoms should be extended. The novel flaunts the conventions of romantic comedy to the extent that a woman's marriage to "a single man in possession of a good fortune"—that is, reaching the altar—is portrayed not as the fulfillment of a goal but as the reward for not being driven by that goal. At the same time, given Jane's and Elizabeth's eminently good luck in marrying men whom they love who also turn out to be very rich, the false universal with which the novel began turns out to be not all that false.

Although Austen's crisp dialogue, skillful plot manipulations, and valorization of female intelligence have made *Pride and Prejudice* a great favorite for over two hundred years, especially with girls and women, it bears noting that the novel's treatment of money matters is insistently myopic. For, while the incomes of the different families figure prominently in the plot, the sources of these incomes, and especially of Darcy's immense fortune, are shielded from view. We are told that Pemberley comprises hundreds of acres; yet the human beings who labor on the land, and who yield the agrarian surplus enabling the rentier Darcy to live as lavishly as he wishes, are completely invisible. As Raymond Williams has observed, Austen is "more exact about income, which is disposable, than about acres, which have to be worked" (R. Williams 1993, 115). While there are housemaids scurrying around in the background, the closest we come to seeing a servant with a name is the loyal Mrs. Reynolds, who testifies to Darcy's beneficence to his tenant farmers ("affable to the poor

... the best landlord and master ... that ever lived" (Austen 1961 [1813], 207–8); while she holds the housekeeping keys, she is an unproductive worker, creating no wealth but presumably being paid out of revenue to maintain discipline among the sizeable staff, who are also paid out of revenue. Any income from the extraction of surplus from the productive laborers on Darcy's estate, or from investments elsewhere in the world that would be deposited into Darcy's London bank account, is similarly effaced. Despite its grandeur, then, Pemberley is, like the money that has gone into its construction and maintenance, a gigantic fetish, seemingly not dependent on value-creating social conditions. The source of the Gardiners' income from "trade," that is, merchant capital, is similarly obscured—even though any marketing in early nineteenth-century London would have been based upon the merchant's buying cheap and selling dear commodities having their source in exploited labor, either in England or elsewhere in its global capitalist networks.

In *Pride and Prejudice*, the class struggle, such as it is, occurs entirely on the level of those propertied classes freed from the obligation to labor for others; it is fought out in the drawing-room realm of the novel of manners. Austen's insistence on individual probity as the basis of moral judgment masks the sources of the wealth that enables moral judgment to be (or appear to be) a matter of free choice for free subjects. The reader who finds herself cheering for the humbling of Lady Catherine and the removal of barriers between Elizabeth Bennet and Fitzwilliam Darcy is rendered complicit in this fantasy of an ethics independent of economic compulsion. The text's interpellation of its reader as a pleased participant in the conventions of romantic comedy requires that the conditions enabling the extraction of surplus—whether from peasant or proletarian labor—be omitted from view. Yet, set in a time and place when enclosure had created hardship for large sectors of England's rural population, and violent resistance to the seizure of common lands was not infrequent (R. Williams 1993; Kelly 2010), the novel is silent about the impoverishment of those sectors of the population that has enabled the emergence of individuality and choice for others. That Austen's own father was significantly involved in the capitalization of agriculture means that the novelist could not have been unaware of current economic trends (White 2013, 82). At the same time, the fact that capitalist social relations, at the time of Austen's writing, had not yet pervaded the countryside, but remained largely at the level of the formal subsumption of labor, facilitates the text's occlusion of the sources of the wealth constituting the social pyramid. In *Pride and Prejudice*, history does not hurt; there are no haunting ghosts from the past or the future; and any conflict between residual and emergent forces in society is readily contained in a story about love and marriage that makes for eminently pleasurable reading.

But not all satirical novels of manners treating the position of women in the upper echelons of capitalist society are as impervious to the lower levels, or as rosy in their outcomes, as *Pride and Prejudice*. In Wharton's *The House of Mirth*, the men "in possession of a good fortune," single or married, have the power to kill, not least because the rapacity bred on Gilded Age Wall Street permeates urban mansions and country estates alike. Lily Bart, the novel's protagonist, is a complex admixture of craven opportunism and admirable independence; she is torn between making an exchangeable commodity of her extraordinary beauty and refusing to sell herself into a marriage of status, convenience, and security. As the novel progresses, Lily Bart is increasingly at the mercy of the wealthy men who buy up property, play the stock market, and lead her to accumulate debt—over $9000, a staggering amount at the time—that she is unable to repay. Lawrence Selden, the one man who has insight into Lily Bart's situation, thinks, when he encounters her in Grand Central Station, that "she must have cost a great deal to make, that a great many dull and ugly people must, in some mysterious way, have been sacrificed to produce her" (Wharton 1994 [1905], 27). Viewing the "sapphire bracelet slipping over her wrist," he ponders that "she was so evidently the victim of the civilization which had produced her, that the links of her bracelet seemed like manacles chaining her to her fate" (Wharton 1994 [1905], 29). Lily's spontaneous decision to visit Selden's apartment unchaperoned—a violation of sexual double standards—makes her susceptible to blackmail by Mrs. Haddon, a charwoman who sees her leave and, mistaking her for the married woman with whom Selden has in fact had an affair, demands "an exorbitant sum" (Wharton 1994 [1905], 114). Through a series of mishaps, partly of Lily's own making but increasingly engineered by hostile former acquaintances discerning her lowered exchange value, this fate becomes increasingly deterministic in the Darwinian world of Fifth Avenue—a trend conveyed through a naturalistic trope describing her as a rootless plant increasingly swept along by the floods beyond her control. Lily Bart descends the social ladder; near the finale, she is fired from her job sewing spangles onto hats at a milliner's shop—staffed by thin, sallow-faced workers and patronized by Lily's wealthy former acquaintances—where she cannot keep up with the work. Although she finally inherits $10,000 from a wealthy aunt, a sum just sufficient to pay off to the last penny the money she owes to the tycoon who unsuccessfully sought her sexual favors as the price for debt cancellation, she has gained in moral stature but lost the will to live.

Conjoining the conventions of the novel of manners with those of literary naturalism and narrative tragedy, *The House of Mirth* displays the sordid underside of the gender-class-money triad resulting in such a different outcome in *Pride and Prejudice*. Where Fitzwilliam Darcy emerges as a morally upright exemplar of the class of paternalistic rentier aristocrats, the predatory men who inhabit Wharton's realm of finance capital are creatures of tooth and claw, economically parasitical and morally bankrupt. Where Jane and Elizabeth Bennet are assigned an inborn integrity, Lily Bart has been "produced" by the "sacrifices" made by "dull and ugly people." The money that establishes status but obscures exploitation in Austen's novel is grotesquely maldistributed in Wharton's, which is set in an urban environment characterized by far more advanced class polarization (Dimock 1985).

That Wharton could go only so far in connecting the dots between and among the members of different social classes is signaled, however, in a strange scene toward the novel's end that invites symptomatic reading. On the cold streets the scantily clad Lily Bart encounters a working-class woman named Nettie Struther, briefly introduced earlier as a protégé of Lawrence Selden's cousin Gerty Farish, the sole figure in the novel's character system shown to have sympathy for the poor. We now learn, for the first time, that Lily had previously contributed funds to Nettie's "timely rescue" from tuberculosis, and that this had been "one of the most satisfying incidents of [Lily's] connexion with Gerty's charitable work." As Lily holds Nettie's baby on her lap in Nettie's kitchen, she experiences a "vision of human solidarity":

> All the men and women she knew were like atoms whirling away from each other in some wild centrifugal dance; her first glimpse of the continuity of life had come to her that evening in Nettie Struther's kitchen.
>
> The poor little working-girl who had found strength to gather up the fragments of her life and build herself a shelter with them seemed to Lily to have reached the central truth of existence.... It was a meagre enough life ... but it had the frail, audacious permanence of a bird's nest built on the edge of a cliff—a mere wisp of leaves and straw, yet so put together that the lives entrusted to it may hang safely over the abyss. (Wharton 1994 [1905], 297)

Lily's intuition of a moral antithesis between the leisured wealthy and the working poor signals Wharton's recognition that problems of the ruling class cannot be solved by the ruling class; a profound reorientation of the social order is needed. Yet Nettie's sudden appearance has the feel of a *deus ex machina* (that is, an event contrived to produce a resolution that does not flow organically from the action).[7] Although the warmly human description of Nettie's kitchen indicates that people of the working class need not be "dull and ugly"—or, like the charwoman Mrs. Haddon, rapacious—the awkwardly inserted retrospective explanation of how Lily came to know Nettie in the first place testifies to Wharton's difficulties in framing a plot, or even a subplot, that would have incorporated Nettie Struther into the novel's character system. Moreover, the metaphors depicting the lives of the different classes—atomic entropy of the bourgeoisie versus nested domesticity of the proletariat—suggest widely divergent analyses of causality. In its anomalous place in the novel's plot and imagistic patterning, the scene acknowledges the depths of class polarity but cannot imagine its dialectical inversion through abolishing the basis of that polarity. Wharton, like Lawrence Selden, has only a vague sense of how the Lily Barts of the world are actually "produced"; the labor performed by the Nettie Struthers of the world remains unconnected to the money that the Lily Barts are positioned to inherit. Ironically, the text's fetishization of the origins of wealth enables Lily's conscience to be monetized at the novel's end—a conclusion notably at odds with the novel's valorization of her growing awareness of the dishonesty in her earlier self-commodification.

For both Austen and Wharton, the sources of wealth in exploited labor remain to one degree or another occluded, and morality remains a matter of individual choice. Whereas Austen's early nineteenth-century English countryside barely manifests the formal subsumption of labor to the regime of capital, however, Wharton's New York testifies to its real subsumption; the city is full of obscenely rich—and ethically challenged—people living cheek by jowl with impoverished charwomen, millinery workers, and proletarian families perched on the edge of the abyss. Compared to Austen's untroubled handling of class contradictions in *Pride and Prejudice*, the political unconscious in *The House of Mirth* is far more restive, registering the unavoidable impact of the history that hurts.

The reality depicted in Hughes's "Always the Same" would seem to be worlds apart—in just about every sense—from that portrayed in the novels of Austen and Wharton:

It is the same everywhere for me:
On the docks of Sierra Leone,
In the cotton fields of Alabama,
In the diamond mines of Kimberley,
On the coffee hills of Haiti,
The banana lands of Central America,
The streets of Harlem,
And the cities of Morocco and Tripoli.

Black:
Exploited, beaten and robbed,
Shot and killed.
Blood running into

Dollars
Pounds
Francs
Pesetas
Lire

For the wealth of the exploiters –
Blood that never comes back to me again.
Better that my blood
Runs into the deep channels of Revolution,
Runs into the strong hands of Revolution,
Stains all flags red,
Drives me away from

Sierre Leone
Kimberley
Alabama
Haiti
Central America
Harlem
Morocco
Tripoli

And all the black lands everywhere.
The force that kills,
The power that robs,
And the greed that does not care.

Better that my blood makes one with the blood
Of all the struggling workers in the world –
Till every land is free of
Dollar robbers
Pound robbers
Franc robbers
Peseta robbers
Lire robbers
Life robbers –

Until the Red Armies of the International Proletariat
Their faces, black, white, olive, yellow, brown,
Unite to raise the blood-red flag that
Never will come down!

(Hughes 1994, 165–66)

Hughes's speaker strips away any illusions his readers may have about the source of "the wealth of the exploiters"; money is a measure of the vast amounts of surplus value extracted from the labor performed by the dark-skinned workers of the world. Even as different commodities are produced at the geographically specified sites of labor, the statement that "It is the same everywhere" stresses the abstraction of labor, that is, the law of value rendering the workers' expenditures of labor power equivalent to one another, even as profits are counted up in the currencies of the different imperialist nations. The racialized violence sustaining this expropriation of surplus labor is explicit ("beaten ... shot ... killed"); the colon following "Black" indicates that exploitation and physical coercion constitute the very definition of blackness in the age of empire. The "blood running into" recalls Marx's statement that capital "comes dripping from head to foot, from every pore, with blood and dirt." In Hughes's poem, money is completely demystified. It cannot be thought of as the medium of equal exchange of wages for labor power; it at once embodies and represents the essence of social inequality.

As the speaker contemplates the draining off of his blood into vampire capital, however, the image of blood is negated and sublated as the blood that energizes Revolution, whose "channels" at once signal the trade routes of the globe and personify the arteries and veins of a collective proletariat possessing a single set of hands. As Marx predicted, the world market makes possible the unity of the workers of the world, as well as the class struggles portending that "all flags" will be "stained red." Joining all workers in their common struggle against "life robbers," the "blood-red flag" of the "Red Armies of the International Proletariat" is held up by those whose faces are not just "black" but also "white, olive, yellow, and brown." While the poem clearly draws its poetry from the future, that future must be brought into being through purposive human activity. Multi-racial working-class revolution, the "not-yet in the now" that can negate the exploitation and misery of the present, is not just desirable but necessary, not just possible but probable. But also not inevitable. In order to get through and past the regime of the "life robbers," those readers open to interpellation (some will not be) are urged to see that the utopia anticipated in the poem will be hastened or delayed by the decisions they make: will they lift the flag, or leave this task to someone else?

How does the treatment of money in Hughes's "Always the Same" relate to its featuring in *Pride and Prejudice* or *The House of Mirth*, except to emphasize that the creators of these texts inhabit nearly incommensurable ideological realms? Here is where a Marxist pedagogy premised upon "thinking totality" comes into the picture—although from outside the picture, to be sure. At a moment toward the end of Austen's romantic comedy, Elizabeth Bennet is shown to be performing the conventional female role of pouring after-dinner coffee and wondering whether Fitzwilliam Darcy will come back for a refill; at stake in this scene is whether the foundering courtship between these two tongue-tied lovers will resolve itself as both of them clearly desire (Austen 1961 [1813], 285–86; Volz 2017). In Wharton's novel of manners, jewels are constantly featured, from the bracelet of sapphires chaining Lily Bart to her fate to the immense diamond pendant bestowed as a wedding gift by the social climber Simon Rosedale upon a couple well-situated in the New York aristocracy. Wharton's implied moral judgment of the gift, refracted through the standpoints of Lily and Gerty, is that the display of wealth is grotesque; Gerty says it is "as big as a dinner plate" (Wharton 1994 [1905], 90). In both novels, the moral yardstick by which the characters' actions are judged is supplied by the conventions internal to the texts' genres; that the occluded origins of Austen's coffee or Wharton's diamond should come up for ethical consideration is beyond the limits either novel sets for itself. Thinking—and reading—historically entails that we recognize such limits. Yet, once juxtaposed with *Pride and Prejudice* and *The House of Mirth*, the questions raised by "Always the Same" cannot be simply excluded from view. Whose hands picked the beans or mined the diamonds, and under what conditions of labor? To raise the issue of commodity fetishism is not to impose anachronistic moral judgments upon either Austen or Wharton. But it is to reaffirm the hard truth of Walter Benjamin's statement that there is no document of civilization that is not at the same time a document of barbarism.

Race and Racism

As our textual analyses have been demonstrating, it is frequently impossible to separate out considerations of race and gender from considerations of class and capital when we address such matters as alienation and rebellion, nation and money. We now focus upon two works of prose fiction in which the representation of race figures centrally: Mark Twain's classic novel *Adventures of Huckleberry Finn* (1995 [1886]; in Graff and Phelan 1995) and Ralph Ellison's short story "A Party Down at the Square" (written in 1937 or 1938, in Ellison 1996). While Ellison's text is temporally located nearly a century later than Twain's, both works, set in the US South, feature the standpoint of a young white boy attempting to come to terms with the oppression of an adult black man. The fact that Ellison's work was directly influenced by Twain's brings intertextuality to the fore when we bracket the texts for analysis. Their pairing also permits us to consider how the Althusserian notion of "structure in dominance" can be helpful in theorizing the complexities of narrative causality.

Twain's novel is no doubt familiar to many readers—not least for the controversies aroused by the omnipresent use of the word "nigger," Twain's problematic portrayal of Jim, and the jarring effect of Huck's apparent reversion to Tom Sawyeresque exploitation of Jim for entertainment in the novel's controversial closing section. What can Marxist critics and teachers contribute to this controversy, which often takes the form of debates over how—or whether—to teach the novel? Regarding the frequent appearance of the "n-word," the novel's defenders routinely argue that Twain's language is historically accurate: Huck would have used no other word to describe enslaved people of African descent, and Jim would have been likely to use it as well. The 2011 revised version of the novel, in which the word "slave" is substituted for the "n-word," is decried for sacrificing truth to a misguided attempt at political correctness (C. Smith 2014). Moreover, some critics urge, close attention to the text reveals that the crucial passage where Huck decides to "go to hell" rather than turn Jim over to the slavecatchers is notable for its absence of the "n-word"; the novel is thus ironically self-critical in its usage of the term, exposing it as a slur rather than validating it as a descriptor (Henry 1991). According to this reading, the novel is Huck's *Bildungsroman*; the changing function of the "n-word" signals Huck's growing freedom from the confines of the dominant racist ideology.

Some of the novel's defenders further propose that Twain's portrayal of Jim challenges rather than confirms racialized stereotypes. The relationship that develops between Huck and Jim on the raft, which famously takes shape as a symbol of freedom, demonstrates that, when sequestered from the toxic influence of the shore, the two experience an egalitarian relationship enabled by the natural setting; their trip down the river takes them through what is—or at least ought to be—the nation's democratic heartland. Jim, the only adult male in the novel capable of selfless love, substitutes for Huck's abusive father, nurturing the boy and giving him moral guidance. In the comic scenes where Huck and Jim argue about Solomon's justice and Frenchmen speaking French, moreover, Jim subverts Huck's logic with a superior folk wisdom (D. Smith 1991). When Jim reverts to a state of passivity in the closing Phelps farm section, proponents of his portraiture—albeit often through some fairly convoluted interpretive moves—suggest that he is just playing along with the boys for tactical purposes, and that he cagily acts the fool in order to manipulate Tom and effect his escape into the swamp. That at the novel's end he saves Tom rather than running for freedom further manifests a nobility withheld from the novel's other adult characters (Hill 1995).

The critics who view *Adventures of Huckleberry Finn* as irretrievably racist, or at best deeply flawed in its representation of race, sharply disagree. Although conceding that the novel's use of the "n-word" is historically accurate, these critics still find its appearances numerically excessive (Sloane 2014). Jim, moreover, remains two-dimensional, whether noble savage or Sambo. He is never shown to be working; as a fugitive, he jokes about being rich for owning himself, but he never evinces anger at the institution of slavery that quantifies his value in dollar terms or forces him into flight away from his family. Upon leaving Missouri, he does not take the obvious course of simply crossing the river into the free state of Illinois; nor does he try to turn back north on the Ohio River after he and Huck pass Cairo in the fog (Smiley 1996). Moreover, the scenes where Jim argues with Huck, rather than testifying to his intelligence, depict him as a wise fool in a minstrel show (a genre of popular entertainment that was, it is noted, dear to Twain's heart) (Briden 1995). Finally, Jim's passivity at the Phelps farm shows him losing whatever manhood he gained on the river; while his decision to rescue Tom rather than escape identifies personal virtue with not resistance to oppression but loyalty to the master (Lester 1995). For many of the novel's critics, it is primarily these matters of characterization, and not simply the prolix use of the "n-word," that make the text deeply flawed (Wallace 1991). If *Huck Finn* is taught alongside a text like Frederick Douglass's 1845 *Narrative of the Life of an American Slave*, Twain's portraiture of both slavery and racism displays his entrapment within the dominant ideologies that his text appears to contest.

The debate over the representation of race in *Huck Finn* is an important one; I teach it when I teach the novel. From the standpoint of historical materialism and ideology critique, however, an ethical assessment of where Twain personally stood on the question of racism, given the potentialities and limitations for a white man of his background in his time, is less interesting than a consideration of the historical forces giving rise to the novel's ideological contradictions in the first place. Biographical information is relevant here: not just Twain's relatively privileged childhood in Hannibal, Missouri, but especially his discovery, upon returning to his birthplace midway through the writing of the novel, that the conditions of both former slaves and poor whites had not substantially changed since the Civil War. Stalled in his writing for nearly two years, in 1885 he took up the manuscript again, sending Huck and Jim past Cairo in the fog, taking them deeper into slave territory, and wrecking their raft. To historicize the text, then, is to read it as at once a representation of slavery and a reaction to the post-Reconstruction South. The entire Phelps farm section, where the white supremacist Tom Sawyer resumes his imperious command over both Huck and Jim, signals Twain's ironic recognition of the reinstated power of the plantation-owning class and the institutionalization of Jim Crow (Nilon 1991; Schmitz 1971); the $40 Tom cynically pays Jim at the end allude to the promised 40 acres never transferred to the freedmen. In the closing chapters, Jim's reversion to stereotype and Huck's apparent betrayal of his friend call for symptomatic reading, indicating not so much Twain's inability to transcend his own personal racism as his troubled attempt to suture over in fiction the arrested historical dialectic he perceived to be operative in the moment of the novel's creation. Negation as movement forward was, in Twain's eyes, impossible; the text's reification of Jim, especially in its closing chapters, corresponds with Twain's deeply pessimistic view that the only available negation was movement backward. The text's formal contradictions, manifested in its abandonment of the character-driven structure of the *Bildungsroman* and resort to the episodic structure of the picaresque satire, mediate the larger historical contradictions shaping the late nineteenth-century US South.

"Is it racist trash or an American classic?" one critic of the novel has bluntly asked (Bell 1991, 124). This query invites an assessment not just of *Huck Finn*, and of whether or not it should be taught, but also of the heavily freighted term "American classic." Many of the novel's defenders implicitly assert that a literary work beloved by so many cannot contain any problematic, let alone reactionary, moral positions: Twain's text cannot be "great" if it violates the mythology of continuing American progress toward democracy and equality. Conversely, not a few of the critics who fault the text for its shortcomings do so out of disappointment: how can a novel presumably articulating a distinctly American vision of freedom and possibility fail to extend this vision equally to all its characters? For defenders and critics alike, the meaning of the nation itself is often what is at stake in an assessment of the text's moral and political stance. If, as Ernest Hemingway wrote, "All modern American literature comes from one book by Mark Twain called *Huckleberry Finn*" (Hemingway 1935, 22), what does it say about American literature—and "America"—if the seedbed is corrupt?

Ellison's short story invites us to review the issues raised by Twain's novel, albeit through a very different ideological lens. The nameless narrator is a young white boy from Chicago who is visiting his Uncle Ed's family in a town in the Deep South. A black man—referred to by the boy only as "that Bacote nigger" (Ellison 1996, 11)—is being lynched in the town square presided over by a statue of a Civil War general. No reason is advanced for the lynching; his blackness is reason enough (Muhammed 2011). There has been a blackout; the pilot of an airplane overhead mistakes the light from the fire for the airport lights of Birmingham, Alabama, his intended destination. Swooping downward, the plane hits an electrical wire, heading upward just in time to avoid crashing. A white woman, electrocuted by the thrashing cable, is "turned ... almost as black as the nigger" (Ellison 1996, 7). Meanwhile, the man who is being burned alive begs, "Will somebody please cut my throat like a Christian?" He is told, "Sorry, but ain't no Christians around here tonight.... We're just one hundred percent Americans" (Ellison 1996, 8). The few onlookers who attempt to leave are steered back by the sheriff and his deputies. Although he vomits in horror, the boy admires the burning man, who refuses to cry out in pain. There is a brief coda: a week later, two white sharecroppers discuss the incident at the general store; when one—who "looked hungry as hell" and cannot get credit from the store owner—says that "it didn't do no good to kill niggers 'cause things don't get no better," he is silenced. The story ends with the young narrator thinking to himself, "It was my

first party and my last. But God.... That Bacote nigger was some nigger"
(Ellison 1996, 11).

Throughout his career Ellison would acknowledge his debt to Twain,
whom he valued for his willingness to foreground the issue of racism in
US history (Ellison 1995); indeed, it was with *Huck Finn* in mind Ellison
declared the genre of the American novel to be a "raft of hope" (Ellison
1996, 483). Ellison's debt to Twain is apparent in "A Party Down at the
Square." The boy, whose human instincts are constrained by his inability
to think beyond "nigger," recalls Huck; while the lynched man, like Jim,
has greater moral stature than any of the white men who victimize him.
Significantly influenced during the late 1930s by communist politics,
however, Ellison creates a class-conscious allegory illustrating the ways
in which white supremacist ideology functions to normalize violence and
legitimate the power of the state and the elites it serves (Foley 2010,
113–15). Although the principal victim of the lynching is, clearly, the
black man whose burning body exhibits the extreme reification of racism,
white people are hurt by their complicity with the dominant ideology
and its corresponding practice. The woman who is killed by the falling
electrical wire is an indirect victim of the bonfire; her turning black shows
she hardly enjoys any privilege of whiteness, even if the defense of white
womanhood probably supplied the unstated pretext for the lynching. The
plane's misdirection from its course invites further allegorical reading:
the powerlines should signify the progress of modernity, but the blackout
and bonfire signal the regressive historical movement, both abroad and at
home, that is fettering human development in atavistic and vicious ways.
(It was for good reason that the *Crisis* in 1940 referred to the "thousands
of little Hitlers down South" [*Crisis* 1940, p. 323]). The role of the state in
enforcing ruling-class hegemony is stressed by the presence of the sheriff
and his deputies, who, in the shadow of the Confederate war memorial,
safeguard the ritual—simultaneously ideological and coercive—taking
place down at the square.

Notably, however, the white sharecropper at the story's end has a lean
and hungry look; the vicarious barbeque of the lynching, while intended
to produce a cross-class affirmation of whiteness, has not fed his stomach.
The boy is being offered admission to membership in the violent white
manhood of "100 percent Americanism." But although the "n-word"
serves, as for Huck, to constrain his consciousness within the bounds
of dominant ideology—to the end, he thinks, "That Bacote nigger was
some nigger!"—the boy's statement that this is "my first party and my
last" suggests that he may end up rejecting the misrecognition supplied

by a white identity. Ruling-class ideological hegemony is not as stable as first appears: reacting out of class interests, the hungry white share-croppers may end up joining with their black counterparts and rising in rebellion, as in fact was happening in some of the left-led multi-racial sharecroppers' unions forming in the1930s South (Hudson 1972; Kelley 2015). The story's narrative present contains the concrete potentiality of its future negation. But whatever happens with the boy, the story's readers are interpellated as class-conscious critics of racial violence and the mythologies by which it divides the working class and reinforces ruling-class hegemony. As in "Boy with His Hair Cut Short," readers are invited to infer the totality of social forces shaping the text's harsh portrayal of a present that contains the possible seeds of an alternative future. The historical contradictions viewed as insoluble in *Adventures of Huckleberry Finn* are here susceptible to negation and sublation.

Twain's classic novel can be taught alongside any number of texts enabling a broadened discussion of history and ideology: Douglass's 1845 *Narrative*, for instance, or John Keene's recent *Counternarratives* (2016), which includes a remarkable story titled "Rivers" set after the Civil War and told from the standpoint of a mature and thoughtful Jim unimag-inable by Twain. One advantage of choosing Ellison's story for pairing with *Huck Finn* is that its clear influence by Twain provides insight into the kinds of political possibilities available to the later writer in large part through his participation in left politics; he was empowered to view the present from the standpoint of a possible better future, rather than viewing the past as foreclosed from a better world to come, as Twain was constrained to do. A second advantage of taking these texts as a cluster is that this procedure demonstrates the theoretical importance that biography can play in textual analysis: in their mediations of their historical moments, both Twain and Ellison are intermediaries whose particular experiences drew upon the range of dialectical possibilities available to each of them. Finally, a comparison of the two texts invites us to explore what it means to view racism as a "structure in dominance," that is, a relatively autonomous ideology and practice, determined "in the last instance" by class-based relationships, but possessing its own definitive capacity to determine situations and events. Twain's novel displays a con-sciousness—on the part of both author and narrator—acceding to racism as a structure in dominance. White supremacy, as embodied in Tom, is clearly a ruling-class project; in the absence of significant opposition, however, it enjoys essentially undisturbed hegemony. Ellison's story, by contrast, also shows racism to be a project defended by the state, but in continual need of shoring up. As a structure in dominance, it shapes attitudes and behaviors to the point of murder; yet its autonomy is relative, not absolute, susceptible to challenge from below.

Gender and Sexuality

While gender and sexuality have figured significantly—indeed, centrally—in several of the texts examined up to this point, we now place these matters front and center. The rationale for the cluster of texts explored here will emerge as we proceed.

Our point of entry is E.L. James's blockbuster 2011 novel, *Fifty Shades of Grey*. While this text would not accord with anyone's definition of great literature—there are numerous websites listing its stylistic bloopers—the novel has garnered a huge following, giving rise to three more novels and a series of movies. That the novel had its genesis in the *Twilight* series of fan fiction no doubt boosted its popularity, giving its readers a sense of investment in the characters and plot even after these were taken over for publishing purposes by James (Illouz 2014, 20–21). Translated into 52 different languages and selling more than 150 million copies by the fall of 2017, the *Fifty Shades* franchise has made its creator a wealthy writer indeed.[8]

The plot of *Fifty Shades* draws upon a series of romance novel conventions, going back at least as far as *Pride and Prejudice*, in which a woman of modest origins wins over the heart (and eventually the hand) of a fabulously wealthy bachelor. It is hard to describe the plot without being snarky, so I hope my readers will stay with me. Anastasia Steele, a (presumably) talented English major on the verge of graduation, is gorgeous (of course) but—alas—still a virgin; she has never even explored the pleasure zones in her body, much less found Mr. Right. But when she interviews the 27-year-old multimillionaire Christian Grey for the campus newspaper, she is swept off her feet. He is gorgeous (of course) and quite the opposite of a virgin; his penthouse Seattle apartment features a "Red Room of Pain" full of sadomasochistic equipment. In a nod to present-day mass-cultural versions of feminism, Ana is portrayed as smart and spunky, capable of earning her own way in the world (and, of course, of attracting any man she wishes). There occurs a pseudo-struggle within Ana between her repressive superego and her would-be-liberated "inner goddess" about whether or not to submit to Christian's request that she sign a contract agreeing to be his "submissive." But she gives in, partly because he has courted her with helicopter rides, glider trips, and an extremely rare first edition of *Tess of the d'Urbervilles*, her favorite novel; but also because she simply cannot contain her sexual desire for him, which is repeatedly brought to the reader's attention through the novel's no-so-soft pornographic narration. As a latter-day hi-tech Byronic hero, however, Christian is a man with dark secrets and a tragic past; hints that his actions are to be explained in Freudian terms are sprinkled generously throughout the text. The novel ends with his going past the boundaries of their pact and her returning to her humble (actually, not-so-humble) Seattle abode (her rich roommate's father pays the rent). It is left open for additional novels in the series to explore the depths of these characters' mutual obsession; needless to say, the novel's open-endedness is less a function of postmodernist indeterminacy than of the money-making opportunities embodied in the sequels.

The exchange value of *Fifty Shades* is self-evident; what is its use value? Antonio Gramsci, referring to Alexandre Dumas's best-selling *The Count of Monte Cristo* (2003 [1844–5]), observed that "the success of a work of commercial literature indicates ... the 'philosophy of the age,' that is, the mass of feelings and conceptions of the world predominant among the 'silent' majority." The work may be a "popular 'narcotic,'" but it "must not be disregarded in the history of culture" (Gramsci, 1985, 348). *Fifty Shades* has been celebrated as a self-help sexual manual, a site of safe fantasy about forbidden practices, and a Cinderella story (Illouz 2014); its popularity points to a "mass of feelings and conceptions of the world" that constitute, or at least contribute to, its use value. But while the novel, like others in the romance genre, may offer a utopian space fulfilling real needs (Radway 1991; Booth 2015), this utopia is far from anticipatory, and questionably compensatory; for it binds its readers all the more closely to the reification giving rise to those needs in the first place. Christian Grey is rendered equivalent to his fine clothes, luxurious apartment, thrilling airplanes, and sizeable sexual organ; his helicopter (which of course he pilots himself) is transparently symbolic of male potency. (In *The Great Gatsby*, the millionaire hero's mansion, speedboat, car, and closetful of shirts are trivial by comparison.)

But Christian's hungry gaze, mirrored in Ana's narration, positions the reader as voyeur; we are always aware of how nicely her clothes fit her curves. The text turns possessions—from the fancy sports car that Christian bestows upon Ana to the fine soft sheets on his bed—into objects of displaced desire; reading *Fifty Shades* is like flipping through the pages of a magazine detailing the adventures of the rich and famous. Readers with limited access to these finer things of life can thus enjoy them vicariously through identification with Ana's seduction; one pleasure compounds the other. The fact that the implements hanging on the walls of the Red Room of Pain figure as items of luxury consumption invites the reader to participate simultaneously in kinky sexual pleasure and sexist objectification. And although the text clearly indicates the unequal status of its male and female characters, heteronormative gender dualism is valorized; the reader is positioned to take pleasure in identifying with one or another of the dominant/submissive roles on display. The fact that the novel is consistently told from the standpoint of Ana helps James to fulfill the writing workshop mandate that writers should "show not tell." There are no narratorial interventions interrupting the seamlessness of the narration, no Brechtian signals that one must go outside the text to understand the text. That the text is saturated in dominant ideologies is the premise of its "showing"; it need not engage in procedures of "telling" when millions of readers clearly are ready to embrace its fantasy as the common sense—that is, the common-sense fantasy—of everyday life.

Two features of the ideological work undertaken by *Fifty Shades* warrant particular notice. First, the contract outlining the dominant/submissive relationship between Christian and Ana is complete with individual sub-clauses requiring independent ratification. Ana's initial reluctance to sign—acknowledging, perhaps, the reader's skepticism about such an arrangement—is overcome by her realization that the contract posits her participation as legitimate and freely chosen. In this blatant fetishization of unequal power relations, one recalls Marx's sardonic commentary on the "freedom" of the worker—that is, freedom from ownership of any means of production—that compels entry into the contract for sale of labor power. Second, Christian figures throughout the novel as not simply the possessor but the embodiment of capital. We learn that, when a child, he was adopted by a family that was wealthy, but not fabulously so: his untold millions (we never see his tax return) have accrued not through inheritance, but through his willingness to take unspecified risks as an entrepreneur in Seattle's hi-tech information industry. There is no exploitation of labor in the world of Christian Grey, only capital willing to place itself on the market and, through creative application, expand itself indefinitely (even though the computers it deploys were probably made in China). The helicopter, the sheets, the glass-encased high-rise apartment: these commodities are so far removed from the labor processes generating them that capital cannot be thought of as a vampire sucking the blood out of living labor. Labor does not mediate between constant capital and the product that rolls off the assembly line.

Capital is, rather, embodied in accoutrements that are detached from social relations of any kind; its mystification is complete. Christian is himself Capital as pure money in seductive human form. And although he occasionally takes time off from his obsession with Anastasia to make and receive a flurry of phone calls—we are told that he "works" so hard that he has little time for sleep—he is shown to be more concerned about the activities of his Gates-style philanthropic foundation, which is busy saving countless lives in Africa, than with overseeing the business empire that magically generates his wealth. Christian's proclivity for violence is purely personal. There is nothing violent about the methods by which his capital has accumulated; he bears no responsibility for the suicides of Foxconn workers like Xu Lizhi. Christian's fetishism is thus merely sexual, for the fetish character of his wealth is a given. The Red Room of Pain may be the site of sadomasochistic distress; but there is no history that hurts.

There would not seem to be much of a political unconscious in *Fifty Shades of Grey*, no repressed recognition of social injustice struggling for displaced expression and rupturing the seamlessness of the narrative. There is an odd moment, however, when something strange emerges from the lower reaches (one hesitates to call them "depths") of the text. Early in the courtship between Christian and Ana, she embarrasses herself by blurting out something awkward and then remarks, "I feel the color in my cheeks rising again. I must be the color of *The Communist Manifesto*" (James 2011, 28). Listed among their favorites by several of the novel's blooper-collectors, this statement violates the convention that confines first-person narration to the visual field of the narrator (unless she happens to be looking in a mirror).⁹ That problem aside, however, the statement is just plain odd in the context of the novel, since neither before nor after this outburst does Ana—whose acquaintance with literature seems restricted to one novel by Thomas Hardy—evince the slightest interest in the ideas of Marx. Does this outburst call for symptomatic reading, revealing James's cloaked awareness of the power of capital projected through the character of Christian Grey? Is it a muted call for the workers of the world to unite and throw off their chains? Or is Ana's description of her blush simply evidence of—if there can be such a thing—the novel's pseudo-political unconscious?

The relationship between capital, gender, and personal violence is explored far more searchingly in Ann Petry's 1946 short story "Like a Winding Sheet." Evidently set during World War II, when both women and African Americans were drawn temporarily into the industrial labor force, the story opens with a black couple, Johnson and his wife Mae, getting out of bed and ready for work. He complains that his legs are aching as usual; as she puts on her overalls, she teases him for staying under rumpled covers that resemble "a winding sheet—a shroud" (Petry 2007, 586). Although they bicker about whether or not she should go to work—it is pay day, but it is also Friday the thirteenth—"he couldn't bring himself to talk to her roughly or threaten to strike her.... He wasn't made that way" (Petry 2007, 587). The scene moves to his workplace, where his legs hurt from having to push around a cart for ten hours; he thinks, "[I]f this was his plant he'd make a lot of changes in it." His supervisor is a white woman with a red-lipsticked mouth; "It was funny," he thinks, "to have a woman for a boss in a plant like this" (Petry 2007, 587). When she chastises him for lateness and states, "I'm sick of you niggers," he is enraged, and a "vein stood out on his forehead, thick." Although he "couldn't bring himself to hit a woman," his hands tingle, and "he had the queer feeling that his hands were not exactly part of him anymore—they had developed a separate life of their own over which he had no control" (Petry 2007, 588). The scene shifts once again, to the café where he stands in line for a cup of coffee before going home. The young white woman behind the counter has a red-lipsticked mouth; when his turn comes, she tosses her hair and tells him that there is no more coffee. Although he thinks she is lying, unwilling to serve him because he is black, the reader is shown his error, for the woman turns from the counter to refill the urn. His hands begin to tingle again; "he wanted to hit her so hard that the scarlet lipstick would smear and spread over her nose"; but "he could not even now bring himself to hit a woman.... All the anger-born energy ... had spread through him and piled up like a poison" (Petry 2007, 590). When Johnson returns home, Mae greets him affectionately, looks in the mirror, pats her hair, and teases him for being "an old hungry nigger trying to act tough." He flies out of control and smashes her lipsticked mouth: "He had lost all control over his hands.... This thing ... that was happening to him ... was like being enmeshed in a winding sheet.... And even as the thought formed in his mind his hands reached for her face again and yet again" (Petry 2007, 591).

Petry's story offers a compelling opportunity for thinking through the roles of race, gender, and class, as well as historically specific circumstances, in the causality of interpersonal violence. Clearly contributing to the tale's tragic arc is the alteration in gender roles accompanying the wartime work situation, which has some women wearing overalls and others placed in supervisory capacities. Johnson's investment in an ideology of gender dualism—taking the form of his chivalric conviction that he is not a man who would beat a woman—is out of sync with the new division of labor no longer based (at least for the duration of the war) on the patriarchy of the wage. The fact that the three women he encounters all have red-lipsticked mouths, and that two of them fuss with their hair, draws attention to his felt need to homogenize them on the basis of shared female attributes (literally, the level of appearance). This unthinking conflation makes it possible for him to turn upon his wife in the horrific closing scene; his warped consciousness is indeed a "winding sheet," wrapped around both his wife and himself.

That Johnson's attack on Mae also stems from the systemic racism shaping and confining his life is abundantly clear. The supervisor's use of the "n-word" is the catalyst precipitating his rage, as well as his awareness of the tingling in his hands; he feels emasculated by his supervisor's racist taunt but—for reasons going back to the plantation and beyond—powerless to retaliate. This readiness to anticipate racism in anyone who is white in turn shapes his response to the actions of the young woman in the cafeteria, whose color and gender prevent him from seeing what the reader sees—namely, that she really has run out of coffee and needs to make more. (This is a key moment in the plot, at first readily missed because the reader is largely confined to Johnson's point of view.) She may look like his supervisor—she is white, she is female—but she is in fact just another worker doing her job, like Johnson himself. When Mae uses the "n-word" in a fond, teasing way, he cannot hear the difference from the way the word was uttered earlier in the day out of another red-lipsticked mouth: again, he is arrested at the level of appearances. But his wife is a black woman, dispensable in the eyes of the law and society at large; he can vent upon her his rage at the abuse heaped upon him as a black man.

As proximate causes, sexism and racism constitute the principal psychological motivators of the physical violence that Johnson enacts upon the body of Mae. Petry complicates her portrayal of causality, however, by supplying a further level of motivation to Johnson's actions. The fact that his legs constantly ache and that the vein stands out on his head indicates that he suffers from high blood pressure; the built-up numbness in his hands suggests the role played by workplace stress and inadequate medical care in causing what might otherwise seem to be pathological behavior of a purely mental kind. More fundamentally, however, Johnson's lack of control over his hands, coupled with his lack of control over his conditions of work, signals a root cause of his anger in his alienation, construed in a classically Marxist sense as the severing of mental from manual labor. His hands have no connection with his mind; he is separated not only from the product of his concrete labor (what he does or what he makes, notably, is never even specified), but also from what Marx called his species being, his fellow workers, and himself. His labor is entirely abstract, identified only by its interchangeability with his wage; his living labor is controlled by the dead labor embodied in the cart he pushes around, rendering him half-dead, indeed zombie-like, all day long. The home, the site of the daily reproduction of labor power, is invaded by alienation; rather than functioning as a haven in a heartless world, it becomes the place where he can exercise the only freedom he has—the freedom to beat and kill, the freedom to reproduce in his own actions, in the seemingly private sphere of marriage and home, the dynamic of the intrinsically violent social relations of capitalism. Which of course is not freedom at all, but entrapment in the folds of a destructive ideological winding sheet.

The story's treatment of class thus figures not primarily at the level of simple economics—while eager to collect their paychecks, Johnson and Mae are not in a state of poverty—but at the level of the social relations of production. Class is, in Petry's story, not primarily a matter of identity; instead, it designates the warped and warping patterns of exploitation and alienation that shape and confine the lives of the proletariat, producing subjects whose actions reveal their subjection to the Subject, capital, as Althusser would put it. At the same time, the story's dominant trope of hands—we may recall the poems of Rukeyser and Hughes—designates not only the alienation of labor but also the relatively autonomous gendered and racialized forms of oppression by which that exploitation is daily reinforced. Racialized heteronormative patriarchy supplies the structure in dominance in the story's narrative causality: it is because Johnson "sees" only gender and race—the common-sense categories of appearance in capitalist society—that he, and his wife, end up strangled in the winding sheet. Yet it is, arguably, the "dull compulsion of economic relations," embodied in his numb and numbing hands, that supplies the "determination in the last instance" shaping the story's tragic outcome. Johnson's lack of class consciousness manifests itself in his misperception of the worker in the cafeteria; but its essence is his inability to break away from the reified categories of gender and race that make him unable to see totality. The story's masterful conjunction of organic form with historical materialist categories of analysis, however, provides the reader with the dialectical understanding that Johnson cannot achieve.

Considerations of social class also figure prominently in the representation of gender and sexuality in Annie Proulx's "Brokeback Mountain," the 1997 *New Yorker* short story upon which Ang Lee's eponymous 2005 movie is based. Set in Wyoming and Texas between approximately 1963 and 1983, the story details the love relationship between two ranch-hands, Jack Twist and Ennis del Mar, "both high-school drop-out country boys with no prospects, brought up to hard work and privation, both rough-mannered, rough-spoken, inured to the stoic life" (Proulx 1997, 74). They discover their mutual lust and love one summer when they are hired to herd sheep on the slopes of Brokeback Mountain, a place where "[y]ou forget how it is bein' broke all the time" (Proulx 1997, 83). Both end up in heterosexual marriages where they have children and live claustrophobic lives; after his divorce, Ennis inhabits a series of cramped domestic spaces whose spatial constriction signals the repression of his sexuality and selfhood. Jack and Ennis have passionate rendezvous in wilderness settings at far-flung intervals but can never be together: "One thing never changed: the brilliant charge of their infrequent couplings was darkened by the sense of time flying, never enough time, never enough" (Proulx 1997, 83). Unlike Ennis, who sticks by his initial insistence that "I'm not so queer" (Proulx 1997, 76), Jack over the years takes risks in fulfilling his sexual desires; he ends up being brutally murdered (it is strongly implied) by homophobes. After Jack's death, Ennis visits Jack's parents and finds in his closet, layered one within the other, shirts each of them had worn that first summer on Brokeback Mountain, where they had shared a "dozy embrace [that] solidified in his memory as the single moment of artless, charmed happiness in their separate and difficult lives" (Proulx 1997, 83). At the end, the trailer-trapped Ennis remains fixed in the past: "There was some open space between what he knew and what he tried to believe, but nothing could be done about it, and if you can't fix it you've got to stand it" (Proulx 1997, 85). Ennis's "open space" is ambiguous, as is also what he means by "it." He could have in mind the circumstances surrounding Jack's death; he could be referring to the entire situation in which he finds himself, a source of suffering that yields neither knowledge nor self-knowledge.

The dominant theme in "Brokeback Mountain" is the internalized self-hatred and emotional paralysis pervading a rural working-class environment premised on hypermasculine assertions of gender identity: these are people who, in addition to "bein' broke all the time," have had their backs broken (Tuss 2006). While the 1969 Stonewall revolt, marking the beginning of the Gay Pride movement, occurred during the timespan covered in the narrative, it has not made its way to the spacious skies and majestic purple mountains of the plains; Proulx's West is a place where the love that dare not speak its name remains unspoken. Proulx draws persuasive connections between psychology and sociology, portraying both men's working-class families, especially the fathers, as mired in domestic violence, ignorance, and deadening heteronormativity. Jack's father, who beat him ruthlessly when he peed in bed, is humiliated that his son has viewed his uncircumcised penis, a symbol of his flawed manhood. Ennis, describing his childhood experience of being taken by his gleeful father to see the mangled body of a gay man lynched with a tire iron, recalls, "Hell, for all I know *he* done the job" (Proulx 1997, 79). Although Jack's mother sympathizes with the grieving Ennis, she is clearly beaten down by her husband, who rules the ideological roost "with the hard need to be the stud duck in the pond" (Proulx 1997, 84). The reader is invited to contemplate how homophobia, which clearly underpins the causality shaping the characters' tragic lives, plays out the frustrations accompanying a hardscrabble working-class existence premised upon survival and little more.

While "Brokeback Mountain" suggestively links sexuality to class, however, it does not, unlike Petry's story, link class to capital; the history that hurts is equivalent to the lived experience of rural working-class patriarchy and psychic repression. The text thus pauses at mid-level analytics, positing culture as causality. At the end of "Like a Winding Sheet," Johnson is caught in a destructive and self-destructive spiral of violence; but the text's representation of his hands, so potent a symbol in proletarian literature, reminds the reader that the standpoint of the proletariat is conditioned by more than what appears on the surface of things. For Petry, "structure in dominance" is accompanied by "determination in the last instance." By contrast, the "open space between what [Ennis] knew and what he believed" constitutes an arrested dialectic for both him and the reader, whose empathetic reaction is not accompanied by greater understanding of "why." Homophobia's other consists not in its potential negation, but in the compensatory utopia of "Brokeback Mountain", a site exempt from the pressures of waged labor and biological reproduction. Same-sex love is linked with the timeless magnificent landscapes of the West—an impression strongly reinforced by the camera work in Ang Lee's highly romantic film adaptation. The smothering world of heteronormativity, marriage, and children is conflated with the time- and space-bound realm of the social, as embodied in Ennis's cramped trailer. Ennis's "open space" symptomatically signals social contradictions insoluble not only in history—the United States West of the early

1980s—but also within the experientially bound theorization of class that frames the tale.

By contrast, homophobic repression is placed in a Marxist analytical framework in Leslie Feinberg's 1993 transgender proletarian *Bildungs-roman Stone Butch Blues*, where multiply mediated connections are drawn between homophobia and the gendered ideologies reinforcing capitalist class rule. Based in part on Feinberg's own experience in the 1960s–80s as a working-class radical initially self-identifying as a "he-she" butch lesbian, the book details the protagonist's struggle with a series of antagonists, both external and internal. (Feinberg, who described herself as "an anti-racist white, working-class, secular Jewish, transgender, lesbian, female, revolutionary communist," expressed a general preference for the pronouns "*zie/hir.*" While she used different pronouns in different contexts, "she"/"her" is used throughout *Stone Butch Blues* [Pratt 2014].) These antagonists include not only the power of the state (displayed in recurring instances of police brutality) and the boss (displayed in numerous episodes of sexuality-based scapegoating and physical injury), but also the spontaneous violence enacted by male fellow workers deeply invested in heteronormative identities. Yet Jess Goldberg, as a class-conscious radical, also experiences solidarity with straight fellow workers who support her as both an organizer and a person marked by sexual difference. In particular, her friend Duffy clearly discerns how her being targeted as "other" consolidates the hold of the employer on all the workers in the plant: gender dualism and homophobia are clearly linked with the divide-and-conquer ideological strategies accompanying the drive to capital accumulation. In *Stone Butch Blues*, the relative autonomy of ideology is illustrated in the motivations of gay-bashers, who clearly do not realize the extent to which their actions reinforce ruling-class hegemony. But the analysis supplied by the text overall does not treat homophobia as a structure in dominance, but instead as direct mediation—or, more precisely, a series of mediations—of capitalist class rule. The distinction is an important one, involving not causal hair-splitting but the designation of causality guiding Feinberg's portrayal of both systemic and personal violence.

The text displays the centrality of class consciousness to Jess's sense of identity: she is in fact more at home with some of her straight fellow union members, as well as with Native Americans and other racial minorities, than with other white people of same-sex orientation who cannot discern their own positioning within the regime of capital. It is significant that the novel opens with her profound sense of alienation in a blind date with a middle-class white lesbian who is far less concerned with police violence against the homeless than with "problems with her co-op and how she's so opposed to rent control." Feinberg sardonically adds, "Small wonder—Daddy is a real estate developer" (Feinberg 1993, 1). Although *Stone Butch Blues* portrays sexually nonconforming people in all social strata as victims of heteronormative discrimination and abuse, the class-conscious query posed by 1930s labor organizers—"Which Side Are You On?"—cuts across gender- and sexuality-based categories of identity, demonstrating not only that working-class queers are far more likely to be targeted for violence than their more class-sheltered counterparts but also that queerness does not in and of itself supply an oppositional identity, much less an anti-capitalist politics.

Stone Butch Blues explores the ways in which heteronormative conceptions of maleness and femaleness have historically warped relationships within the very community of those identified by sexual difference. Jess at first subscribes to a rigid butch–femme dyad, describing women to whom she is attracted as "*chicks* or *broads* or *hooters* or *headlights*" (Feinberg 1993, 83; italics in original). Unable to conceive of one butch being drawn to another butch, she embraces the gender dualism that is a principal source of her alienation. The availability of a greater range of possible sexual identities in the post-Stonewall period contributes to her broadened acceptance of different modes of queerness; active participation in movement-based resistance—unavailable to the Ennis of "Brokeback Mountain," who insists that "I'm not so queer"—enables the dialectical expansion of limits. But Jess's engagement with historical materialist anthropological writings describing the valorized social status of sexually ambiguous figures in pre-class societies also figures crucially in the process; she is able to link her nonconformist sexuality identity to her felt need, as a revolutionary proletarian organizer, to negate capitalist modernity by a return, on a higher level, to the egalitarianism of the primitive communalist mode of production. Although early in the novel Jess grudgingly admires Duffy in spite of, rather than because of, his being a self-described communist, toward the end she accepts Duffy's Marxist challenge to "imagine a world worth living in … a world worth fighting for" (Feinberg 1993, 328). Her closing dream of being encircled by people of whom "*it was hard to say who was a woman, who was a man*" (Feinberg 1993, 329; italics in original) departs from the gritty realism of the preceding narrative; repurposing the genre of the *Bildungsroman* for collectivist political ends, this gesture toward an anticipatory utopia—the "not-yet in the now"—entails imagining through and past current possibilities for human interaction. That for some readers the novel may, in drawing its poetry from the future, press uncomfortably against the limits of an intrinsically individualistic genre, says as much about the ideological constraints imposed by inherited literary form as about the plausibility of the concrete potentiality envisioned in the text.

The four texts included in this cluster contain a large range of formulations about the relationship between and among gender, sexuality, class, race, and capital. *Fifty Shades* not only affirms the unequal power relations in a classed and gendered binary opposition but in fact makes domination—by capital, by male violence—feel good. "Like a Winding Sheet" registers the toxic effects of gender- and race-based reification, which together constitute a structure in dominance enacting the imperatives of capitalist social relations of production. "Brokeback Mountain" displays a close alignment of sexuality-based and class-based oppressions, but these remain essentially disarticulated from an analysis of capital. *Stone Butch Blues* explores the relationship between a series of gender-, sexuality-, and race-based oppressions and capitalist exploitation. While these texts display intersections of various kinds—of vectors of causality, of identities—their very different formulations of the relationships involved indicate the difficulty of theorizing intersectionality in more than descriptive terms. Intersectionality may usefully account for the various factors or elements involved in a given process but does not supply an adequate theoretical model for thinking about totality in dialectical terms (Foley 2018).

Nature

Up to this point we have been considering the literary representation of categories of experience based in historically specific social formations. These have been linked to the different levels of generality contained in Ollman's levels two through four. To refresh your memory: after (1) the context surrounding a given individual, these are (2) the immediate phase of capitalism relevant to the moment in question; (3) the longer span of the capitalist mode of production; and (4) the much longer era of class society. Our hermeneutic of suspicion has made us alert to false universals that purport to transcend social divisions by evading the realities of inequality, oppression, and exploitation—that is, modes of analysis bypassing levels two through four. But now we will tackle the question of universals from another angle: is there anything that people from all social strata and zones of existence can be said legitimately to have in common? Are there any shared experiences that point to what it simply means to be human, regardless of class position or historical situation? These questions encompass Ollman's level five, the span of the existence of *Homo sapiens*. If communism is envisioned as a mode of production aimed at the fulfillment of universal human needs, can this impulse toward future universality be embodied in works of literature produced in class society without papering over the contradictions fettering movement into such a future?

This question is often brought to the fore in literary works representing human encounters with the nonhuman natural world. These texts address Ollman's levels six and seven, encompassing, respectively, what humans have in common with all other living things, and what they share with everything, organic and inorganic, in the universe. As noted previously in our discussion of naturalization as ideology, positing parallels or analogies between human and natural processes is fraught with peril, since such maneuvers frequently conflate historically generated beliefs and behaviors with a presumably timeless human essence. Even to posit the existence of a natural world beyond human intervention, however, requires caution, especially in the light of today's heightened awareness of environmental devastation. While societies have always been shaped by the pressures and limits imposed by nature, human beings increasingly inhabit an environment that they have made, for better or for worse. To posit that one can commune with an environment untouched by human labor—much less by the depredations wrought by capital's incessant drive to accumulation—is, to say the least, a naïve proposition. Current designations of the contemporary era as "Anthropocene," as well as of the need for "post-human" paradigms analyzing the relationship between human beings and the rest of the planet in more humbling terms, make it a temptation always to place the words "nature" or "natural" within quotation marks (Foster et al 2010; Angus 2016). Arguably, however, it is also anti-materialist to proclaim that everything is social and nothing is natural. Humans share many things in common with all organic life; the earth rotates on its axis without regard to the organic life it carries with it.

Whether or not it posits that nature should be spelled with a capital N, a good deal of the literature associated with the Romantic and Transcendentalist movements proposes that human encounters with the natural world perform a restorative function. This idea is clearly displayed in "I Wandered Lonely as a Cloud" (1965 [1807]) by the English Romantic poet William Wordsworth, where during a countryside walk the poet comes across thousands of daffodils growing wild by the side of a lake:

I wandered lonely as a cloud
That floats on high o'er vales and hills,
When all at once I saw a crowd,
A host, of golden daffodils;
Beside the lake, beneath the trees,
Fluttering and dancing in the breeze.

Continuous as the stars that shine
And twinkle on the milky way,
They stretched in never-ending line
Along the margin of a bay:
Ten thousand saw I at a glance,
Tossing their heads in sprightly dance.

The waves beside them danced; but they
Out-did the sparkling waves in glee:
A poet could not but be gay,
In such a jocund company:
I gazed—and gazed—but little thought
What wealth the show to me had brought:

For oft, when on my couch I lie
In vacant or in pensive mood,
They flash upon that inward eye
Which is the bliss of solitude;
And then my heart with pleasure fills,
And dances with the daffodils.

(Wordsworth 1965 [1807], 149)

The speaker's initial sense of lonely detachment is alleviated by the vision of the flowers, which have taken on human qualities, now constituting a "crowd," a "host," a "jocund company" that put on a "show" in which they "dance" and "toss their heads." The memory of this encounter, which has made his own heart "dance," remains with him when "in vacant or in pensive mood" he is once again alone; the image recalled by his "inward eye" transforms his "solitude" into a state of "bliss." The poem displays a quintessential Romantic view of nature as compensatory utopia, as well as the poet's function in conveying "emotion recollected in tranquility," as Wordsworth wrote in his famous 1800 Preface to the *Lyrical Ballads* (in Wordsworth 1965, 740).

"I Wandered Lonely as a Cloud" aptly captures the feeling of renewal that all but the most intransigently dour people experience when coming across an unexpected display of botanical splendor, especially when not planted by human hands in a park or a garden. Even as it provides entry to such a shared experience, however, the poem invites being read symptomatically as what Adorno called "a form of reaction against the reification of the world" (Adorno 1974, 58). For the speaker's initial sense of isolation is a given; he is capable of being touched by the flowers' "sprightly dance" to the extent that he lacks the "jocund company" of human beings. "I saw," "saw I," and "I gazed—and gazed": his position as a viewing subject is defined by his separation from the landscape before him; objectification is the precondition for a fuller sense of subjectivity. The fact that the memory of "ten thousand" flowers constitutes unanticipated "wealth," and that he can "gaze—and gaze" on them without buying or consuming them, indicates his alienation from the money-obsessed world of getting and spending (registered, we will recall, in his sonnet titled "The World Is Too Much with Us"). Like the stars in the Milky Way, the flowers cannot be subjected to the rule of the market.

It bears noting, however, that Wordsworth's insistence on the wildness of the scene entails closing his mind to the fact that, as one historian has noted, "there was no pristine nature left in Britain by the end of the eighteenth century.... The romantic distinction between wild and cultivated nature was a myth" (White 2013, 3). The poet portrays himself as a wandering cloud, but on the ground he would have had to climb over any number of stiles separating one farm from the next and testifying to the controlling existence of private property. Indeed, the very notion that he contemplates a landscape aligns his standpoint with the school of landscape artists hired to capture on canvas from a high point the vast estates of wealthy landowners (Heffernan 1985). Wordsworth may have wished to democratize access to natural beauty, especially in his beloved Lake District; there is nothing inauthentic in his response to the daffodils, or in his view that the poet should share his experience with others. Nonetheless, his response, like that of Matthew Arnold in "To Marguerite—Continued," does as much to suture over alienation as dispel it.

Some writers simply insist from the outset that descriptions of the natural realm cannot be exempt from the social determinations embedded in language. Take, for instance, "Sunset," by the South African poet Oswald Mbuyiseni Mtshali:

> The sun spun like
> a tossed coin.
> It whirled on the azure sky,
> It clattered into the horizon,
> It clicked in the slot,
> and neon-lights popped
> and blinked "Time expired,"
> as on a parking meter.
>
> (Mtshali 2012 [1975], 24)

Mtshali's comparison of a setting sun to a coin put into a parking meter, and of stars with neon lights, defamiliarizes and trivializes the grand movement of nature, as well as the poetic conventions associating sunset with some kind of transhistorical cosmic process. Even the sun, an entity beyond the reach of the almighty dollar (or, in this case, the solid gold Krugerrand), cannot be described in language other than that of markets and money. Where the speaker in "I Wandered Lonely as a Cloud" discovers in his encounter with the daffodils an unexpected "wealth" that presumably has nothing to do with the cash nexus, here the sunset signals the omnipresent hegemony of exchange value.

But the poem's seemingly playful tone belies its critical commentary on racialized super-exploitation, especially when the poem is located in the historical and geographical context of apartheid-era South Africa and is read alongside other poems in the volume where it first appeared, Mtshali's *Sounds of a Cowhide Drum* (2012 [1975]). "Sunset" is a companion poem to "The Song of Sunrise," where the rising sun is a bell tolling, "Arise! All Workers! To Work!" (1972, 36), as well as to "Reapers in a Mieliefield," which describes black laborers, whom "the sun lashes ... with a red-hot rod" (Mtshali 2012 [1975], 12). In an association at once metaphorical and physical, the sun is a timekeeper and an instrument of torture, shortening the lives of laborers for whom time prematurely expires. Yet, in "Sunset," the sun's sinking below the horizon suggests that its hegemony in the sky—rule by the Krugerrand, racial apartheid, British rule—is coming to an end: even for those with money, parking spaces are only available on a temporary basis. While the hubristic claim that the sun never set on the British Empire was literally true in the nineteenth and early twentieth centuries, in that the UK controlled territories all around the globe, here the geographical descriptor is re-metaphorized to signal the end of an era. "Sunset," along with its companion poems, suggests that nature cannot be described in terms separable from modes of perception generated in the realm of capitalist money-making and racial oppression—even if much of the natural world is beyond social intervention, and the sun is still the sun.

While parallels between human and natural processes can be ideologically freighted, literary works written from a consciously Marxist standpoint can also suggest provocative correlations between historical materialism and physical materialism, which Engels described as the dialectics of nature. In Tillie Olsen's novel *Yonnondio: From the Thirties* (1974), which documents the harsh lives of Midwest US working-class families, the natural world does not constitute a utopian alternative to the social world; but neither is it informed by principles of a different order. The elderly mentor character Elias Caldwell attempts to explain to his "stargazing companion," the young Mazie Holbrook, the scientific laws governing change in the universe, the "vastness of eternal things that had been before her and would be after her" (Olsen 1974, 47). Such knowledge, he urges, should produce not passivity, but "rebel[lion] against that which will not let life be" (1974, 52–53). This connection between natural and social processes re-emerges when Anna Holbrook, Mazie's mother, takes her children to pick dandelion greens on a bluff adjoining a wealthy neighborhood above the meat-packing hell of Omaha. Here the mother can display affection for daughter, Mazie, in a way impossible in their shack below, where Anna's hands are confined to the daily and generational reproduction of labor power:

> The fingers stroked, spun a web, cocooned Mazie into happiness and intactness and selfness. Soft wove the bliss round hurt and fear and want and shame—the old worn fragile bliss, a new frail selfness bliss, healing transforming. Up from the grasses, from the earth, from the broad tree trunk at their back, latent life streamed and seeded. The air and self shone boundless. (Olsen 1974, 102)

The natural setting is hardly exempt from constraints of the social world; although the wild dandelion greens constitute a use value that can nourish the family for free, Mazie feels a "weedy sense of not belonging" (Olsen 1974, 98) across from the mansions of the wealthy, whose easy living is clearly enabled by the labor—both productive and reproductive—of families like the Holbrooks. Moreover, the moment is brief; Anna soon reverts to the demands placed on her "bounded body" by proletarian motherhood. Nonetheless, "the new frail selfness bliss" is possible when mother and child are removed from the immediate pressures of survival in the alienated realm of capitalist production and reproduction. This is not the "bliss of solitude," as in Wordsworth, but the bliss of negating, however temporarily, social experiences of "hurt and fear and want and shame." The "latent life" that "streamed and seeded" signifies not a compensatory utopia to which the proletariat can escape, but an anticipatory utopia that is dialectically embedded in life processes; it waits to be realized but is fettered by "what which will not let life be." Through this portrayal of continuity between human and other forms of organic life, the text gestures toward the realm of freedom precluded by the daily grind of necessity. But its realization is contingent upon the negation and sublation of capitalist social relations. The "not-yet" exists as a concrete potentiality in the "now," but its coming into being is contingent upon the class struggle; it will take revolutionary human praxis to bring into being a world where no one has to think of herself as a weed.

Mortality

But what of mortality? Even if the language used to describe any process is irretrievably social, isn't it also true that all living things, including humans, undergo an organic movement through birth, growth, aging, and death? Isn't this single truth testament to a universal experience warranting treatment in works of literature? The New England poet Robert Frost confronts this question in "Nothing Gold Can Stay":

> Nature's first green is gold,
> Her hardest hue to hold.
> Her early leaf's a flower;
> But only so an hour.
> Then leaf subsides to leaf,
> So Eden sank to grief,
> So dawn goes down to day
> Nothing gold can stay.

(Frost 1979 [1926], 222–23)

Linking the cycles of nature in the seasons and the course of a day, the poem's four rhymed couplets capture the relentless antinomies of beauty and transiency: gold/hold, flower/hour, leaf/grief, day/stay. Usually thought of as impervious to change, gold here signifies what is most precious but also most fleeting, the life of a leaf turning from its original yellowish hue to its familiar green, followed by autumn, when it falls to the ground and dies.

This deservedly famous lyric can be described as a "nature poem"; indeed, "Nature" is personified in its first word. The mention of "Eden" in the sixth line, however, significantly expands the poem's metaphorical and propositional domain. The allusion here, of course, to the Fall of Man in the Bible's Book of Genesis, when, against God's prohibition, Adam and Eve ate a piece of fruit from the Tree of Knowledge. This original sin of disobedience exiled them from the Golden Age of the Garden of Eden, eternally in bloom, into the realm of history, where sin, labor, pain, and death would be the price henceforth paid by humanity for its exercise of free will. Readers familiar with the Abrahamic tradition are invited to draw the conclusion—powerfully enhanced by the poem's autotelic form—that the natural and human worlds obey the same cyclical pattern: one loss and decline is as inevitable as the other.

The reader can choose to remain on the surface of things, associating Nature's loss of its fleetingly gold phase with humanity's loss of its mythic golden age of prelapsarian innocence. ("Prelapsarian" refers to the situation of Adam and Eve before their fall ["lapse"] into sin.) Yet the poem's treating the loss of Eden as a vehicle chosen to describe its tenor— the cycle of nature—is not ideologically innocent. After all, the doctrine of original sin has functioned powerfully for more than two millennia as a rationale for hierarchical social control: how can altering social relations in the world of fallen humanity make any difference, if the human stain is intrinsic to us all? What appears to be a simple lyric linking natural with human processes of change is itself stained, if you will, by a key tenet of dominant ideology, one so central to Western culture as to be practically invisible. To point this out is not to accuse Frost of preaching submission to church authority, much less taking a position against social revolution (although a good deal of Frost's oeuvre has a decidedly conservative bent). But the allusion to the Fall of Man does not simply illustrate the inevitability of mortality; the key images—of the tree, of the day— reciprocally reinforce the naturalness of the notion of original sin and the immutability of the human condition. The realization that there is no not-yet in the now, rendered with such beauty, becomes a source of melancholy pleasure.

No melancholy pleasure can be derived from the comparison of botanical and human cycles of life and death in the poem "Strange Fruit" (1939), written by Abel Meeropol and famously sung by Billie Holiday. The grotesque physical details encapsulate the embedded narrative: "Southern

trees bear [the] strange fruit [of] black bodies swinging in the … breeze";
the "blood on the leaves" corresponds to the "blood at the root" of slavery
and Jim Crow. The "pastoral scene" of a "gallant south," conventionally
symbolized by the "scent of magnolias, sweet and fresh," is belied by the
"bulging eyes and the twisted mouth" of the lynched man, as well as the
residual "smell of burning flesh" (morbidly rhyming with "fresh"). Very
possibly murdered because of false accusations that he sexually violated
a white woman presumably embodying the myth of southern purity and
innocence, the man is now "fruit for the crows to pluck," for the "sun to
rot, for the trees to drop." He is the "strange and bitter fruit" of a violent
regime of extreme racist reification (Meeropol 2006 [1939], 902).

By contrast with "Nothing Gold Can Stay," there is, in "Strange Fruit,"
no golden age of prelapsarian innocence, no Garden of Eden before the
fall: the lynching tree is the Tree of Knowledge, and the bodies suspended
from its branches are the harvested fruits of economic terrorism. The
mortal sins enacted in the plantation regime—sins, not sin, for the poem
describes not one body, but many—are not timeless and original, but
historically specific, rooted in the racialized political economy of agrarian
capitalism. Any mythology intimating a shared human condition
between murderers and murdered—including their all being mortal, all
ultimately doomed to die—ends up supplying ideological legitimation to
social formations, past and present, based upon extreme exploitation and
coercion. It might be tempting to teach "Strange Fruit" alongside *Gone
with the Wind*, which appeared on the screen in the same year that Billie
Holiday recorded the song.

The poems by Frost and Meeropol discussed above present largely
incompatible—or at least dramatically polarized—approaches to the representation of mortality in poetry. Shakespeare's Sonnet 65 invites us to
consider another standpoint:

> Since brass, nor stone, nor earth, nor boundless sea
> But sad mortality o'er-sways their power,
> How with this rage shall beauty hold a plea,
> Whose action is no stronger than a flower?
> O, how shall summer's honey breath hold out
> Against the wrackful siege of batt'ring days,
> When rocks impregnable are not so stout,
> Nor gates of steel so strong, but time decays?
> O fearful meditation! where, alack,
> Shall time's best jewel from time's chest lie hid?

Or what strong hand can hold his swift foot back?
Or who his spoil of beauty can forbid?
O, none, unless this miracle have might,
That in black ink my love may still shine bright.

The speaker contemplates the inevitable fading of his lover's beauty; the poem is haunted by the knowledge of mortality. The only force potentially capable of opposing the onslaught of time and decay is the poem itself. First noting the remorselessness of change even in those features of the inorganic world seemingly beyond its reach—brass, stone, earth, and sea—the sonnet moves through a series of curiously mixed metaphors comparing evanescent natural entities, both organic and inorganic, to destructive forces operative in the human world: a flower making a plea before a court, a summer breeze attempting to hold off a battering-ram assault upon a steel-gated city. Some rhymes are especially apposite: "sea" with "plea," "flower" with "power." In the last quatrain, the sonnet intensifies its "fearful meditation" ("O" and "Or" are insistently repeated); "Time" is here suggestively personified—as a hoarder, a racer, a deliberate "spoiler" of beauty. The couplet proclaims the speaker's hope for a "miracle": that the "black ink"—the scrawl of the poet's pen, the printed text—will withstand the predations of time. Or at least that it *may* manage to do so: "unless" in line thirteen suggests that the poem's preservative power is by no means guaranteed.

The poem's treatment of mortality makes a strong claim to universality, equating processes occurring in the inorganic universe, the organic world, different phases in human history, and the poet's personal situation: Ollman's levels one, two, four, six, and seven are gestured toward in the course of the poem's fourteen lines. Although the poem gains in urgency toward its end, none of these loci of change is privileged over another; all demonstrate the inexorability of time, decay, and death. Yet it bears noting that, in lines three through eight, the manmade forces antagonistic to beauty's survival are metaphorically conjoined with social institutions and practices—courts and warfare—rendering people helpless in the face of state power; the image of the battering-ram, used in medieval but also early modern warfare, suggests ongoing practices of military aggression. In line ten, the speaker's designation of his lover's beauty as "time's best jewel," which he wishes to keep hidden from "time's chest" (presumably a coffin), compares the rapacity of time to the actions of a hoarder who values a jewel not for its beauty—its present use value—but for profit—its future exchange value. Insofar as hoarding was frequently associated with usury, this metaphor relates suggestively to the competing practices of usury, hoarding, and investment in the nascent capitalist economic practices of Shakespeare's day. (It also perhaps bears noting that the bard was himself brought to trial for profiteering from the hoarding of grain during a time of shortage [Duncan-Jones 2010, 121–22].) The closing personified images of time as an all too rapid runner and an unspecified "spoiler," while not linked to any historically specific social practices, build upon the earlier metaphors linking mortality with law, warfare, and money.

Even as it treats a concern—the ability of art to elude the grip of mortality—that draws upon a range of natural and historical processes at once timeless and timebound, Shakespeare's sonnet remains linguistically embedded in metaphors largely premised upon social practices prevalent in his time. And even though the poem holds up its autotelism as a mode of resistance—its organic form possesses a compensatory utopia that presumably counters the onslaught of time—it makes no claim to independence from history.

Art

The claim (or at least the bid) to art's transcendence of time presented in the couplet of Shakespeare's sonnet brings us, finally, to a consideration of literary works that are in some sense about their own literariness—that is, about the act of using language to represent a world beyond language. What do writers see themselves doing when they take up their pens (or, more recently, turn on their laptops)? While some writers gain sustenance from the fact that the literary text, like many a work of art, endures long after its creator is gone—a truth that is captured in the Latin phrase, *ars longa, vita brevis*—others, like "Strange Fruit," would seem to be more concerned with doing away with aspects of the human condition that prompted them to write in the first place. Some texts go further, calling into question the very possibility that certain social realities can be represented in art.

For an instance of this skepticism, we examine a very short poem by Langston Hughes titled "Johannesburg Mines":

> In the Johannesburg mines
> There are 240,000 natives working.
>
> What kind of poem
> Would you make out of that?

> 240,000 natives working
> In the Johannesburg mines.
>
> (Hughes 1994 [1925], 43)

The representation of imperialist exploitation in Hughes's in "Always the Same" reminds us that "Johannesburg Mines" can hardly be taken as Hughes's final word about the power—or impotence—of poetry. But in this text he interrogates the limits of literary representation. The poem's stripped-down, non-imagistic language; its repetition of the number "240,000" in Arabic numerals; its reiteration of the title in the first and last lines, as well as of the paternalistic phrase "natives working"; its targeting of European ownership in the name "Johannesburg": all these features suggest that what happens to workers in the mines of South Africa fetters not only human development but the very production of poetry. The query inserted in the middle of the poem—"What kind of poem/ Would you make out of that?"—defies hegemonic assumptions about poetry on the part of both its creators and its readers. Where Shakespeare's Sonnet 65 contemplates the power of poetry to vanquish—or at least offer consolation for—mortality, Hughes's "Johannesburg Mines" proposes that the socially produced mortality of black South African miners cannot be the topic of poetic treatment. And yet, in its relentless symmetry, the poem adheres, indeed quite rigorously, to principles of organic form. Perhaps it is not as easy, at least for Hughes, to write an anti-poem poem as he would have us believe. A further irony consists in the fact that "Johannesburg Mines" is frequently anthologized.

Diametrically opposed to "Johannesburg Mines" is the conception of the nature of poetry contained in Archibald MacLeish's "Ars Poetica" (1952 [1926]). Translated as "the art of poetry," the title draws upon a tradition of instructions about the nature of poetry going back to the 1st-century BCE Roman poet Horace. MacLeish writes:

> A poem should be palpable and mute
> As a globed fruit,
>
> Dumb
> As old medallions to the thumb,
>
> Silent as the sleeve-worn stone
> Of casement ledges where the moss has grown—

A poem should be wordless
As the flight of birds.

      *

A poem should be motionless in time
As the moon climbs,

Leaving, as the moon releases
Twig by twig the night-entangled trees,

Leaving, as the moon behind the winter leaves,
Memory by memory the mind—

A poem should be motionless in time
As the moon climbs.

      *

A poem should be equal to:
Not true.

For all the history of grief
An empty doorway and a maple leaf.

For love
The leaning grasses and two lights above the sea—

A poem should not mean
But be.

(MacLeish 1952 [1926], 40–41)

MacLeish's poem is richly imagistic; indeed, its central point (for it does have a "point") is that a good poem, a real poem, is one that relies upon concrete images, rather than proclamations or assertions, to convey its effect. It is does not speak; it is "mute," "dumb," "silent," even—albeit paradoxically—"wordless." Like a "globed fruit," it is at once real and artificial, a source of aesthetic nourishment as well as an autonomous object of contemplation. But its relation to the past is mysterious, unknowable: like old medallions and window casements worn down by people long forgotten, it transcends its moment of origin. Just as the climbing moon traces its eternally repeated voyage through the nighttime sky, leaving behind the tangled trees of the earth, the poem moves without seeming to move, ascending past both individual and collective memory. The last stanza forthrightly affirms that poetry makes no claim to truth-telling: "A poem should be equal to, not true." Poetry's power of generalized assertion resides in specific evocations of tactile and visual experience that, rather than conveying cognition, reverberate with strong but unspecified affect: grief is signified by "an empty doorway and a maple leaf," love by "the leaning grasses and two lights above the sea." It is through its powers of non-referential implication that a poem can manage not to "mean" but to "be." MacLeish's "Ars Poetica" exemplifies to perfection the doctrine, widely taught in creative writing programs, that a literary work should "show not tell."

"Ars Poetica" has often been seen as a kind of manifesto for the modernist poetic movement called—unsurprisingly—Imagism, which aimed to transcend the limitations of proposition-laden poetry by insisting upon "no ideas but in things," as the poet William Carlos Williams put it (W. Williams, 1992, 6). In the hands of the New Critics—who, we will recall, elevated formalism to the level of political and cultural orthodoxy during the Cold War—over the decades MacLeish's poem would come to stand in for a critique of the entire tradition of socially committed poetry that had exercised widespread influence during and beyond the Depression years. The poem also inspired John Ciardi's highly influential literature textbook, *How Does a Poem Mean?* (Ciardi 1959). Yet the poem offers a specious antidote to intrusive didacticism. "Ars Poetica" appears to thrive on the richly paradoxical nature of its claims: how can a poem, made of words, be wordless? How can a climbing moon be motionless? The key contradiction in the poem, however, resides not so much in its teasing and ambiguous images or its evasive syntax (the second stanza verges on grammatical incoherence) as in its relentless deployment of the phrase "A poem should." Ostensibly a critique of the notion of art as propaganda, "Ars Poetica" sets forth a doctrine about what constitutes good and (by extension) bad art that itself constitutes a militantly propagandistic act of "telling." Poems should be beyond history; they should contain not formulable ideas, but ineffable experiences; they should eschew abstraction and reside entirely in the realm of the concrete. Because the version of concreteness displayed in "Ars Poetica" entails the detachment of particulars from any imaginable shared and general "meaning," however, what results is not an expanded appreciation of the rich reality behind the image, but instead a fetishization of immediacy and rejection of totality—along with a strict reminder that this is what poetry, *qua* poetry, is supposed to do. While the high modernist doctrine with which this poem is associated has gone the way of all flesh, its legacy remains alive and well in the doctrines of New Formalism and surface reading enjoying considerable popularity in twenty-first-century literary study.

We'll end our examination of this cluster of poems about poetry by considering a Depression-era work titled "A Bed for the Night" by Bertolt Brecht:

> I hear that in New York
> At the corner of 26th Street and Broadway
> A man stands every evening during the winter months
> And gets beds for the homeless there
> By appealing to passers-by
>
> It won't change the world
> It won't improve relations among men
> It will not shorten the age of exploitation
> But a few men have a bed for the night
> For a night the wind is kept from them
> The snow meant for them falls on the roadway.
>
> Don't put down the book on reading this, man.
>
> A few people have a bed for the night
> For a night the wind is kept from them
> The snow meant for them falls on the roadway
> But it won't change the world
> It won't improve relations among men
> It will not shorten the age of exploitation.
>
> (Brecht 1976, 181)

The poem poses both a problem in dialectics and a query about poetry that are intimately interconnected. The speaker has heard of a charitable man who, standing at a street corner, regularly attempts to solicit funds so that homeless people will, at least for one night, be sheltered from the wind and snow. This information leads the speaker to contemplate the relationship between reform and revolution and to ask the reader to make a choice: which outlook is more realistic? Stanza two poses the reformist position: while the man's charitable act cannot "change the world," it makes a difference, in the short term, to those who are its recipients. Stanza four, by contrast, reminds the reader that charitable acts, however well intended, will not "shorten the age of exploitation." The fact that stanza four gets the final word strongly implies Brecht's conviction that revolution is necessary in order to do away with the condition—capitalism's need for a reserve army of unemployed labor—that produces homelessness in the first place. The ending phrase, "age of exploitation," implies that the era we inhabit is temporary: it came into being in time and can go out of being in time. The key device conveying this conclusion is repetition-with-a-difference, since the second and fourth stanzas contain lines that are nearly identical but rearranged. As a commentary on the dialectical powers of language, Brecht's formulation reminds us of the rhetorically weighting power of "but." There is, after all, a world of difference between my saying, "I admire your honesty, but I have to disagree" and my saying, "I have to disagree, but I admire your honesty." There is no way to present both sides of any question without ideologically privileging one side over the other: no naïve way to engage in showing without also telling. Rearranging the short series of assertions to convey the critical shift in emphasis, Brecht's poem uses organic form to explore dialectical contradiction and inversion.

But—what do we make of stanza three, consisting of the single line, "Don't put down the book on reading this, man"? Like Hughes's "What kind of poem / Would you make out of that?", this jolting query comes from a place outside of the poem's frame. The speaker's designation of the reader as "man" links us not just to the "man" collecting funds but also to the "men" and "people" noted in the text. Not only are we being brought into the political debate set forth in the poem; we are also being addressed as readers who approach poems with certain common-sense expectations about poetry, and indeed literature more generally. Many poets, Brecht implies, would stop at the end of stanza two, content with implying approval of the philanthropist's selfless gesture, or at least conveying a resigned acceptance of the necessarily piecemeal and modest nature of any efforts to "change the world." Many readers, similarly, are accustomed to drawing comfort from an empathetic engagement with literary works that verify and reinforce taken-for-granted notions about the limits to transformative political possibility—to finding beauty in works that foreclose contradictions and project compensatory utopias.

In "A Bed for the Night," Brecht directs attention to the fact that, in most literary works produced in capitalist society, revolution—if considered at all—is portrayed as wish-fulfilling fantasy: reform is the only realistic option. His poem would have us think otherwise: not only about the world—reform is fantasy, revolution is realism—but also about the role that literature can play in representing the world, and thereby transforming it. "Art is not a mirror held up to reality, but a hammer with which to shape it": as an organic intellectual, the poet supplies an alternative common sense by coming, as Lenin put it, "from outside" the everyday common sense of life in capitalist society. As poet, communist, and revolutionary humanist, Brecht would have us recall Marx's early statement of mission: "The philosophers have only interpreted the world in various ways; the point is to change it."

Let's allow Brecht—and Marx—to have the final word.

Notes

Prologue

1. www.google.com/search?q=world+bank+founding&ie=utf-8&oe=utf-8&client=firefox-b-1
2. See www.cgdev.org/blog/chart-week-1-elephant-graph-flattening-out

1   Historical Materialism

1. See www.nybooks.com/articles/2012/06/21/how-texas-inflicts-bad-textbooks-on-us/

2   Political Economy

1. See www.nytimes.com/2015/12/16/world/asia/china-air-restaurant-clean-charge.html
2. See 'Steel industry' entry at conservapedia.com/

4   Literature and Literary Criticism

1. See www.dw.com/en/controversies-that-have-dogged-the-nobel-prize-for-literature-awards/a-40819676
2. See https://study.com/academy/lesson/gone-with-the-wind-themes-setting.html
3. See for example www.booksthatgrow.com/what-to-a-slave-is-the-fourth-of-july-guide/
4. See www.penguin.com/static/pdf/teachersguides/ animalfarm.pdf
5. See www.gradesaver.com/native-son
6. See www.shmoop.com/bartleby-the-scrivener/title.html
7. See www.reference.com/world-view/individual-vs-society-9e766ff82f4e10f0
8. See www.questia.com/library/literature/literary-themes-and-topics/identity-in-literature
9. See www.scholastic.com/teachers/blog-posts/jeremy-rinkel/hunger-games-novel-study/

5   Marxist Literary Criticism

1. See https://history.howstuffworks.com/historical-figures/why-is-ayn-rand-so-popular-today.htm

6   Marxist Pedagogy

1. See www.nytimes.com/2010/06/07/business/global/07suicide.htm

2. See www.nytimes.com/2012/01/22/business/apple-america-and-a-squeezed-middle-class.html

3. https://techcrunch.com/2018/06/10/after-report-on-appalling-conditions-foxconn-will-investigate-plant-that-makes-amazon-devices/

4. http://study.com/academy/lesson/yeats-the-second-coming-a-poem-of-postwar-apocalypse.html

5. http://constitutionus.com/

6. www.britannica.com/event/Battle-of-Verdun

7. https://literarydevices.net/deus-ex-machina/

8. http://global.penguinrandomhouse.com/announcements/e-l-jamess-darker-fifty-shades-darker-as-told-by-christian-to-be-published-november-28-2017/

9. www.thestranger.com/blogs/slog/2015/02/14/21710269/fifty-terrible-lines-from-fifty-shades-of-grey

Bibliography

AAUW (2018) "It's Time to Close the Gender Pay Gap," 12 September. www.aauw.org/article/its-time-to-close-the-gender-pay-gap/

Abrams, Nathan D. (2008) "Antonio's B-boys: Rap, Rappers, and Gramsci's Intellectuals." *Popular Music and Society* 19(4): 1–19.

Adorno, Theodor (1974) "Lyric Poetry and Society." *Telos* 20–21: 56–71.

—— (1977a) "Commitment." Trans. Francis McDonagh. In Theodor Adorno et al. *Aesthetics and Politics: Theodor Adorno, Walter Benjamin, Ernst Bloch, Bertolt Brecht, Georg Lukács.* London: Verso, pp. 177–95.

—— (1977b) "Reconciliation under Duress." Trans. Rodney Livingstone. In Theodor Adorno et al. *Aesthetics and Politics: Theodor Adorno, Walter Benjamin, Ernst Bloch, Bertolt Brecht, Georg Lukács.* London: Verso, pp. 151–76.

Aguilar, Delia (2015) "Intersectionality." In *Marxism and Feminism.* Ed. Shahrzad Mojab. London: Zed Books, pp. 203–20.

Alexander, Michelle (2010) *The New Jim Crow: Mass Incarceration in the Age of Color-blindness.* New York: New Press.

Allen, Theodore (2012) *The Invention of the White Race.* 2nd edn. New York: Verso.

Althusser, Louis (1969) *For Marx.* Trans. Ben Brewster. London: Allen Lane.

—— (1971) *Lenin and Philosophy.* Trans. Ben Brewster. New York: Monthly Review.

—— (2014) *On the Reproduction of Capitalism.* Trans. G.M. Goshgarian. London: Verso.

Amado, Jorge (1945 [1943]) *The Violent Land (Terras Do Sem Fim).* Trans. Samuel Putnam. New York: Alfred A. Knopf.

Anderson, Kevin (2010) *Marx at the Margins: On Nationalism, Ethnicity, and Non-Western Societies.* Expanded edn. Chicago: University of Chicago Press.

Angelou, Maya (1987) *I Know Why the Caged Bird Sings.* New York: Virago Modern Classics.

Angus, Ian (2016) *Facing the Anthropocene: Fossil Capitalism and the Crisis of the Earth System.* New York: Monthly Review Press.

Anievas, Alexander, and Kamran Matin (2016) *Historical Sociology and World History: Uneven and Combined Development over the Longue Durée.* London: Rowman and Littlefield.

Anzaldúa, Gloria (1999) "We Call Them Greasers." In *Borderlands/La Frontera*, 2nd edition, ed. with an introduction by Sonia Saldívar-Hull. San Francisco: Aunt Lute Books, pp. 156-57.

Aristotle (2013) *Poetics.* Trans. Anthony Kenny. Oxford: Oxford World's Classics.

Arnold, Matthew (1965) *The Poems of Matthew Arnold.* Ed. Kenneth Allot. New York: Barnes and Noble.

Arthur, C.J. (1986) *Dialectics of Labour: Marx and His Relation to Hegel.* Oxford: Basil Blackwell.

Austen, Jane (1961 [1813]) *Pride and Prejudice.* New York: New American Library.

"Author's Field Day" (1934) *New Masses* 12(8), 3 July: 27–32.

Badiou, Alain (2015) *The Communist Hypothesis.* Trans. David Macey. London: Verso.

Balibar, Étienne (2007) *The Philosophy of Marx*. Trans. Chris Turner. London: Verso.
—— and Pierre Macherey (1996) "On Literature as an Ideological Form." In *Marxist Literary Theory: A Reader*. Ed. Terry Eagleton and Drew Milne. Oxford: Blackwell.
Balzac, Honoré de (1999) *Old Goriot (Père Goriot)*. Trans. A.J. Krailsheimer. Oxford: Oxford World's Classics.
Baptist, Edward (2016) *The Half Has Never Been Told: Slavery and the Making of American Capitalism*. New York: Basic Books.
Barnard, Alan (2007) *Anthropology and the Bushman*. Oxford: Berg.
Barnett, David (2015) *Brecht in Practice: Theatre, Theory, Performance*. London: Methuen.
Barthes, Roland (1972) *Mythologies*. Trans. Annette Lavers. London: Jonathan Cape.
—— (1974) *S/Z*. Trans. Richard Miller. New York: Hill and Wang.
Bartoloni, Paolo, and Anthony Stephens (2010) "Introduction to Ambiguity in Culture and Literature." CLCWeb: *Comparative Literature and Culture* 12(4): https://doi. org/10.7771/1481-4374.1669
Beard, Charles (1957 [1913]) *An Economic Interpretation of the Constitution of the United States*. New York: Macmillan.
Beech, Dave (2015) *Art and Value: Art's Economic Exceptionalism in Classical, Neoclassical and Marxist Economics*. Chicago: Haymarket Books.
Behn, Aphra (2004 [1688]) *Oroonoko; or, The Royal Slave*. London: Penguin.
Bell, Bernard (1991) "Twain's 'Nigger Jim': The Tragic Face behind the Minstrel Mask." In *Satire or Evasion? Black Perspectives on Huckleberry Finn*. Ed. James S. Leonard et al. Durham, NC: Duke University Press, pp. 124–40.
Belsey, Catherine (1980) *Critical Practice*. New York: Methuen.
Benjamin, Walter (1969) *Illuminations*. Trans. Harry Zohn. New York: Schocken Books.
Bennett, Lerone (1975) *The Shaping of Black America*. Chicago: Johnson Pub. Co.
Bennett, Tony (1990) *Outside Literature*. London: Routledge.
Berlant, Lauren (2004) "Introduction: Compassion (and Withholding)." In *Compassion: The Culture and Politics of an Emotion*. Ed. Laurent Berlant. New York: Routledge.
Best, Stephen, and Sharon Marcus (2009) "The Way We Read Now." *Representations* 108(Fall): 1–21.
Bewes, Timothy (2002) *Reification; or, The Anxiety of Late Capitalism*. London: Verso.
Blake, William (1953) *Selected Poetry and Prose of William Blake*. Ed. Northrop Frye. New York: Modern Library.
Bloch, Ernst (1986) *The Principle of Hope*. Trans. Neville Plaice, Stephen Plaice, and Paul Knight. Cambridge, MA: MIT Press.
Booth, Naomi (2015) "The Felicity of Falling: *Fifty Shades of Grey* and the Feminine Art of Sinking." *Women: A Cultural Review* 26(1–2): 22–39.
Bosteels, Bruno (2011) *The Actuality of Communism*. London: Verso.
Boswell, James (1964 [1791]) *Boswell's Life of Johnson, LL.D.* Ed. G.B.Hill, rev. L.F. Powell, 6 vols. Oxford: Clarendon Press.
Bourdieu, Pierre (1990) *In Other Words: Essays Towards a Reflexive Sociology*. Trans. M. Adamson. Stanford, CA: Stanford University Press.
Brass, Tom (2010) "Capitalism, Primitive Accumulation and Unfree Labour." In *Imperialism, Crisis and Class Struggle: The Enduring Verities of Capitalism – Essays Presented to James Petras*. Ed. H. Veltmeyer. Leiden, Netherlands: Brill, pp. 67–149.
Brecht, Bertolt (1964) *Brecht on Theatre: The Development of an Aesthetic*. Trans. John Willett. New York: Farrar, Straus and Giroux.

—— (1965) "Praise of Communism." In *The Mother*. Trans. Lee Baxandall. New York: Grove Press.

—— (1976) *Poems*. Ed. John Willett et al. New York: Methuen.

—— (1977) "Against Georg Lukács." Trans. Stuart Hood. In *Aesthetics and Politics: Theodor Adorno, Walter Benjamin, Ernst Bloch, Bertolt Brecht, Georg Lukács*. London: Verso, pp. 68–85.

—— (1991) *Mother Courage and Her Children*. Trans. Eric Bentley. New York: Grove Press.

—— (1999) *The Good Person of Setzuan*. Trans. Eric Bentley. Minneapolis: University of Minnesota Press.

Brennan, Timothy (2007) *Wars of Position: The Cultural Politics of Left and Right*. New York: Columbia University Press.

Briden, Earl F. (1995) "Kemble's 'Specialty' and the Pictorial Countertext of *Huckleberry Finn*." In *Mark Twain "Adventures of Huckleberry Finn": A Case Study in Critical Controversy*. Ed. Gerald Graff and James Phelan. Boston, MA: Bedford/St. Martin's, pp. 383–406.

Brontë, Emily (2009 [1847]) *Wuthering Heights*. Oxford: Oxford World's Classics.

Brooks, Cleanth (1947) *The Well Wrought Urn: Studies in the Structure of Poetry*. New York: Reynal and Hitchcock.

Brooks, Peter (1984) *Reading for the Plot: Design and Intention in Narrative*. Cambridge, MA: Harvard University Press.

Brown, Malcolm, ed. (2007) *Meeting in No Man's Land: Christmas 1914 and Fraternization in the Great War*. London: Constable.

Brown, Nicholas (2012) "The Work of Art in the Age of Real Subsumption under Capital." http://nonsite.org/editorial/the-work-of-art-in-the-age-of-its-real-subsumption-under-capital

Bulosan, Carlos (2007) "If You Want to Know What We Are." In *American Working-Class Literature: An Anthology*. Ed. Nicholas Coles and Janet Zandy. New York: Oxford University Press, pp. 592–94.

—— (2014 [1946]) *America Is in the Heart*. Seattle: University of Washington Press.

Bunyan, John (2008 [1678]) *The Pilgrim's Progress from This World to That Which Is to Come; Delivered under the Similitude of a Dream*. New York: W.W. Norton.

Burgis, Tom (2015) *The Looting Machine: Warlords, Oligarchs, Corporations, Smugglers, and the Theft of Africa's Wealth*. New York: Public Affairs.

Burke, Kenneth (1941) *The Philosophy of Literary Form: Studies in Symbolic Action*. Baton Rouge: Louisiana State University Press.

Buzgalin, Aleksandr, and Andrey Kolganov (2013) "The Anatomy of Twenty-first Century Exploitation: From Traditional Extraction of Surplus Value to Exploitation of Creative Activity." *Science & Society* 27(4): 486–511.

Cabral, Amilcar (1966) "The Weapon of Theory." www.marxists.org/subject/africa/cabral/1966/weapon-theory.htm

Calvino, Italo (1983 [1963]) *Marcovaldo: or, The Seasons in the City*. Trans. William Weaver. San Diego: Harvest Books.

Carlyle, Thomas (1970 [1843]) *Past and Present*. London: Everyman's Library.

Caudwell, Christopher [Sprigg, Christopher St. John] (1937) *Illusion and Reality: A Study of the Sources of Poetry*. New York: International Publishers.

—— (1971) *Studies and Further Studies in a Dying Culture*. New York: Monthly Review Press.

Chakrabarty, Dipesh (2007) *Provincializing Europe: Postcolonial Thought and Historical Difference*. Princeton, NJ: Princeton University Press.

Chatman, Seymour (1978) *Story and Discourse: Narrative Structure in Fiction and Film*. Ithaca, NY: Cornell University Press.

Chattopadhyay, Paresh (2012) "The Myth of Twentieth-Century Socialism and the Continuing Relevance of Karl Marx." In *Marx for Today*. Ed. Marcello Musto. London: Routledge, pp. 36–58.

Chesler, Phyllis, and Nathan Bloom (2012) "Hindu vs. Muslim Honor Killings." *Middle East Quarterly* 9(3): 43–52.

Chibber, Vivek (2013) *Postcolonial Theory and the Specter of Capital*. London: Verso.

Chung, Sheng Kuan (2004) "Zen (Ch'an) and Aesthetic Education." *In Teaching for Aesthetic Experience: The Art of Learning*. Ed. Gene Diaz and Martha McKenna. New York: Peter Lang, pp. 33–48.

Ciardi, John (1959) *How Does a Poem Mean?* Boston, MA: Houghton Mifflin.

Cleaver, Eldridge (1967) *On the Ideology of the Black Panther Party*. San Francisco: Black Panther Party.

Cleghorn, Sara (2007) "The Golf Links Lie So Near the Mill." In *American Working-Class Literature: An Anthology*. Ed. Nicholas Coles and Janet Zandy. New York: Oxford University Press, p. 309.

Cohan, George F. (1917) "Over There." www.encyclopedia.com/history/dictionaries-thesauruses-pictures-and-press-releases/lyrics-over-there-1917-george-m-cohan

Coles, Nicholas, and Janet Zandy (2007) *American Working-Class Literature: An Anthology*. New York: Oxford University Press.

Collins, Suzanne (2008) *The Hunger Games*. New York: Scholastic Press.

Combahee River Collective Statement (1983 [1979]) In *Home Girls, A Black Feminist Anthology*. Ed. Barbara Smith. New York: Kitchen Table: Women of Color Press, Inc., pp. 264-74.

Commission on the Humanities and Social Sciences (2013) *The Heart of the Matter*. Cambridge, MA: American Academy of Arts & Sciences. www.humanitiescommission.org/_pdf/hss_report.pdf

Cooper, James Fenimore (2005 [1841]) *The Deerslayer; or, The First Warpath*. New York: Barnes and Noble Classics.

Cooper, Thomas (1995 [1845]) "'Merrie England'—No More!" In *The Literature of Struggle: An Anthology of Chartist Fiction*. Ed. Ian Haywood. Aldershot: Scola, pp. 53–59.

Crehan, Kate (2016) *Gramsci's Common Sense: Inequality and Its Narratives*. Durham, NC: Duke University Press.

Crisis (1940) "Editorial of the Month." October: 323.

Damon, Maria (2011) *Postliterary America: From Bagel Shop Jazz to Micropoetries*. Iowa City: University of Iowa Press.

Daniels, Lee (director and co-producer) (2009) *Precious: Based on the Novel 'Push' by Sapphire*. Film.

Davis, Angela Y. (1983) *Women, Race and Class*. New York: Random House.

—— (1994) "Afro-images: Politics, Fashion, and Nostalgia." *Critical Inquiry* 21(Autumn): 37–45.

Davis, Lennard J. (1983) *Factual Fictions: The Origins of the English Novel*. New York: Columbia University Press.

—— (1987) *Resisting Novels: Ideology and Fiction*. London: Methuen.

Dawahare, Anthony (2018) *Tillie Olsen and the Dialectical Philosophy of Proletarian Literature*. Lanham, MD: Lexington Books.

De Ste. Croix, G.E.M. (1981) *The Class Struggle in the Ancient Greek World*. Ithaca, NY: Cornell University Press.

—— (1987) *Resisting Novels: Ideology and Fiction*. London: Methuen.

Dean, Jodi (2012) *The Communist Horizon*. London: Verso.

—— (2016) *Crowds and Party*. London: Verso.

Defoe, Daniel (2003 [1722]) *A Journal of the Plague Year*. London: Penguin Classics.

Delany, Sheila (1990) *Medieval Literary Politics: Shapes of Ideology*. New York: St. Martin's Press.

D'Emilio, John (1998 [1983]) *Sexual Politics, Sexual Communities: The Making of a Homosexual Minority in the United States, 1940–1970*. Rev. edn. Chicago: University of Chicago Press.

Dickens, Charles (2003 [1854]) *Hard Times*. London: Penguin Classics.

Dickinson, Emily (1976) *Complete Poems*. Boston, MA: Back Bay Books.

Dimock, Wai Chee (1985) "Debasing Exchange: Edith Wharton's *The House of Mirth*." *PMLA* 100(5, October): 783–92.

Donne, John (1959) *Devotions on Emergent Occasions*. Ann Arbor: University of Michigan Press.

Dos Passos, John (1937) *U.S.A.* New York: Modern Library.

Douglass, Frederick (1996) *The Oxford Frederick Douglass Reader*. Ed. William L. Andrews. New York: Oxford University Press.

Douzinas, Costas, and Slavoj Žižek, eds (2010) *The Idea of Communism*. London: Verso.

Dreiser, Theodore (1967 [1912]) *The Financier*. New York: New American Library.

—— (1994 [1900]) *Sister Carrie*. New York: W.W. Norton.

Du Bois, W.E.B. (1998 [1935]) *Black Reconstruction in America 1860–1880*. New York: Free Press.

—— (2000 [1926]) "Criteria of Negro Art." *Crisis* 32(October): 290–97. In *African American Literary Theory: A Reader*. Ed. Winston Napier. New York: New York University Press, pp. 17–23.

Dumas, Alexandre (père) (2003 [1844–5]) *The Count of Monte Cristo*. Trans. Robin Buss. London: Penguin Classics.

Dunbar-Ortiz, Roxanne (2014) *An Indigenous People's History of the United States*. Boston, MA: Beacon Press.

Duncan-Jones, Katherine (2010) *Shakespeare: An Ungentle Life*. London: Bloomsbury Arden Shakespeare.

Durkheim, Émile (2002) *Suicide: A Study in Sociology*. London: Routledge.

Dylan, Bob (2016) *The Lyrics: 1961–2012*. New York: Simon and Schuster.

Eagleton, Terry (1976) *Marxism and Literary Criticism*. Berkeley: University of California Press.

—— (1984) *The Function of Criticism: From the* Spectator *to Post-Structuralism*. London: Verso.

—— (1990) *The Ideology of the Aesthetic*. Oxford: Basil Blackwell.

—— (1991) *Ideology: An Introduction*. London: Verso.

—— (2006) *How to Read a Poem*. Oxford: Wiley-Blackwell.

—— (2011) *Why Marx Was Right*. New Haven, CT: Yale University Press.

—— (2012) *The Event of Literature*. New Haven, CT: Yale University Press.

—— (2013) *How to Read Literature*. New Haven, CT: Yale University Press.

Ebert, Teresa, and Mas'ud Zavarzadeh (2008) *Class in Culture*. Boulder, CO: Paradigm Publishers.

Egan, Daniel (2016) *The Dialectic of Position and Maneuver: Understanding Gramsci's Military Metaphor*. Leiden, Netherlands: Brill.

Eliot, T.S. (1971) *The Complete Poems and Plays, 1909–1950*. New York: Harcourt, Brace and World, Inc.

—— (2014) *The Complete Prose of T.S. Eliot: The Critical Edition: Apprentice Years, 1905–1918*. Ed. Ronald Schuchard and Jewel Spears Brooker. Baltimore, MD: Johns Hopkins University Press.

Ellison, Ralph (1995) *The Collected Essays of Ralph Ellison*. Ed. John F. Callahan. New York: Modern Library.

—— (1996) *Flying Home and Other Stories*. Ed. John F. Callahan. New York: Random House.

Engels, Friedrich. "Progress of Communism in Germany." In *Writings for the* New Moral World (*NMW*). www.marxists.org/archive/marx/works/subject/newspapers/moral-world.htm

—— (1969 [1845]) *The Condition of the Working Class in England* (*CWCE*). www.marxists. org/archive/marx/works/1845/condition-working-class/

—— (1947 [1877–8]) *Herr Eugen Dühring's Revolution in Science (Anti-Dühring)* (*A-D*). www.marxists.org/archive/marx/works/1877/anti-duhring/

—— (1995 [1872]) *The Housing Question* (*HQ*). www.marxists.org/archive/marx/works/1872/housing-question/

—— (2010 [1884]) *On the Origin of the Family, Private Property, and the State* (*OFPPS*). www.marxists.org/archive/marx/works/1884/origin-family/index.htm

—— (1970 [1880]) *Socialism: Utopian and Scientific* (*SUAS*) www.marxists.org/archive/marx/works/1880/soc-utop/index.htm

Estrada, Gabriel S. (2011) "Two Spirits, Nádleeh, and LGBTQ2 Navajo Gaze." *American Indian Culture and Research Journal* 35(4): 167–90.

Euripides (1963 [431 BCE]) *Medea*. Trans. Philip Vellacott. London: Penguin Classics.

Everett, Percival (2001) *Erasure*. Lebanon, NH: University Press of New England.

Faith, Rosamund (1981) "The Class Struggle in Fourteenth-Century England." In *People's History and Socialist Theory*. Ed. Raphael Samuel. London: Routledge and Kegan Paul, pp. 50–60.

Fanon, Frantz (1963) *The Wretched of the Earth*. Trans. Constance Farrington. New York: Grove Press.

—— (2008 [1952]) *Black Skin, White Masks*. Trans. Richard Philcox. New York: Grove Press.

Federici, Silvia (2004) *Caliban and the Witch: Women, the Body, and Primitive Accumulation*. New York: Autonomedia.

Feinberg, Leslie (1993) *Stone Butch Blues: A Novel*. Ithaca, NY: Firebrand Books.

Felski, Rita (2008) *The Uses of Literature*. Oxford: Blackwell.

—— (2015) *The Limits of Critique*. Chicago: University of Chicago Press.

Ferguson, Stephen (2015) *Philosophy of African American Studies: Nothing Left of Blackness*. New York: Palgrave Macmillan.

Fielding, Helen (1996) *Bridget Jones's Diary*. London: Picador.

Fields, Barbara (1990) "Slavery, Race and Ideology in the United States of America." *New Left Review* 181(May/June).

Fisher, Mark (2009) *Capitalist Realism: Is There No Alternative?* Winchester, UK: Zero Books.

Fitzgerald, F. Scott (1925) *The Great Gatsby*. New York: Scribner.

Floyd, Kevin (2009) *The Reification of Desire: Toward a Queer Marxism*. Minneapolis: University of Minnesota Press.

Foley, Barbara (1986) *Telling the Truth: The Theory and Practice of Documentary Fiction*. Ithaca, NY: Cornell University Press.

—— (1992) "Class." *Rethinking Marxism* 5(Summer): 117–28.

—— (1993) *Radical Representations: Politics and Form in US Proletarian Fiction, 1929–1941*. Durham, NC: Duke University Press.

—— (2000) "From Wall Street to Astor Place: Historicizing Melville's 'Bartleby'." *American Literature* 72(March): 87–116.

—— (2002) "From Situational Dialectics to Pseudo-Dialectics: Mao, Jiang, and Capitalist Transition." *Cultural Logic* 5(3). http://eserver.org/clogic/2002/foley.html

—— (2003) *Spectres of 1919: Class and Nation in the Making of the New Negro*. Urbana: University of Illinois Press.

—— (2010) *Wrestling with the Left: The Making of Ralph Ellison's Invisible Man*. Durham, NC: Duke University Press.

—— (2013) "Biography and the Political Unconscious: Ellison, Toomer, Jameson, and the Politics of Symptomatic Reading." *Biography* 36(4): 649–71.

—— (2014) *Jean Toomer: Repression, Race, and Revolution*. Urbana: University of Illinois Press.

—— (2018) "Intersectionality: A Marxist Critique." *Science & Society* 82(2): 269–75.

—— (2019) "Racism." *Bloomsbury Companion to Marxism*. Ed. Jeff Diamanti, Andrew Pendakis and Imre Szeman. London: Bloomsbury Academic, pp. 607–12.

—— and Peter Gardner (2017) "Retrospective Radicalism: Politics and History in Ernest Hemingway's *A Farewell to Arms*." *College Literature: A Journal of Critical Literary Studies* 44(1): 1–29.

Foster, John Bellamy, Brett Clark, and Richard York (2010) *The Ecological Rift: Capitalism's War on the Earth*. New York: Monthly Review Press.

Frank, Anne (1995 [1947]) *The Diary of a Young Girl*. Trans. Susan Massotty. New York: Doubleday.

Franklin, Benjamin (2016 [1793]) *The Autobiography of Benjamin Franklin*. New York: Bedford.

Fredrickson, George (1987) *The Black Image in the White Mind: The Debate on Afro-American Character and Destiny, 1817–1914*. Middletown, CT: Wesleyan University Press.

Freeman, Joseph (1935) "Introduction." In *Proletarian Literature in the United States: An Anthology*. Ed. Granville Hicks et al. New York: International Publishers.

Frosch, Mary (2007) *Coming of Age in America: A Multicultural Anthology*. New York: New Press.

Frost, Robert (1979) *The Poetry of Robert Frost*. Ed. Edward Connery Lathem. New York: Holt, Rinehart and Winston.

Funaroff, Sol (1938) *The Spider and the Clock: Poems*. New York: International.

Fuss, Diana (2017) "But What About Love?" *PMLA* 132(2): 352–55.

Gabriel, Mary (2011) *Love and Capital: Karl and Jenny Marx and the Birth of a Revolution.* Boston, MA: Little, Brown.

Garcia, Matt (2012) *From the Jaws of Victory: The Triumph and Tragedy of Cesar Chavez and the Farm Worker Movement.* Berkeley: University of California Press.

Gardner, Peter (2005) "The Seductive Politics of *Mary Barton.*" *Victorians Institute Journal* 33: 45–67.

Gaskell, Elizabeth (1997 [1848]) *Mary Barton.* London: Penguin Classics.

Genette, Gérard (1980) *Narrative Discourse: An Essay in Method.* Trans. Jane E. Lewin. Ithaca, NY: Cornell University Press.

Gimenez, Martha (2005) "Capitalism and the Oppression of Women: Marx Revisited." *Science & Society* 69(1): 11–32.

Gogol, Nikolai (2004 [1892]) *Dead Souls.* Trans. Robert A. Maguire. New York: Penguin Classics.

Gold, Mike (1929) "Go Left, Young Writers." *New Masses* 4(8): 3–4.

—— (2004 [1930]) *Jews without Money.* Carroll and Graf.

Golding, William (2003 [1954]) *Lord of the Flies.* London: Penguin Books.

Goldsmith, Oliver (2002 [1775]) *The Deserted Village.* Oldcastle: Gallery Books.

Gomberg, Paul (2007) *How to Make Opportunity Equal: Race and Contributive Justice.* Oxford: Blackwell.

González, Marcial, and Carlos Gallejo (2018) *Dialectical Imaginaries: Materialist Approaches to U.S. Latino/a Literature in the Age of Neoliberalism.* Ann Arbor: University of Michigan Press.

Gowdy, John (2004) "Hunter-gatherers and the Mythology of the Market." *Cambridge Encyclopedia of Hunters and Gatherers.* Cambridge: Cambridge University Press.

Graff, Gerald and James Phelan, eds (1995) *Mark Twain "Adventures of Huckleberry Finn": A Case Study in Critical Controversy.* Boston, MA: Bedford/St. Martin's.

Gramsci, Antonio (1971) *Selections from the Prison Notebooks of Antonio Gramsci.* Ed. and trans. Quintin Hoare and Geoffrey Nowell-Smith. New York: International Publishers.

—— (1985) *Selections from Cultural Writings.* Ed. David Forgags and Geoffrey Nowell-Smith. Trans. William Boelhower. London: Lawrence and Wishart.

Grant, Madison (1918) *The Passing of the Great Race; or, The Racial Basis of European History.* New York: Charles Scribner's Sons.

Griffith, D.W. (1915) *The Birth of a Nation.* Film. David W. Griffith Corporation.

Groden, Michael, Martin Kreiswirth and Imre Szeman (2012) *Johns Hopkins Guide to Literary Theory and Criticism.* Baltimore, MD: Johns Hopkins University Press.

Halberstam, Jack J. (2011) *The Queer Art of Failure.* Durham, NC: Duke University Press.

Hardt, Michael (2010) "The Common in Communism." In *The Idea of Communism.* Ed. Costas Douzinas and Slavoj Žižek, London: Verso, pp. 131–44.

—— and Antonio Negri (2004) *Multitude: War and Democracy in the Age of Empire.* New York: Penguin.

Hardy, Thomas (2009 [1895]) *Jude the Obscure.* Oxford: Oxford World's Classics.

Hartsock, Nancy (2004) "The Feminist Standpoint." In *The Feminist Standpoint Theory Reader.* Ed. Sandra Harding. London: Routledge, pp. 35–54.

Harvey, David (1990) *The Condition of Postmodernity: An Inquiry into the Origins of Cultural Change.* Oxford: Blackwell.

—— (2003) *The New Imperialism.* Oxford: Oxford University Press.

—— and Hector Agredano Rivera. "Explaining the Crisis." *International Socialist Review* 73(September).

Hawthorne, Nathaniel (2017 [1850]) *The Scarlet Letter*. New York: W.W. Norton.

Heaven, Pamela (2011) "Marx Was Right; Capitalism Can Destroy Itself: Roubini." *Financial Post* 12 August.

Hebdige, Dick (1979) *Subculture: The Meaning of Style*. London: Routledge.

Heffernan, James A.W. (1985) *The Re-creation of Landscape: A Study of Wordsworth, Coleridge, Constable, and Turner*. Hanover, NH: University Press of New England for Dartmouth College.

Hemingway, Ernest (1935) *The Green Hills of Africa*. New York: Charles Scribner's Sons.

Henry, Peaches (1991) "The Struggle for Tolerance: Race and Censorship in *Huckleberry Finn*." In *Satire or Evasion? Black Perspectives on Huckleberry Finn*. Ed. James S. Leonard et al. Durham, NC: Duke University Press, pp. 25–49.

Hicks, Granville (1974) "Revolution and the Novel." In *Granville Hicks and the New Masses*. Ed. Jack Alan Robbins. Port Washington, NY: Kennikat.

Hill, Richard (1995) "Overreaching: Critical Agenda and the Ending of *Adventures of Huckleberry Finn*." In *Mark Twain "Adventures of Huckleberry Finn": A Case Study in Critical Controversy*. Ed. Gerald Graff and James Phelan. Boston, MA: Bedford/St. Martin's, pp. 312–34.

Hindess, Barry and Paul Hirst (1975) *Pre-Capitalist Modes of Production*. London: Routledge and Kegan Paul.

Hobsbawm, Eric J. (2012) *Nations and Nationalism since 1780: Programme, Myth, Reality*. 2nd edn. Cambridge: Cambridge University Press.

Holstun, James (2017) "Buffalo Unsteeled: Connie Porter, Leslie Feinberg, and the Persistence of Proletarian Fiction." *English Language and Literature* 63(1): 23–43.

Homer (2011 [c. 762 BCE]) *The Iliad*. Trans. Richmond Lattimore. Chicago: University of Chicago Press.

Honey, Maureen (1984) *Creating Rosie the Riveter: Class, Gender and Propaganda during World War II*. Amherst: University of Massachusetts Press.

Horkheimer, Max, and Theodor Adorno (1994) *Dialectic of Enlightenment*. Trans. John Cumming. New York: Continuum.

Horne, Gerald (2014) *The Counter-Revolution of 1776: Slave Resistance and the Origins of the United States of America*. New York: NYU Press.

Hudson, Hosea (1972) *Black Worker in the Deep South: A Personal Record*. New York: International Publishers.

Hughes, Langston (1994) *The Collected Poems of Langston Hughes*. Ed. Arnold Rampersad. New York: Vintage Books.

Hugo, Victor (2012 [1833]) *The Hunchback of Notre Dame* (*Notre-Dame de Paris* [1831]). Trans. Jean-Marc Hovasse. London: Everyman's Library.

Hurston, Zora Neale (2006 [1937]) *Their Eyes Were Watching God*. New York: Harper Perennial Classics.

Illouz, Eva (2014) *Fifty Shades of Grey, Best Sellers, and Society*. Chicago: University of Chicago Press.

Irr, Caren (2017) "Introduction: An Althusser for the Twenty-First Century." *Mediations* 30(2): 29–36.

Isenberg, Nancy (2016) *White Trash: The 400-Year Untold History of Class in America*. New York: Viking.

Jacobs, Harriet (2001 [1861]) *Incidents in the Life of a Slave Girl*. New York: Penguin Classics.

James, E.L. (2011) *Fifty Shades of Grey*. New York: Vintage.

Jameson, Fredric (1977) "Conclusion." In Theodor Adorno et al., *Aesthetics and Politics: Theodor Adorno, Walter Benjamin, Ernst Bloch, Bertolt Brecht, Georg Lukács*. London: Verso, pp. 196–213.

——— (1981) *The Political Unconscious: Narrative as a Socially Symbolic Act*. Ithaca, NY: Cornell University Press.

——— (2008) *The Ideologies of Theory*. London: Verso.

Jones, Gayl (1975) *Corregidora*. Boston, MA: Beacon.

Jones, Jack (1934) *Rhondda Roundabout*. London: Faber and Faber.

Joyce, James (1999 [1939]) *Finnegans Wake*. London: Penguin Classics.

——— (2003 [1916]) *A Portrait of the Artist as a Young Man*. London: Penguin Classics.

Junger, Sebastian (1997) *The Perfect Storm*. New York: W.W. Norton.

Kalmring, Stefan and Andreas Nowak (2017) "Viewing Africa with Marx: Remarks on Marx's Fragmented Engagement with the African Continent." *Science & Society* 81(3): 331–47.

Kaplan, Justin (1995) "Born to Trouble: One Hundred Years of *Huckleberry Finn*." In *Mark Twain "Adventures of Huckleberry Finn": A Case Study in Critical Controversy*. Ed. Gerald Graff and James Phelan. Boston, MA: Bedford/St. Martin's, pp. 348–58.

Kaplan, Sandra (2017) "Depth and Complexity Icons." www.romoland.net/cms/lib/CA01902709/Centricity/Domain/21/Kaplan-Depth-and-Complexity-1y4xdgk.pdf

Karanikas, Alexander (1966) *Tillers of a Myth: Southern Agrarians as Social and Literary Critics*. Madison: University of Wisconsin Press.

Keene, John (2016) *Counternarratives*. New York: New Directions.

Kelley, Robin D.G. (2002) *Freedom Dreams: The Black Radical Imagination*. Boston, MA: Beacon.

——— (2015) *Hammer and Hoe: Alabama Communists During the Depression*. 2nd edn. Chapel Hill: University of North Carolina Press.

Kellner, Douglas (2002) "The Frankfurt School and British Cultural Studies: The Missed Articulation." In *Rethinking the Frankfurt School: Alternative Legacies of Cultural Critique*. Ed. Jeffrey Nealon and Caren Irr. Albany: SUNY Press.

Kelly, Helena (2010) "Austen and Enclosure." www.jasna.org/persuasions/on-line/vol30no2/kelly.html

Kendi, Ibram (2016) *The Definitive History of Racist Ideas in America*. New York: Nation Books.

King, Martin Luther (1965) "Our God Is Marching On." www.mlkonline.net/ourgod.html

——— (2018 [1963]) *Letter from Birmingham Jail*. New York: Penguin Random House.

Kipling, Rudyard (1922) *Verse: 1885–1918*. Garden City, NY: Doubleday, Page and Co.

Klein, Naomi (2007) *The Shock Doctrine: The Rise of Disaster Capitalism*. New York: Macmillan.

Laclau, Ernesto, and Chantal Mouffe (1985) *Hegemony and Socialist Strategy: Towards a Radical Democratic Politics*. London: Verso.

Lafargue, Paul (1972 [1890]) "Reminiscences of Marx." www.marxists.org/archive/lafargue/1890/xx/marx.htm

Lamarr, Kendrick (2017) *Damn*. Album. Top Dawg Entertainment. www.youtube.com/watch?v=-O-xqoNdG6o

Langland, William (2007 [1370–90]) *The Vision of Piers Plowman*. Oxford: Oxford World's Classics.

Larsen, Nella (1971 [1928]) *Quicksand*. New York: Collier Books.

Lasch, Christopher (1995) *Haven in a Heartless World: The Family Besieged*. Rev. edn. New York: W.W. Norton.

Lazarus, Neil (2011) *The Postcolonial Unconscious*. Cambridge: Cambridge University Press.

Leacock, Eleanor Burke (1981) *Myths of Male Dominance*. New York: Monthly Review Press.

Lenin, V.I. (1961 [1902]) *What Is To Be Done? Burning Questions of our Movement (WITBD)*. www.marxists.org/archive/lenin/works/1901/witbd/

—— (1999 [1918]) *The State and Revolution (S&R)*. www.marxists.org/archive/lenin/works/1917/staterev/

—— (1975) *On Socialist Ideology and Culture*. Moscow: Progress Publishers.

—— (1965 [1926]) "On Proletarian Culture" (*OPC*). www.Marxists.org/archives/Lenin/works/1920/OCT/08.htm

—— (1964 [1917]) *April Theses*. www.marxists.org/archive/lenin/works/1917/apr/04.htm

Leonard, James S. et al., eds (1991) *Satire or Evasion? Black Perspectives on Huckleberry Finn*. Durham, NC: Duke University Press.

Lerner, Gerda (1987) *The Creation of Patriarchy*. Oxford: Oxford University Press.

Lesjak, Carolyn (2013) "Reading Dialectically." In *Literary Materialisms*. Ed. Mathias Nilges and Emilio Sauri. New York: Palgrave Macmillan, pp. 17–48.

Lester, Julius (1995) "Morality and Adventures of Huckleberry Finn." (1995) In *Mark Twain "Adventures of Huckleberry Finn": A Case Study in Critical Controversy*. Ed. Gerald Graff and James Phelan. Boston, MA: Bedford/St. Martin's, pp. 340–48.

Levinson, Marjorie (2007) "What Is New Formalism?" *PMLA* 122(2): 558–69.

Levitas, Ruth (1990) *The Concept of Utopia*. Syracuse, NY: Syracuse University Press.

Lewis, R.W.B. (1955) *The American Adam: Innocence, Tragedy and Tradition in the Nineteenth Century*. Chicago: University of Chicago Press.

Lifshitz, Mikhail (1973 [1938]) *The Philosophy of Art of Karl Marx*. Trans. Ralph B. Winn. London: Pluto Press.

Lih, Lars (2006) *Lenin Rediscovered: "What Is to Be Done?" in Context*. Leiden, Netherlands: Brill.

Loewen, James W. (2007) *Lies My Teacher Told Me: Everything Your American History Textbook Got Wrong*. Rev. edn. New York: Touchstone Books.

London, Jack (2006 [1908]) *The Iron Heel*. New York: Penguin Classics.

Longinus, Cassius (1957 [n.d.]) *On the Sublime*. New York: Liberal Arts Press.

Loose, Margaret A. (2014) *The Chartist Imaginary: Literary Form in Working-Class Political Theory and Practice*. Columbus: Ohio State University Press.

López, Dennis (2014) "'You Talk 'merican?' Class, Value, and the Social Production of Difference in Helena María Viramontes's *Under the Feet of Jesus*." *College Literature* 41(4): 41–70.

Lovejoy, Arthur O. (1976 [1936]) *The Great Chain of Being: A Study of the History of an Idea*. Cambridge, MA: Harvard University Press.

Lukács, Georg (1962) *The Historical Novel.* Trans. Hannah and Stanley Mitchell. London: Merlin Press.

—— (1963) "The Ideology of Modernism." In *The Meaning of Contemporary Realism.* Trans. John and Necke Mander. London: Methuen, pp. 17–46.

—— (1964) *Studies in European Realism: A Sociological Survey of the Writings of Balzac, Stendhal, Tolstoy, Zola, Gorky, and Others.* New York: Grosset and Dunlap.

—— (1971) *History and Class Consciousness.* Trans. Rodney Livingstone. Cambridge, MA: MIT Press.

—— (1977) "Realism in the Balance." Trans. Rodney Livingston. In Theodor Adorno et al. *Aesthetics and Politics: Theodor Adorno, Walter Benjamin, Ernst Bloch, Bertolt Brecht, Georg Lukács.* London: Verso, pp. 28–59.

Macherey, Pierre (1978) *A Theory of Literary Production.* Trans. Geoffrey Wall. London: Routledge and Kegan Paul.

—— (2012) "Figures of Interpellation in Althusser and Fanon." *Radical Philosophy* 173: 14–17.

MacLeish, Archibald (1952 [1926]) *Collected Poems.* Boston, MA: Houghton Mifflin.

Maerhofer, John W. (2009) *Rethinking the Vanguard: Aesthetic and Political Positions in the Modernist Debate, 1917–1962.* Newcastle: Cambridge Scholars.

Mailer, Norman (1968) *The Armies of the Night: History as a Novel/The Novel as History.* New York: New American Library.

Mao Zedong (1967 [1937]) "On Contradiction." In *Selected Works of Mao Tsetung* (*SW*). 4 vols. Peking: Foreign Languages Press, vol. 1, pp. 311–47.

—— (1940) "On New Democracy." In *SW*, vol. 2, pp. 339–84.

—— (1943) "Talks at the Yenan Forum on Art Literature and Art." In *SW*, vol. 3, pp. 69–98.

Markels, Julian (2003) *The Marxian Imagination: Representing Class in Literature.* New York: Monthly Review Press.

Marx, Karl (1887 [1867] *Capital*, vol. I (*C* I). www.marxists.org/archive/marx/works/1867-c1/

—— (1959 [1894] *Capital*, vol. III (*C* III). www.marxists.org/archive/marx/works/1894-c3/index.htm

—— (1969 [1895]) *The Class Struggles in France* (*CSF*). www.marxists.org/archive/marx/works/1850/class-struggles-france/index.htm

—— (1956) *"Confession"* (*Confession*). www.marxists.org/archive/marx/works/1865/04/01.htm

—— (1970 [1890–1] *Critique of the Gotha Programme* (*CGP*) www.marxists.org/archive/marx/works/1875/gotha/

—— (1970 [1843]) *Critique of Hegel's Philosophy of Right* (*CHPR*) www.marxists.org/archive/marx/works/1843/critique-hpr/

—— (1959 [1932]) *Economic and Philosophic Manuscripts of 1844* (*EPM*) www.marxists.org/archive/marx/works/1844/manuscripts/preface.htm

—— (1869 and 1937 [1852]) *The Eighteenth Brumaire of Louis Bonaparte* (*18 B*) www.marxists.org/archive/marx/works/download/pdf/18th-Brumaire.pdf

—— (1972) *Ethnographical Notebooks.* www.marxists.org/archive/marx/works/1881/ethnographical-notebooks/notebooks.pdf

—— (1973 [1939–41]) *Grundrisse* (*GR*) www.marxists.org/archive/marx/works/1857/grundrisse/

—— (1956 [1845]) *The Holy Family* (*HF*) www.marxists.org/archive/marx/works/1845/holy-family/index.htm

—— (1977 [1859]) Preface to *A Contribution to the Critique of Political Economy* (*PCCPE*) www.marxists.org/archive/marx/works/1859/critique-pol-economy/preface.htm

—— (1955 [1847])*The Poverty of Philosophy* (*PP*) www.marxists.org/archive/marx/works/1847/poverty-philosophy/

—— (n.d. [1842–3]) *Rheinische Zeitung* (*RZ*) www.marxists.org/archive/marx/works/subject/newspapers/rheinische-zeitung.htm

—— (1969 [1863]) *Theories of Surplus Value* (*TSV*) www.marxists.org/archive/marx/works/1863/theories-surplus-value/

—— (1969 [1888]) *Theses on Feuerbach* (*Theses*) www.marxists.org/archive/marx/works/1845/theses/theses.htm

—— (1891 [1849]) *Wage-Labor and Capital* (*WL&C*) www.marxists.org/archive/marx/works/1847/wage-labour/

Marx, Karl, and Friedrich Engels (1969 [1848]) *The Communist Manifesto* (*CM*) www.marxists.org/archive/marx/works/download/pdf/Manifesto.pdf

—— (1976 [1932])*The German Ideology* (*GI*) www.marxists.org/archive/marx/works/1845/german-ideology/index.htm

—— (1870–) *Marx–Engels Correspondence* (*MEC*) www.marxists.org/archive/marx/letters/date/index.htm

—— (1976) *Marx and Engels on Literature and Art* (*MELA*) www.marxists.org/archive/marx/works/subject/art/index.htm

Mavroudeas, S. and F. Papadatos (forthcoming) "Is the Financialisation Hypothesis a Theoretical Blind Alley?" *World Review of Political Economy.*

Mayer, Arno J. (2012) *Why Did Not the Heavens Darken? The Final Solution in History.* London: Verso.

McCrae, John (1919) *In Flanders Fields and Other Poems.* New York: G.P. Putnam.

McElwee, Sean (2014) "Marx Was Right: Five Surprising Ways Karl Marx Predicted 2014." *Rolling Stone*, 30 January.

McEwan, Ian (2007) *On Chesil Beach.* London: Jonathan Cape.

McGurl, Mark (2009) *The Program Era.* Cambridge, MA: Harvard University Press.

McIntosh, Peggy (1989) "White Privilege: Unpacking the Invisible Knapsack of Privilege." *Peace and Freedom*, July–Aug.: 10–12.

McKay, Claude (2004) *The Complete Poems of Claude McKay.* Ed. William J. Maxwell. Urbana: University of Illinois Press.

—— (1979) *The Negroes in America.* Ed. Alan L. McLeod. Trans. Robert J. Winter. Port Washington, NY: Kennikat Press.

McKenna, Tony (2015) *Art, Literature and Culture from a Marxist Perspective.* New York: Palgrave Macmillan.

Meeropol, Abel (2006 [1939]) "Strange Fruit." *International Journal of Epidemiology* 35: 902.

Melville, Herman (1956a [1856]) "Bartleby, the Scrivener: A Story of Wall Street." In *The Shorter Novels of Herman Melville.* New York: Liveright.

—— (1956b) "Benito Cereno." In *The Shorter Novels of Herman Melville.* New York: Liveright, pp. 1–106.

—— (1956c) *Moby-Dick.* Boston, MA: Houghton Mifflin.

Menand, Louis (2016) "Karl Marx, Yesterday and Today." *The New Yorker*, 10 October.

Menchú, Rigoberta (2010 [1983]) *I, Rigoberta Menchú: An Indian Woman in Guatemala.* Trans. Ann Wright. New York: Verso.

Mészáros, István (1995) *Beyond Capital: Toward a Theory of Transition.* New York: Monthly Review Press.

Metscher, Thomas (1979) "Literature and Art as Ideological Form." *New Literary History* 11(1): 21–39.

Meyerson, Gregory (2000) "Rethinking Black Marxism: Reflections on Cedric Robinson and Others." *Cultural Logic* 3(2). https://clogic.eserver.org/gregory-meyerson-rethinking-black-marxism-reflections-cedric-robinson-and-others-1

Milanović, Branko (2018) *Global Inequality: A New Approach to the Age of Globalisation.* Cambridge, MA: Belknap Press of Harvard University Press.

Miller, Arthur (1996 [1949]) *Death of a Salesman.* Harmondsworth: Penguin Books.

Miller, W. Jason (2015) *Origins of the Dream: Hughes's Poetry and King's Rhetoric.* Gainesville: University of Florida Press.

Mills, Charles (2003) *From Class to Race: Essays in White Marxism and Black Radicalism.* Lanham, MD: Rowman and Littlefield.

Milton, John (2003 [1674]) *Paradise Lost.* London: Penguin Classics.

Mitchell, Margaret (1936) *Gone with the Wind.* New York: The Macmillan Co.

Mohanty, Satya (1997) *Literary Theory and the Claims of History: Postmodernism, Objectivity, Multicultural Politics.* Ithaca, NY: Cornell University Press.

Moore, Charles (2015) "The Middle-Class Squeeze." *Wall Street Journal*, 25 October

Morawski, Stefan (190) "The Aesthetic Views of Marx and Engels." *Journal of Aesthetics and Art Criticism* 28(3): 301–14.

Morris, William (1994 [1890]) *News from Nowhere.* London: Penguin Classics.

Morrison, Toni (2009) *A Mercy.* New York: Vintage.

Mouffe, Chantal (2014 [1979]) "Hegemony and Ideology in Gramsci." Trans. Denise Derôme. In *Gramsci and Marxist Theory.* Ed. Chantal Mouffe. London: Routledge and Kegan Paul, pp. 168–204.

Moya, Paula (2002) *Learning from Experience: Minority Identities, Multicultural Struggles.* Berkeley: University of California Press.

Mtshali, Oswald Mbuyiseni (2012 [1975]) *Sounds of a Cowhide Drum.* Auckland Park, South Africa: Jacana Media.

Mueller, Tim B. (2013) "The Rockefeller Foundation, the Social Sciences, and the Humanities in the Cold War." *Journal of Cold War Studies* 15(3): 108–35.

Muhammed, Khalil Gibran (2011) *The Condemnation of Blackness: Race, Crime, and the Making of Modern Urban America.* Cambridge, MA: Harvard University Press.

Mullen, Bill (2013) "Proletarian Literature." www.oxfordbibliographies.com/view/document/obo-9780199827251/obo-9780199827251-0130.xml. 2013

Musto, Marcello (2012) "Revisiting Marx's Concept of Alienation." In *Marx for Today.* Ed. Marcello Musto. London: Routledge, pp. 92–116.

Nammo, Dave (2017) "Socialism's Rising Popularity Threatens America's Future." *National Review*, 18 March. www.nationalreview.com/article/445882/socialism-polls-indicates-its-alarming-rise-public-opinion

Ness, Immanuel (2016) *Southern Insurgency: The Coming of the Global Working Class.* London: Pluto.

Ngai, Sianne (2012) *Our Aesthetic Categories: Zany, Cute, Interesting.* Cambridge, MA: Harvard University Press.

Nguyen, Viet Thanh (2014) "War, Memory, Identity." Podcast. National University of Singapore: Asia Research Institute, August.

—— (2015) *The Sympathizer*. New York: Grove Press.

—— (2016) *Nothing Ever Dies: Vietnam and the Memory of War*. Cambridge, MA: Harvard University Press.

—— (2017) "Your Writing Tools Aren't Mine." *New York Times Book Review*, 30 April: 13.

Nilon, Charles (1991) "The Ending of *Huck Finn*: Freeing the Freed Negro." In *Satire or Evasion? Black Perspectives on Huckleberry Finn*. Ed. James S. Leonard et al. Durham, NC: Duke University Press, pp. 62–76.

Nkrumah, Kwame (1965) *Neo-colonialism: The Highest Stage of Imperialism*. www.marxists. org/subject/africa/nkrumah/neo-colonialism/index.htm

—— (1967) "African Socialism Revisited." In *Africa: National and Social Revolution*. Prague: Peace and Socialism Publishers.

Noel, Urayoan (2010) *Hi-Density Politics*. Buffalo, NY: BlazeVOX Books.

Norris, Frank (1994 [1899]) *McTeague: A Story of San Francisco*. New York: Penguin Classics.

North, Joseph (2017) *Literary Criticism: A Concise Political History*. Cambridge, MA: Harvard University Press.

North, Michael (2013) "The Making of 'Make It New'." *Guernica: A Magazine of Global Arts and Politics*, 15 August. www.guernicamag.com/the-making-of-making-it-new/

Nucleous, Mark (2003) "The Political Economy of the Dead: Marx's Vampires." *History of Political Thought* 24(4): 668–84.

Nussbaum, Martha C. (1997) *Cultivating Humanity: A Classical Defense of Reform in Liberal Education*. Cambridge, MA: Harvard University Press.

N.W.A. (1988) "Fuck tha Police." In *Straight Outta Compton*. Album. Los Angeles: Ruthless Records.

Obama, Barack (2004 [1995]) *Dreams from My Father: A Story of Race and Inheritance*. New York: Broadway Books.

O'Brien, Tim (1990) *The Things They Carried*. Boston, MA: Houghton Mifflin.

Odets, Clifford (1979 [1935]) *Waiting for Lefty*. In *Six Plays*. Ed. Harold Clurman. New York: Grove Press.

Ohmann, Richard (1971) "Speech Acts and the Definition of Literature." *Philosophy and Rhetoric* 4(1): 1–19.

Ollman, Bertell (1993) *Dialectical Investigations*. New York: Routledge.

Olsen, Tillie (1960) *Tell Me a Riddle*. New York: Delta Books.

—— (1974) *Yonnondio: From the Thirties*. New York: Delta.

O'Neill, Eugene (2014 [1956]) *Long Day's Journey into Night*. New Haven, CT: Yale University Press.

Orwell, George (1946) *Animal Farm*. New York: Harcourt, Brace and Co.

Page, Myra (1996 [1935]) *Moscow Yankee*. Urbana: University of Illinois Press.

Painter, Nell (2011) *The History of White People*. New York: W.W. Norton.

Patterson, Tim (1975) "Notes on the Historical Application of Marxist Cultural Theory." *Science & Society* 39(3): 257–91.

Pearl Poet (2016) *Pearl*. Trans. Simon Armitage. New York: Liveright.

Peterson, Jordan (2018) *12 Rules for Life: An Antidote to Chaos*. Toronto: Random House Canada.

Petry, Ann (2007) "Like a Winding Sheet." In *American Working-Class Literature: An Anthology*. Ed. Nicholas Coles and Janet Zandy. New York: Oxford University Press, pp. 586–90.

Piercy, Marge (1976) *Woman on the Edge of Time*. New York: Alfred A. Knopf.

Piketty, Thomas (2013) *Capital in the Twenty-first Century*. Cambridge, MA: Harvard University Press.

Pines, Christopher L. (1993) *Ideology and False Consciousness: Marx and His Historical Progenitors*. Albany: SUNY Press.

PLP (Progressive Labor Party) (1982) "Road to Revolution IV." www.marxists.org/history/erol/1960-1970/rr4.pdf

Poitier, Eugène (1871) "L'Internationale." American English Translation. n.d.

Poulantzas, Nicos (1973) "On Social Classes." *New Left Review* I/78 (March–April): 27–54.

Pound, Ezra (1935) *Make It New: Essays by Ezra Pound*. New Haven, CT: Yale University Press.

—— (1986) *Cantos*. New York: New Directions.

Pratt, Minnie Bruce (2014) "Leslie Feinberg: A Communist Who Revolutionized Transgender Rights." www.workers.org/2014/11/18/leslie-feinberg/

Prescott, John F. (1985) *In Flanders Fields: The Story of John McCrae*. Erin, Ontario: Boston Mills Press.

Proulx, Annie (1997) "Brokeback Mountain." *The New Yorker*, 13 October: 74–85.

Proust, Marcel (2003 [1913–27]) *Remembrance of Things Past. [In Search of Lost Time]*. Trans C.K. Scott Moncrieff and Terence Kilmartin. New York: Modern Library Classics.

Rabinowitz, Peter J. and Michael W. Smith (1998) *Authorizing Readers: Resistance and Respect in the Teaching of Literature*. New York: Teachers College Press.

Radway, Janice A. (1991) *Reading the Romance: Women, Patriarchy, and Popular Literature*. 2nd edn. Chapel Hill: University of North Carolina Press.

Rand, Ayn (1957) *Atlas Shrugged*. New York: Random House.

Read, Jason (2017) "Ideology as Individuation, Individuating Ideology." *Mediations*, 30(2): 75–82. www.mediationsjournal.org/articles/IndividuatingIdeology

Resch, Robert Paul (1992) "Structure in Dominance and Determination in the Last Instance." In *Althusser and the Renewal of Marxist Social Theory*. Berkeley: University of California Press.

Reveley, James (2013) "The Exploitative Web: Misuses of Marxism in Critical Social Media Studies." *Science & Society* 77(4): 512–35.

Richards, I.A. (1930) *Principles of Literary Criticism*. 4th edn. New York: Harcourt, Brace.

Ricoeur, Paul (2008) *Freud and Philosophy: An Essay on Interpretation*. Trans. Denis Savage. New Haven, CT: Yale University Press.

Riefenstahl, Leni (1935) *The Triumph of the Will*. Film. Berlin: Reichsparteitag-Film.

—— (1938) *Olympia*. Film. Berlin: Olympia-Film.

Riesman, David, with Nathan Glazer and Reuel Denney (2001 [1950]) *The Lonely Crowd*. 1950. Rev. edn. New Haven, CT: Yale University Press.

Ritchie, Andrea J. (2017) *Invisible No More: Police Violence Against Black Women and Women of Color*. Boston, MA: Beacon Press.

Robbins, Bruce (2017) "Not So Well Attached." *PMLA* 132(March): 371–76.

Roediger, David (2017) *Class, Race and Marxism*. New York: Verso.

Rose, Peter (2006) "Divorcing Ideology from Marxism and Marxism from Ideology: Some Problems." *Arethusa* 39: 101–36.

—— (2012) *Class in Archaic Greece.* Cambridge: Cambridge University Press.

Ross, Robert J.S. (2013) "Bread and Roses: Women Workers and the Struggle for Dignity and Respect." *Working USA: The Journal of Labor & Society* 16 (March): 59–68.

Rousseau, Jean-Jacques (1953 [1782–89]) *The Confessions of Jean-Jacques Rousseau.* Trans J.M. Cohen. London: Penguin.

Rubin Jr, Louis D. (1978) Introduction to Twelve Southerners, *I'll Take My Stand: The South and the Agrarian Tradition.* Ed. Louis D. Rubin. Baton Rouge: Louisiana State University Press, pp. xi–xxxvi.

Rubinstein, Annette T. (1969) *The Great Tradition in English Literature from Shakespeare to Shaw.* 1953. New York: Monthly Review Press.

Rukeyser, Muriel (1978) *Collected Poems.* New York: McGraw-Hill.

Said, Edward (1994) *Culture and Imperialism.* New York: Random House.

San Juan Jr., E. (1976) "Art against Imperialism, for the National Liberation Struggle of Third World Peoples." In *Weapons of Criticism: Marxism in America and the Literary Tradition.* Ed. Norman Rudich. Palo Alto, CA: Ramparts Press, pp. 147–60.

Sánchez Vázquez, Adolfo (1973 [1965]) *Art and Society: Essays in Marxist Aesthetics.* Trans. Maro Riofrancos. New York: Monthly Review Press.

Sandburg, Carl (1950) *The Complete Poems of Carl Sandburg.* New York: Harcourt, Brace and Co.

Sapphire (1996) *Push.* New York: Alfred A. Knopf.

Saricks, Joyce (2009) *The Readers' Advisory Guide to Genre Fiction.* 2nd edn. Chicago: ALA Editions.

Schlauch, Margaret (1967) *English Medieval Literature and Its Social Foundations.* Warszawa, Panstwowe Wydawnictwo Naukowe.

Schmertz, Joanna (2006) "Exploring Ambiguity and Intention: Higher Learning for First-Year Readers and Writers." *Pedagogy* 6(1): 123–27.

Schmitz, Neil (1971) "Twain, Huckleberry Finn, and the Reconstruction." *American Studies* 12(1): 59–67.

Sembène, Ousmane (1962 [1960]) *God's Bits of Wood.* Trans. Francis Price. London: William Heinemann.

Shakespeare, William (1972 [1605–6]) *King Lear.* London: Bloomsbury—Arden Shakespeare.

—— (2011 [1596–99]) *The Merchant of Venice.* London: Bloomsbury—Arden Shakespeare.

—— (1997 [1609]) *Sonnets.* London: Bloomsbury—Arden Shakespeare.

—— (2008 [1605–8]) *Timon of Athens.* London: Bloomsbury—Arden Shakespeare.

Shandro, Alan (2015) *Lenin and the Logic of Hegemony: Political Practice and Theory in the Class Struggle.* Chicago: Haymarket Books.

Shankar, Subramanian (2012) *Flesh and Fish Blood: Postcolonialism, Translation, and the Vernacular.* Berkeley: University of California Press.

Shapiro, James (2015) *The Year of Lear: Shakespeare in 1606.* New York: Simon and Schuster.

Shelley, Mary (2018 [1818]) *Frankenstein; or, the Modern Prometheus.* London: Penguin Classics.

Shelley, Percy Bysshe (1951) *Shelley: Selected Poetry and Prose.* Ed. Carlos Baker. New York: Modern Library.

Shklovskij, Viktor (1998) "Art as Technique." In *Literary Theory: An Anthology*. Ed. Julie Rivkin and Michael Ryan. Malden: Blackwell.

Sidney, Sir Philip (1970 [1595]) *The Defence of Poesie*. London: Macmillan.

Silone, Ignacio (1960 [1933]) *Fontamara*. Trans. Harvey Fergusson. New York: Atheneum.

Sinclair, Upton (2010) *The Jungle*. New York: Oxford World's Classics.

Singh, Nikhal P. (2017) "On Race, Violence and So-called 'Primitive Accumulation.'" In *Futures of Black Radicalism*. Ed. Gaye Theresa Johnson and Alex Lubin. London: Verso, pp. 39–58.

Sloane, David E.E. (2014) "The N-word in *Adventures of Huckleberry Finn* Reconsidered." *The Mark Twain Annual* 12: 70–82.

Smiley, Jane (1996) "Say It Ain't So, Huck: Second Thoughts on Mark Twain's 'Masterpiece.'" *Harper's Magazine*, 292(1748): 61–67.

Smith, Cassander (2014) "'Nigger' or 'Slave': Why Labels Matter for Jim (and Twain) in *Adventures of Huckleberry Finn*." *Papers on Language and Literature* 50 (March): 182–206.

Smith, David L. (1991) "Huck, Jim, and American Racial Discourse." In *Satire or Evasion? Black Perspectives on Huckleberry Finn*. Ed. James S. Leonard et al. Durham, NC: Duke University Press, pp. 103–23.

Smith, John (2016) *Imperialism in the Twenty-First Century: Globalization, Superexploitation, and Capitalism's Final Crisis*. New York: Monthly Review Press.

Sophocles (1990 [c. 441 BCE]) *Antigone*. Trans. Richard Emil Braun. Oxford: Oxford University Press.

Squiers, Anthony (2014) *An Introduction to the Social and Political Philosophy of Bertolt Brecht: Revolution and Aesthetics*. Amsterdam: Rodopi.

Stackhouse, Julie (2017) "Why Didn't Bank Regulators Prevent the Financial Crisis?" 23 May. www.stlouisfed.org/on-the-economy/2017/may/why-didnt-bank-regulators-prevent-financial-crisis

Standing, Guy (2011) *The Precariat: The New Dangerous Class*. New York: Bloomsbury USA.

Starosta, Guido (2012) "Cognitive Commodities and the Value Form." *Science & Society* 76(3): 365–92.

Stasi, Paul (2015) "Georg Lukács Reconsidered." *Mediations* 28(2): 139–51.

Stoddard, Lothrop (1920) *The Rising Tide of Color against White World-Supremacy*. New York: Charles Scribner's Sons.

Taylor, Keeanga-Yamahtta (2016) *From #BlackLivesMatter to Black Liberation*. Chicago: Haymarket Books.

Thomas, Angie (2017) *The Hate U Give*. New York: Balzer and Bray.

Thomas, Dylan (1957) *Collected Poems*. New York: New Directions.

Thomas, Gwyn (1986) *Sorrow for Thy Sons*. London: Lawrence and Wishart.

Thompson, Michael J. (2011) *Georg Lukács Reconsidered: Critical Essays on Politics, Philosophy and Aesthetics*. London: Continuum.

Thomson, George (1968 [1940]) *Aeschylus and Athens: A Study in the Social Origins of Drama*. New York: Grosset and Dunlap.

Thoreau, Henry David (2000 [1854]) *Walden; or, Life in the Woods*. Boston, MA: Beacon Press.

Tomasi di Lampedusa, Giuseppe (1960) *The Leopard* [*Il Gattopardo*]. Trans. Archibald Colquhoun. New York: Pantheon.

Tressell, Robert (2012 [1914]) *The Ragged-Trousered Philanthropists*. Hertfordshire: Wordsworth Classics.

Trollope, Anthony (2016 [1875]) *The Way We Live Now*. Oxford: Oxford World's Classics.

Trumbo, Dalton (1989) *Johnny Got his Gun*. 1939. New York: Bantam Books.

Tuss, Alex J. (2006) "Brokeback Mountain and the Geography of Desire." *Journal of Men's Studies* 14(2): 243–46.

Twain, Mark (1995 [1886]) *Adventures of Huckleberry Finn*. In *Mark Twain "Adventures of Huckleberry Finn": A Case Study in Critical Controversy*. Ed. Gerald Graff and James Phelan. Boston, MA: Bedford/St. Martin's.

Twelve Southerners (1978 [1931]) *I'll Take My Stand: A Tract against Communism*. Ed. Louis D. Rubin. Baton Rouge: Louisiana State University Press.

Van Rooden, Aukje (2015) "Reconsidering Literary Autonomy: From an Individual towards a Relational Paradigm." *Journal of the History of Ideas* 76(2): 167–90.

Viramontes, Helena Maria (1985) "The Cariboo Café." In *The Moths and Other Stories*. Houston, TX: Arte Publico Press, pp. 65–82.

—— (1995) *Under the Feet of Jesus*. New York: Dutton.

Vogel, Lise (2014) *Marxism and the Oppression of Women: Toward a Unitary Theory*. Rev. edn. Chicago: Haymarket Books.

Volz, Jessica (2017) "Coffee, Tea and Visuality: The Art of Attraction in *Pride and Prejudice*." https://janeaustenlf.org/pride-and-possibilities-articles/2017/2/21/issue-8-coffee-tea-and-visuality

Vonnegut, Kurt (1973) *Breakfast of Champions; or, Goodbye, Blue Monday*. New York: Delacorte.

Wa Thiong'o, Ngũgĩ (1989 [1986]) *Matigari*. Oxford: Heinemann.

Wakefield Master (1910 [c. 1500]) *The Second Shepherds' Play*. In *The Second Shepherds' Play, Everyman and Other Early Plays*. Trans. Clarence Griffin Child. Boston, MA: Houghton Mifflin.

Walker, Alice (1992 [1982]) *The Color Purple*. Boston, MA: Houghton Mifflin Harcourt.

Wallace, John H. (1991) "The Case Against *Huck Finn*." In *Satire or Evasion? Black Perspectives on Huckleberry Finn*. Ed. James S. Leonard et al. Durham, NC: Duke University Press, pp. 16–24.

Warwick Research Collective (2015) *Combined and Uneven Development: Towards a New Theory of World-Literature*. Liverpool: Liverpool University Press.

Waugh, Patricia (1984) *Metafiction: The Theory and Practice of Self-Conscious Fiction*. London: Routledge.

Wharton, Edith (1994 [1905]) *The House of Mirth*. Ed. Shari Benstock. Boston, MA: Bedford/St. Martin's.

Whitman, Walt (1961 [1855]) *Leaves of Grass*. New York: Penguin Classics.

White, Simon J. (2013) *Romanticism and the Rural Community*. London: Palgrave Macmillan.

Wiesel, Elie (1960 [1950]) *Night*. Trans. Stella Rodway. New York: Hill and Wang.

Williams, Eric (1994 [1944]) *Capitalism and Slavery*. Chapel Hill: University of North Carolina Press.

Williams, Jeffrey (2015) "The New Modesty in Literary Criticism." *Chronicle of Higher Education*, 5 Jan. www.chronicle.com/article/the-new-modesty-in-literary/150993

Williams, Raymond (1977) *Marxism and Literature*. Oxford: Oxford University Press.

—— (1993) *The Country and the City*. London: Hogarth Press.

Williams, William Carlos (1992 [1946–1958]) *Paterson*. Ed. Christopher McGowan. New York: New Directions.

Wimsatt, William K. and Monroe C. Beardsley (1954) *The Verbal Icon: Studies in the Meaning of Poetry*. Lexington: University Press of Kentucky.

Wittgenstein, Ludwig (1953) *Philosophical Investigations*. Oxford: Basil Blackwell.

Woloch, Alex (2005) *The One v. the Many: Minor Characters and the Space of the Protagonist in the Novel*. Princeton, NJ: Princeton University Press.

Wood, Ellen Meiksins (1998) *The Retreat from Class: A New "True" Socialism*. Rev. edn. London: Verso.

—— (1995) "Rethinking Base and Superstructure." In *Democracy against Capitalism: Renewing Historical Materialism*. Cambridge: Cambridge University Press, pp. 49–75.

Woolf, Virginia (2008 [1975]) *To the Lighthouse*. Oxford: Oxford University Press.

Wordsworth, William (1965) *The Poetical Works of William Wordsworth*. Ed. Thomas Hutchinson. London: Oxford University Press.

Wright, Richard (1937) "Blueprint for Negro Writing." *New Challenge* 2(Fall): 58–65.

—— (1965 [1940]) *Uncle Tom's Children*. New York: Harper Perennial.

—— (1993 [1940]) *Native Son*. New York: Library of America.

Xu Lizhi (2017) "I Swallowed an Iron Moon." In *Iron Moon: An Anthology of Chinese Worker Poetry*. Ed. Qin Xiaoyu. Trans. Eleanor Goodman. Buffalo: White Pine Press, p. 198.

Yeats, William Butler (1956) *The Collected Poems of W.B. Yeats*. New York: Macmillan.

—— (2013 [1925]) *A Vision*. In *The Collected Works of W.B. Yeats*, vol. 14. Ed. Catherine E. Paul and Margaret Mills Harper. New York: Simon and Schuster.

Zinn, Howard (2015 [1980]) *A People's History of the United States*. New York: Harper Perennial Classics.

Žižek, Slavoj, ed. (2013) *The Idea of Communism 2: The New York Conference*. London: Verso.

Zweig, Michael (2011) *The Working-Class Majority: America's Best-kept Secret*. 2nd edn. Ithaca, NY: ILR Press.

Index

CPSIA information can be obtained
at www.ICGtesting.com
Printed in the USA
BVHW011650050822
643908BV00021B/219